Philosophy of Wittgenstein
Indian Responses

Hyderabad Studies in Philosophy, no. 1

Philosophy of Wittgenstein
Indian Responses

Edited by
R.C. Pradhan

Decent Books
New Delhi

Published and printed by:
Decent Books
'Suryodaya', D-36/A-1, Mohan Garden
Najafgarh Road
New Delhi – 110 059
Ph. (011) 2535-3435

Distributed by:
D.K. Printworld (P) Ltd.
Regd. office : *'Vedaśrī,'* F-395, Sudarshan Park
(Metro Station: Ramesh Nagar)
New Delhi - 110 015
Phones : (011) 2545 3975, 2546 6019; *Fax* : (011) 2546 5926
e-mail : indology@dkprintworld.com
Web : www.dkprintworld.com

ISBN 978-81-86921-15-9

First Published in India in 2001
Second impression published in 2013

Acknowledgements

THE papers included in this volume except those of A. Dasgupta and R.C. Pradhan were presented in a National Seminar on "Wittgenstein's Philosophy of Language" held in February 24-26, 1999. The Seminar was organised under the UGC Special Assistance Programme of the Department of Philosophy, University of Hyderabad. We are grateful to the UGC and the Indian Council of Philosophical Research for providing funds for organising the Seminar.

The present volume entitled *The Philosophy of Wittgenstein : Indian Responses* is the first volume under the general series **Hyderabad Studies in Philosophy**. We are grateful to the UGC for providing funds for publication under the Special Assistance Programme.

We are grateful to the Vice-Chancellor and the Chairman of the SAP Advisory Committee, Professor P. Rama Rao for giving us all encouragements in all our academic activities. We are thankful to Professor P.K. Mohapatra, External Member of the SAP Advisory Committee and Professor A. Ramamurti, the former Co-ordinator, SAP and Member of the Advisory Committee for guiding us regarding the publication of this volume.

We are thankful to Professor A. Das Gupta, Head, Department of Philosophy and Co-ordinator, SAP for extending all help in the publication of this volume and also in organising the Seminar. We are also thankful to all our colleagues: Dr. Chinmoy Goswami, Dr. S.G. Kulkarni, Dr. A. Raghuramaraju, Dr. K.S. Prasad and Mr. Anand V. Wazalwar for extending their help in making this publication possible.

We are thankful to Decent Books, New Delhi, for undertaking this composition for publication. We are thankful to Mr. Gupta for preparing the manuscript.

Hyderabad
2000

R.C. Pradhan

Contents

Abbreviations

B.B.	:	*The Blue and Brown Books*
LFM	:	*Lectures on the Foundations of Mathematics*
PI	:	*Philosophical Investigations*
PG	:	*Philosophical Grammar*
RFM	:	*Remarks on the Foundations of Mathematics*
TLP	:	*Tractatus Logico-Philosophicus*

Introduction

THE essays included in this volume reflect the contemporary evaluation of Wittgenstein's philosophy, especially his philosophy of language. Wittgenstein is a key figure in the development of contemporary philosophy in the West. He has influenced the very course of philosophy in the twentieth-century West by the force of his imaginative and creative thinking. Wittgenstein remains a beacon light for generations to come for the freshness of his thinking and his open-ended philosophical quest. This volume is an effort on the part of Indian philosophers to evaluate and reassess Wittgenstein's thoughts.

I

Wittgenstein's cultural roots lie in the West, especially in the spiritual traditions of Europe. The European cultural traditions as represented in philosophy, literature, music, painting, sculpture, etc., have a deep influence on him. However, he belonged at heart to the classical age of the European civilization rather than to the scientific civilization of the twentieth-century West. This is reflected in his trenchant criticism of the modern West in his *Culture and Value* in the following words:

> . . . the fact remains that I have no sympathy for the current of European civilization and do not understand its goals, if it has any. So I am really writing for friends who are scattered throughout the corners of the globe. (p.6e.)

These words sound prophetic in view of his criticism of the scientific spirit of the modern West and his glorification of the quest for spiritual liberation rather than for construction of new patterns of thought on the model of science and mathematics. He adds:

> I am not interested in constructing a building, so much as in having a perspicuous view of the foundations of possible buildings. (p.7e)

Thus, for him, what matters most is the spiritual vision of things as a whole rather than the scientific analysis of the phenomena. This view is foreign to the contemporary culture of the West which is wedded to the idea of progress.

Suresh Chandra in his paper 'Attacking Modern Western Civilization: Mahatma Gandhi and Ludwig Wittgenstein' has highlighted how both Gandhi and Wittgenstein have taken to task the modern civilization based on science and technology. He has shown that Gandhi and Wittgenstein share the common apathy for the anti-spiritual nature of the scientific and materialist culture of the West. Gandhi in his *Hind Swaraj* has exposed the hollowness of the materialist civilization of the West. For Gandhi, the modern Western civilization is soulless and it suffers from the bankruptcy of the spiritual values. According to Suresh Chandra, Wittgenstein has also revolted against the anti-spiritual nature of the Western civilization as he finds in it nothing but the urge for the material development of man. The fine nuances of the human spirit are lacking in this technology-addict culture. Suresh Chandra, however, argues that while Gandhi not only challenged the West but also has offered an alternative model of culture based on the Indian spiritual heritage, Wittgenstein has failed to give an alternative model. Hence, it is argued, Wittgenstein remained within the Western civilization even though he was dissatisfied with it. Suresh Chandra concludes that Wittgenstein was 'a child of Gandhian thinking — but only a child'. Though many may not agree with this view, it is important to note that Wittgenstein was not as revolutionary as Gandhi in his approach to Western civilization. But it is not to be inferred that Wittgenstein had no alternative vision of culture and life. It is embedded, as he repeatedly reminded us, in his view that liberation of the mind from the linguistic and conceptual puzzlements is the goal of philosophy. This view of philosophy reminds us of the Upanishadic ideal that the ultimate goal of our quest is the end of all bondage.

Wittgenstein's attitude towards silence and quietude is noteworthy in view of his aspiration for 'complete clarity' and the end of all 'bewitchment of intelligence by means of language'. The philosophical quest in this sense is not one of saying something or discovering truth but of 'showing' the deep sources of all truths. This idea of showing is Wittgenstein's equivalent of silence in the face of the urge to express the limits of language and thought. It is the limits which have to be in the realm of silence, that is, are to be shown, because we cannot express the limits in language itself. Srinivasa Rao in his paper, 'Speech and Silence in Western Philosophy: A Critique of Wittgenstein from an Indian Point of view' has argued that the silence Wittgenstein talks about is not about a realm beyond language and the world. According to him, Wittgenstein's concept of silence is a limiting concept which reminds us of the fact that the limits of language and the world are themselves not the subject-matter of another language. Citing parallels from the Indian philosophical systems, Rao holds that for a Nayayika language expresses everything that can be named and so no positive content can be ascribed to silence in the system of Nyaya. Only in Vedanta, according to him, there is place for silence which has more than a negative meaning. In Vedanta there is the urge to posit a realm of silence that is beyond the limits of language. Language in Vedanta is unable to express the ultimate truth because the truth concerns the limits of all existence. Rao brings Wittgenstein closer to Nyaya rather than to Vedanta on the issue of silence because he thinks that Wittgenstein invests only negative meaning on silence. But it may be contended that Wittgenstein's notion of silence has a positive content also in view of the fact that in the *Tractatus* he is definitely aware of the realm of the mystical that defies all canons of linguistic expression. The inexpressible or the mystical has a positive role to play in the development of Wittgenstein's philosophical outlook. He is sensitive to the fact that the limits of language are not empty boundaries, that is, boundaries that bound nothing. Hence, the parallel between Wittgenstein and Vedanta may be more illuminating than the one Rao draws.

II

Wittgenstein is interested not only in the limits of language but also in its structure so far as the structure can be logically mapped. It is out of this interest that he develops the concept of grammar that is supposed to provide the perspicuity of language and its rules. For Wittgenstein, the rules define the meaning of language. The later Wittgenstein, especially, highlights the use of language, i.e., the language-games which provide the broad spectrum of how the rules are applied in actual practice or forms of life. Nizar Ahmed in his paper 'Language-game, Grounding and the Metaphysics of Meaning' has highlighted this issue by suggesting that the rules of language and meaning emerge from the forms of life and, therefore, do not have a Platonist or essentialist root. They are a part of the historical structure of language. The language-games themselves, according to Ahmed, do not have any grounding either in reason or experience. They are groundless in the sense that no explanation is forthcoming either for their existence or for their non-existence. The world-picture which is associated with them is also groundless. This leads us back to the view that beyond language there is no separate realm of reason for explaining why language functions the way it does. Thus, Ahmed is right in pointing out that the question of a metaphysics of meaning does not arise because there is nothing that a theory of meaning can do as there is no scope for explanation of meaning. Meaning can only be described and shown how it emerges from use of language. Besides, meaning is not a cognitive concept at all; it is a grammatical notion as much as the rules themselves. Thus, considered, meaning has to be located in the grammar of language. Metaphysics of meaning is a misnomer because there is no essence left in the concept of meaning except the nuances of forms of life. Thus, there is no fund of grammatical structures which are not explicit in the use of language. This has been construed as a kind of post-modernist thinking by Ahmed because Wittgenstein seems to have given up the very ground of metaphysics of meaning. But to construe Wittgenstein as a post-modernist is to make him belong to an ultra radical group that has no roots in the tradition of philosophy of language. Wittgenstein, however, believes that human language has a structure and that meaning can be shown in the network of language-games.

The question of criteria has dominated Wittgenstein's philosophy of language for more than one reason: it provided the much needed mechanism for relating language to human behaviour and also provided an operationalistic explanation of meaning. It is beyond doubt that Wittgenstein emphasised the operational aspects of language in his bid to defeat mentalism in theory of language and meaning. But whether he took a completely behaviourist turn is a matter of debate. Amitabha DasGupta in his paper 'Criteria and The Conceptual Structure' has criticised Wittgenstein's operationalism in philosophy of language and has argued for a Chomsky-Fodorian defence of mentalism in language and meaning analysis. He argues that Wittgenstein's notion of criterion fails to avoid the behaviouristic implications because it tries to understand language in terms of the behaviour associated with it. But, according to him, our language-learning depends not on the manifest behaviour but on the in-built mechanism of linguistic competence. Taking clue from Chomsky and Fodor, he argues that there are mental mechanisms which go into the process of language-learning. These mechanisms constitute the conceptual structure which underlies our language use. These structures have to be relocated while understanding language and meaning. Thus, DasGupta seeks to emphasise the mentalistic approach to language which Wittgenstein seems to have underplayed.

Wittgenstein was mainly concerned with the basic question how meaning and interpersonal communication are possible. He made it easier to understand how human beings come together to understand one another by introducing the notion of language-game. Language-games are the instruments through which a whole lot of interpersonal activities are undertaken. In that case the idea of communicative discourse becomes a prominent feature of philosophy of language. The social dimension of language is made the sole dimension of linguistic activities. From this emerges the idea of forms of life which dominates Wittgenstein's later philosophy of language. It is a unique feature of this idea that we can bring the contemporary philosophy of communication under the common theme of communicative competence and communicative rationality à là Habermas. S. Panneerselvam in his paper 'On the Problem of Communication: Wittgenstein and Habermas' has highlighted the interface between Wittgenstein's notion of forms of life and Habermas's idea of communicative competence. According to him, both Wittgenstein and Habermas agree on the fact that language is a social phenomenon and that communication is the basic feature of language. But whereas Wittgenstein is more concerned with the grammar of language, Habermas goes into the intersubjective communicative interest of the linguistic community and derives a universal pragmatics for the sake of understanding the logical structure of human speech. Habermas develops a critical social theory by undertaking an analysis of language in its social and communicative context. This brings in the idea that language is not a transcendental reality and that it is a historico-social reality which encompasses the whole spectrum of human activities including the social actions. It is the social actions which are the hallmark of the social dimension of language. Panneerselvam argues that Habermas has brought in a truly social revolution in our understanding of language by projecting the underlying ideal conditions of speech. Wittgenstein, according to him, has failed to realise the social structure of language because of his commitment to a fragmentary approach to the language-games. Habermas has definitely made his social theory of language the fulcrum of his philosophy of language, but it is Wittgenstein who for the first time made us aware of the social dimension of language. His concept of forms of life brings in the much needed social context for philosophy of language and communication.

The question of private language which dominated Wittgenstein's later philosophy takes a new dimension in view of the communicative context of language and meaning. Wittgenstein's attack on the idea of a private language is not only a grammatical and normative one but is also based on the idea of intersubjective character of language. The intersubjective nature of language rules out the possibility of a private language exclusively meant for the individual. Kripke has shown recently that language has a social and communitarian base because of which the functioning of language is secured against all possible odds. That language has no other foundation except those of the social conventions is itself a reminder of the fact that all that we claim as normative in language has its source in communitarian sanctions. Kripke's sceptical interpretation of Wittgenstein has been the main theme of P.R. Bhat's paper 'Wittgenstein on Private Language'. Bhat has suggested that Kripke has not done justice to Wittgenstein's notion of language by imposing a sceptical interpretation on rule-following. Rule-following is not a matter of mere social convention, no is it a matter of sheer fortuitous individual choices. It is grounded on grammar that vouchsafes for the regularity and necessity of rule-following. Basing on this argument Bhat goes further to show that private language is not possible because we cannot imagine what the grammatical rules of such a language would be. If the grammatical rules be such that one can follow them without there being the possibility that he can go wrong, then there is no provision in that grammar for going wrong. Thus, such a language becomes impossible to imagine. Bhat has done well to have suggested that the private language argument has many versions of which the one based on the idea of rule-following is the strongest. Besides, according to him, the idea of privacy has no epistemic content to support a purely sensational language as a private language. The sensational language itself is public because of its being intelligible to others. Thus, there are no mental states including our intentions which can support the possibility of being unintelligible in the sense of being private. The so-called argument in support of private language cannot derive strength from Kripke's sceptical idea that we can go wrong in not only knowing other's intention but also knowing our own intentions. Such failures if any can be taken care of within the limits of our public languages.

III

Kripke's interpretation of Wittgenstein has led to a series of studies on Wittgenstein's concept of rule following. One of them is Collin McGinn's. McGinn has refuted the sceptical interpretation and has opted for a normative account of rule-following which is based on the natural forms of life. G.P. Das in his paper 'Kripke-McGinn Controversy on Rule and Rule-Following' has highlighted the Kripke-McGinn debate on the nature of rule-following and has shown that McGinn is closer to Wittgenstein in his interpretation of rule-following. McGinn has taken a non-sceptical stand on rule-following because he believes that rule-following is as much a natural form of life as language-use is. Thus, seen in the context of natural habits of language use, rule-following does not seem mysterious at all. Nor for that matter is meaning a mysterious entity. Meaning and rules have their natural home in the language-game and the forms of life. Therefore, there is no place for the sceptical doubt that our rule-following may break down at any point because there is no solid foundation on which it stands. The idea of a community cannot supply the much needed support for rule-following if rule-following itself is not backed by the individual's natural ability to follow a rule. In this debate McGinn's interpretation is clearly on the safer grounds because language is not based on theoretical considerations. It is mostly a natural form of life.

Wittgenstein's concept of rule-following has a wider application, namely, in the realm of mathematics and logic. He was keenly interested in understanding the language of mathematics and logic because he believed that it has a whole lot of concepts which can throw light on the nature of language. Besides, some of the problems such as those relating to objectivity, necessity, etc., are bound to crop up in the realm of mathematics. Wittgenstein has been dissatisfied with the standard theories of philosophy of mathematics such as Platonism, formalism, conventionalism, etc., which have dominated the philosophical discussions. He has tried to do away with some of these theories in a bid to see mathematics as it is. Sadhan Chakraborti in his paper 'Wittgenstein on Necessity and Objectivity in Mathematics and Logic' has drawn our attention to these problems and has offered the view that Wittgenstein is a realist in his philosophy of logic and mathematics. Chakraborti does not believe that Wittgenstein has dissolved all theories in the philosophy of mathematics. He thinks that no philosophy of mathematics is possible if we do not admit the objectivity of mathematical truths. Besides, these truths have a necessity which is rarely ascribable to non-mathematical truths. Hence, there must be an independent realm of mathematical truths. This Wittgenstein concedes by showing that the language of mathematics and logic is normative and is based on certain rules which are embedded in all our mathematical activities. There is no doubt that mathematical truths are not Platonic entities nor are they mere linguistic conventions. They are part of our frame-work of thinking logically. Thus, we cannot be anti-realist about mathematics. Chakraborti argues that between hard realism and anti-realism, there is a soft realism that can account for the respectability of the mathematical truths.

Wittgenstein's concept of necessity of mathematical and logical truths has been variously interpreted by philosophers in the post-Wittgensteinian period, namely, by Dummett who appeals to conventionalism and by Putnam who appeals to a form of naturalism. For Dummett, Wittgenstein is a 'full-blooded' conventionalist because he takes mathematical truths as linguistic conventions which are accepted as true by conscious decisions. Dummett holds that the necessity of mathematical truths is dependent on the human decisions. Putnam, on the other hand, holds that mathematical truths for Wittgenstein are based on the forms of life of the people and, therefore, there is a natural and empirical source of necessity in these forms of life. Both these interpretations have been found inadequate because both miss Wittgenstein's idea of necessity as embedded in the grammar of the mathematical propositions. I have argued in my paper 'Logical Necessity, Conventionalism and Forms of Life: Wittgenstein's Philosophy Revisited' that logical necessity in Wittgenstein has its source in the grammar of mathematics but not in the conscious decisions nor in the empirical forms of life. Both Dummett and Putnam have missed the Wittgensteinian point that necessity is normativity associated with the way we think and use language in mathematics. This is not a matter of our deciding it nor is it a matter of our contingent forms of life. There is something very constitutive about these truths as they lie at the bedrock of our language and thought. This may be called a transcendental argument for necessity which overcomes the conventionalist overtones attributed to Wittgenstein by many interpreters.

IV

Wittgenstein's philosophy of language has many-sided implications. There is not only the problem of necessity but also there is the problem of how society is affected by language, especially how language can contribute to the domination of one group by another. Language has been a tool of social domination and also a tool of power in the hands of the most powerful. Thus, the feminists feel that language has been the instrument of suppression of women, Shefali Moitra in her paper 'Wittgenstein's Philosophy of Language : A Feminist Response' has drawn our attention to how in Wittgenstein language has been projected as a liberating force rather than as an instrument of suppression. While the early Wittgenstein may appear to be against the liberty of the suppressed groups because of his transcendental approach to language and thought, his later philosophy makes room for different forms of life and different ways of thinking. This spirit for accommodation encourages the moderate feminist to derive comfort from Wittgenstein against the hegemonistic tendencies of the patriarchal society. Moitra accepts that pluralism and relativism found in the later Wittgenstein can go long way in helping the post-modernist battle against essentialism, puritanism and patriarchism. The feminist response to Wittgenstein, thus, lies in making language available as a tool of liberation rather than of bondage. Wittgenstein has been a champion of liberation of all kinds.

Sanil V. in his paper 'The Language of Face: Wittgenstein in Cinema' has brought a new dimension of Wittgenstein's philosophy of language by relating language to cinema. Cinema itself has a language which presents the visual images of people and their emotions through a transparent language of face. According to Sanil, Wittgenstein has brought language back into the human form of life so as to capture the different moods and emotions as expressed in human language. There is a transparency about the human forms of life and the language-games associated with them. They reveal the aspects of life so that one can see those aspects mirrored in language. Wittgenstein emphasises the 'seeing of aspects' to highlight the visuality of the phenomena like duck-rabbit pictures. Wittgenstein has a deep respect for the visual phenomena such as the linguistic formations which play a significant role in the development of meaning. Meaning itself is something visual, something that can be seen and experienced. This brings language closer to the language of face and, thus, to the language of pictures or cinema. In this sense Sanil has highlighted the Wittgensteinian concept of picture in a radically different way than is traditionally understood.

The language of emotions is a powerful language that dominates all forms of art including the visual arts. Emotions are powerful so far as human life is concerned. Therefore, the language of emotions needs a proper understanding. G.P. Ramachandra in his paper 'Exploring the Grammar of Emotion Words' has brought out the grammar of the language of emotions as developed by Wittgenstein. According to Ramachandra, the emotion words are not designatory of any object, so they are not names of anything. They only express the forms of life. Like other mental words, the emotion words are expressions of forms of life rather than names of any entities. Thus, the grammar of emotion words shows that there is nothing descriptive about this language and that we can better appreciate the nature of the fictional and poetic discourse by taking recourse to the non-cognitive aspects of language. Wittgenstein's philosophy of mind has abundantly shown that any ontological view of mind will mislead us about the language of mind itself. This idea contains in itself a new vision of language, especially of the language of emotions and other deeper feelings of human beings.

In these essays there has been a fresh attempt to re-look at Wittgenstein's philosophy with an open mind. It is an exercise in understanding, evaluating and assimilating his philosophy from a contemporary point of view.

R.C. Pradhan

1

Attacking Modern Western Civilisation

Mahatma Gandhi and Ludwig Wittgenstein*

Suresh Chandra

THE position of Wittgenstein in the context of early twentieth-century Anglo-American philosophy is not very different from the position of Gandhi in the context of early twentieth-century political thinking of the world. Gandhi provided to the world a new method of political revolt, the method of civil resistance. Wittgenstein provided to the world of philosophy a new way of doing philosophy. Philosophy should remain within the bounds of language. If Wittgenstein has shown the futility of writing in a fashion that does not care for the boundaries of language, Gandhi has shown the futility of armed revolts against the alien or native rulers. Of course, Wittgenstein was aware of the fact that the philosophers have hardly cared for the boundaries of their thought and language. (Incidentally, Wittgenstein himself suffered from his disease of thought.) So was Gandhi aware of the fact that armed conflicts among the rulers of the world was a common feature of history. History has not stopped moving, so these conflicts have not stopped occurring. Concerning history, as it has so far been written, Gandhi remarked,

> history, as we know it, is a record of the wars of the world. . . . How kings played, how they became enemies of one

* There is nothing odd about comparing Wittgenstein, whose sole occupation was the removal of logico-linguistic confusions, with Gandhi, who was no kind of professor and whose whole occupation was the removal of British from India, for with one voice they condemned the modern Western civilization.

This is the revised version of a paper that was completed during my Resident Fellowship of ICPR, 1997-8. The original paper was used for my lecture on Gandhi at North Bengal University in February 1998.

> another, how they murdered one another, is accurately recorded in history.[1]

The wars of the world, as recorded in history, are certainly not restricted to the kings, sometimes people also revolted against their kings. And the kings were not always alien, sometimes they were natives. The Russian and the Chinese revolts are the recent examples of revolts against the native rulers. The success of armed revolts, whether against the alien or the native rulers, does not mean that we should praise them. These revolts have led to a tremendous loss of both, human beings and human values. Human beings were dehumanised, life was devalued. Gandhi planned to win freedom for India, without dehumanising and devaluing Indians without involving them in an armed revolt. Though history, as defined above by Gandhi, has observed the success of violent revolts, it has never observed the success of a non-violent revolt, as least on such a vast scale as India. What Gandhi planned for the freedom of India was something out of the way, something quite unusual. He wished to remove the alien rule from India by following the non-violent civil resistance. He wished to create history. The revolutionaries of Russia and China, to whatever heights their names might have reached, never tried to create history; they simply followed the dictates of history. Therefore, they justified their revolutions as historically necessary. According to them, history has left for them no other alternative except to involve themselves in a large-scale violence, in a large-scale blood-shed. But Gandhi created history where no history existed. India won freedom without an armed revolt.

Originality of Gandhi has been questioned. Those who have hardly any academic or political achievements have tried to pull Gandhi down in all kinds of ways. It is pointed out by some of them that Gandhi was not original; he derived his views from Tolstoy, Ruskin, Thoreau, Emerson and so many other Western thinkers. Gandhi has mentioned these names.[2] To Tolstoy perhaps Gandhi owed more than to any other Western thinker. In South Africa a time came when he decided to give rural orientation to his agitation. The best

---

1. *Hind Swaraj, Collected Works of Mahatma Gandhi*, vol. X, p. 47. Gandhi is aware of the fact that history has neglected the subaltern classes.
2. *Ibid.*, Preface to *Indian Home Rule,* Johannesburg, 20 March, 1910, pp.188-9.

way was to start living in the countryside. He started living with his family, friends and followers in Tolstoy Farm. The fact that he named the farm after Tolstoy shows that he was influenced by Tolstoy more than by any other Western thinker. Of course, one would hesitate in describing Tolstoy as a Western thinker; Russia before revolution was not given the status of a Western power; the Russians were considered as the Asiatic barbarians. The Western character that the Russians acquired was the result of the barbaric acts of Stalin, not very different from the barbaric acts of the Americans against the red-Indians. Now Russia is a Western power like America. Coming to the question of Gandhi's originality of thinking, questioning the originality of Gandhi was not very unlike questioning the originality of Wittgenstein. It was pointed out by some critics of Wittgenstein that he was not an original thinker, he borrowed his ideas from others. In this context it is worthwhile to note Wittgenstein's reaction. He remarked,

> I believe that my originality (if that is the right word) is an originality belonging to the soil rather than to the seed. (Perhaps I have no seed of my own.) Sow a seed in my soil and it will grow differently than it would in any other soil.[3]

Perhaps Gandhi's originality too belonged to the soil rather than to the seed. Wittgenstein's soil was fertilised by the Austro-German culture with a Jewish touch. Gandhi's soil was fertilised by the 'ancient civilisation of India', as Gandhi himself accepted.[4] Non-violence that Gandhi adopted as a weapon of protest, is as old as Buddha and Mahavira, the two leading pre-Alexander philosophers of India. The sweep of these philosophers was so great on the Indian mind that the foreigners were enticed to invade India; they expected no resistance from the Indians. For 'non-violence' was equated with 'non-resistance'. Soon Alexander invaded and intruded into India, and the later Western invaders had a walk-over in India; there was hardly any resistance. Of course, the history books glorify our resistance, adding a note that the foreigners were ultimately successful. Gandhi picked up the weapon of non-violence from the ancient Indian civilisation, but polished it; its edges were sharpened. The weapon that enticed the Western invaders to India in our ancient times, was used by Gandhi to remove the Western invaders from India in our own times. Gandhi

3. *Culture and Value*, 1939-40, p. 36.
4. Preface to *Indian Home Rule*, p. 189.

converted the weapon of non-violence into the weapon of protest, weapon of resistance. It has no more remained a weapon of non-resistance. Thus, Gandhi clings to our past heritage, but in a new fashion, in an original fashion.

Consider the two situations, the situation of Gandhi's India and the situation of Tolstoy's Russia. India had the heritage of non-violence, Russia had no such heritage. Therefore, there were no takers of Tolstoy's ideas in Russia, the soil of Russia was not suitable for those ideas. Russia saw the bloody revolt in 1917, not to eliminate any alien ruler but to eliminate its own rulers. And what about Ruskin, Emerson and Thoreau? There is no doubt that they are well known, not only to the academicians and politicians of their own country, but also to the academicians and politicians of the outside world? Is their position different from the position of Tolstoy? Could their seed germinate in their own soil? Could they influence the masses of their own soil? Then the seed that they had, has certainly reached them from some alien soil. Should we rule out that India was the possible donor of that seed?

Even if we accept that Gandhi was influenced by some modern Western thinkers, he rejected outrightly the modern Western civilisation. And in this he was followed by Wittgenstein. What Gandhi said in his *Hind Swaraj* in 1909-10 is echoed in Wittgenstein in 1929-30 in the collection of his remarks on *Culture and Value*. Since it is only an echo, details of the original thought are missing. Of course, it is quite possible that Wittgenstein never read Gandhi — though he was a voracious reader and read all kinds of works — it may be sheer coincidence that their views were similar. Though a product of modern Western civilisation, Wittgenstein revolted against this civilisation. As he remarked,

> I have no sympathy for the current of European civilisation and do not understand its goals, if it has any.[5]

How to identify the European civilisation with which Wittgenstein had no sympathy? Referring to the main current of European and American civilisation Wittgenstein remarked,

> The spirit of this civilisation makes itself manifest in the industry, architecture and music of our time, in its fascism

5. *Culture and Value*, p. 6.

and socialism, and it is alien and uncongenial to the author[6].

Though the words are few — Wittgenstein always left to his readers to fill the details — he made his position quite clear. He wishes to alienate himself from the Euro-American civilisation of his time. This is for the reason that he rejects the major products of this civilisation, such products as industry, architecture and music. So also he rejects the political creeds of fascism and socialism which dominated the Europe of his time. If one goes deeper into the remarks of Wittgenstein, one would discover that the civilisation he opposed was the product of Industrial Revolution that occurred in Europe and brought to it what is called the modern age.

Industrial Revolution brought an end to the pre-modern age of Europe, the age which was distinctly different from the modern age of Europe. And the modernisation of Europe coincided with the enslavement of Afro-Asian countries, colonisation of Australia and America and the butchery of red and black skinned people. Paradoxically, this was also the age when the Europeans started talking about liberalism-liberal this and liberal that. So also there was much noise in Europe about liberty, humanity and international brotherhood, etc. But all these noises the Europeans made were for entertaining each other. They were not meant for entertaining the colonised races and tribes of the world. The colonised people had no liberty of any kind. (Incidentally, no Industrial Revolution occurred in India, therefore, India continued living in the pre-modern age. The age in which Europeans were modernising themselves in all kinds of ways, the Indians were trying to become natural slaves of the Europeans. Yet the academicians of free India started talking about post-modernity. Without ever entering into the modern age, we have got ourselves involved in the debate on post-modernism. Are not the Indians strange kind of people, and their academicians stranger than them? They have the capacity to reach the Mount Everest without ever touching the foot-hills of Himalayas. They have taken some sort of a quantum jump. Perhaps they are stimulated by globalisation and market economy. They are trying to produce stuff for the European consumers. The European consumer had undergone the process of modernisation, and he has now entered into the age of post-modernity. But how can the European consumers be enticed to buy goods on post-modernity from Indians who have never undergone

6. *Culture and Value*, p. 64.

the experience of modernity? Perhaps the Indian academicians wish to present something new to the Indian academic world, they find no novelty in the old Indian debates. So they brought the debate on post-modernism from Europe, and are replaying it in India, with the hope that they will be praised for their original research — quite a novel research indeed!).

Wittgenstein distinguishes 'civilisation' from 'culture'. He rejected the Euro-American civilisation because it lacked culture. He mused:

> Perhaps one day this civilisation will produce a culture. — when that happens there will be a real history of the discoveries of the eighteenth, nineteenth and twentieth centuries which will be deeply interesting.[7]

Obviously, culture cannot be generated with retrospective effect, therefore, the three centuries of Western civilisation that attracted Wittgenstein's attention would always remain evil, whatever happens in the future. It is better to forget the history of the discoveries made in these centuries, because those discoveries were misused; they devalued human life. However, if the civilisation of these centuries gives birth to a civilisation which has culture, then these centuries would have historical significance. Wittgenstein is moved by the idea that evil can also generate good. But future for Wittgenstein remains undecided. Whether the modern Western civilisation which has generated only evil since its genesis, can ever produce good? How can one predict about that? Wittgenstein rules out such a prediction. As he remarked,

> When we think about world's future, we always mean the destination it will reach if it keeps going in the direction we can see it going in now; it does not occur to us that its path is not a straight line but a curve, constantly changing direction.[8]

But this shows that the Western civilisation of the modern times cannot even be programmed to generate good. Our programming would fail, it may suddenly take a different direction than that which we have programmed it to take. Does it not mean that one who occupies his position in the modern Western civilisation is cursed to

7. *Culture and Value*, p. 64.
8. *Ibid.*, p. 3.

suffer? He cannot even dream of jumping out of this situation. Or rather, his dream cannot physically transport him to the dreamt *reality*. As Wittgenstein remarked

> You can't *build* clouds. And that is why the future you dream of never comes true.[9]

Wittgenstein finally remarked on this condition,

> we have no reason to think that the future will really develop in the way we dream now. For our dreams are covered in tinsel like paper hats and fancy dress costumes.[10]

Deprived of its glittering paper-hat and the fancy-dress costume, the future reality may even be uglier than the reality of the present. Wittgenstein's position is not very unlike the position of the fly in the fly-bottle. Fly-bottle in this case is the modern Euro-American civilisation.

> The fly flutters and flutters in the fly-glass, strikes against the walls, flutters further. How can it be brought to rest?[11]

Wittgenstein has certainly failed to liberate the fly from the fly-bottle. Western civilisation is bad enough, but it is horrible if one cannot jump out of it, if one wishes to do so.

Industrial revolution gave birth to the capitalist society, which was backed by industry, and industry on its own part was backed by science. Growth of industry in Europe led to the evolution of two distinct classes, the class of those who invested capital in the industry and the class of those who worked in the industry as its wage-earners. The profit motive led the capitalists to exploit the wage-earners. Without the state (the law enforcing agencies) helping the capitalists, it was impossible to exploit the wage-earners. Restrictions were not to be imposed on the quantum of profit on one's capital. So it was natural for the capitalists to support the rulers financially and otherwise. And the rulers on their own part helped the capitalists. Under whose shelter would the industrial wage-earner go? Ideologies

---

9. *Culture and Value*, p. 41.
10. *Ibid*.
11. Wittgenstein's Notes on 'Private Language and Sense-Data' in the *Private Language Argument*, ed. O.R. Jones, London, 1971.

to support the wage-earners were generated by the educated elite — Marx became the most reputed ideologue of his age. Socialism or communism became that ideology which came to the rescue of the wage-earners against the capitalists. This ideology is obviously a result of reaction to capitalism. But how did capitalism help the growth of fascism, say in Italy or Germany? The process is simple. If capitalism was to survive, the communism and socialism had to go. Mussolini attracted the capitalists of Italy by his organising armed gangs against communists and socialist, whom he considered foreign agents. Neither Marx nor Lenin nor their ideology was the product of Italy. Italy for Italians, was the slogan of Mussolini. Big landlords also came to back him; they were afraid of their lands being confiscated if communists came to power in Italy. Thus, Mussolini became the ruler of Italy, through a kind of 'bloodless revolution'; he was invited by the king on October 1922 to form the government. The case of Germany was only slightly different from that of Italy. Hitler narrowed down the definition of nationalism. In his Germany only the Aryans had a right to survive, the non-Aryans were to be eliminated. He too became the Chancellor of Germany on 30th January, 1933, merely with the help of spreading hatred against the Jews and the communists. He too became the Chancellor through a 'bloodless revolution'. Of course, much blood flowed in Germany, so also in Italy, for building up the images of Mussolini and Hitler. Nazis terrorised Germany, as the fascists of Italy terrorised Italy.

Other than the usual grounds, Wittgenstein had his own personal ground for rejecting fascism. Though he took birth in a Christian family and was given a decent Christian burial when he died on 29th August, 1951, at heart he was more Jew than Christian. This has to do something with his ancestors; two of his grandparents were Jews, so the Jew blood flowed into his veins. *Culture and Value* is full of remarks in favour of Jews. His views on religion remained quite ambiguous even to his friends and close associates. They doubted whether it would be right on their part to give Wittgenstein a Christian burial. Drury remembered his conversation with Wittgenstein on the occasion when Wittgenstein was quite appreciative of Tolstoy who gave Christian burial to his brother, in spite of the fact that Tolstoy was a stern critic of the Church. Following Tolstoy, Wittgenstein's friends decided to give him Christian burial. But Drury closes his *Conversation With Wittgenstein*, saying,

> I have been troubled ever since as to whether what we did then was right.[12]

It might have not been right, but it was certainly closer to what was right. For Wittgenstein's friends considered him three-quarters Aryan (Christian) and only one-quarter Jew. In his *Confession* to Fania Pascal, his teacher of Russian language from 1933 to 1935, Wittgenstein disclosed

> that he understood that most people who know him, including his friends, took him to be three-quarters Aryan and one-quarter Jewish. In fact the proportion was the reverse, and he had done nothing to prevent this misapprehension.[13]

It was Wittgenstein's duty, as a moral agent, to correct the impressions of his friends. He failed in his duty, so he confessed. Wittgenstein enjoyed puzzling his friends; duck-rabbit picture-puzzle became quite popular. Even his dead body did not stop puzzling his friends. His dead body was not very unlike his living body.

Wittgenstein's attitude towards fascism in 1933 is understandable. For it is in this very year that Hitler became the Chancellor of Germany, and Germany's process of Aryanisation started with greater vigour. Aryanisation meant the elimination of Jews and the socialists of all kinds. But it is quite difficult to understand Wittgenstein's equation of socialism with fascism, particularly when the socialists were the only force fighting against the growth of Nazism. And Wittgenstein came to reject socialism at a time when he was mastering Russian language to go to Russia for exploring the possibility of settling down there. His remark against socialism in 1933 clarifies one thing that he was not thinking of settling down in Russia because of its socialism. He rejected Marxism as a scientific view, and about Lenin he said,

> When Lenin intervened in 1917 his move was not scientific, it was *tragic*.[14]

Lenin was like the hero in a tragedy. Wittgenstein did accept the ability of Lenin, even of Stalin, to move the people around them, but

---

12. *Ludwig Wittgenstein: Personal Recollections*, ed. Rush Rhees, Oxford, 1981, p.184. M.O.'C Drury was a close friend of Wittgenstein.
13. *Ibid.*, p. 48.
14. *Ludwig Wittgenstein: Personal Recollections, Drury*, p. 223.

this would not convert them into scientists of any kind. The two Russians Wittgenstein liked most were neither politicians nor university professors, they were Tolstoy and Dostoievsky. Wittgenstein thought that these two

> really had something important to say about religion![15]

But Wittgenstein certainly did not plan to settle down in Russia for the sake of reading Tolstoy and Dostoievsky. They had been, and could be, read while one remained in Britain.

Wittgenstein's reason for planning to settle down in Russia was his nostalgia about the past. He wished to run away to the past, he disliked remaining in the modern Western civilisation. This civilisation appeared to him as the cancerous growth which would even destroy the human soul. Russia, in which he planned to live, appeared to him as some kind of copy of the image that he manufactured in his mind about the past. He considered Russians as the primitive people, far away from the infection of the modern Western civilisation. According to Fania Pascal, Russia offered a refuge to Wittgenstein

> when his desire to flee from civilised life gained upper hand.[16]

And this desire was not suppressed by the Russian Revolution of Stalin's purges. When asked to react on the subject of Russian Revolution, Wittgenstein

> had said that a revolution is gradual too. He had also said that Lenin had grabbed the wheel of a runaway car; this was no more than a cliché of those times.[17]

Nothing was serious to Wittgenstein in 1933 except his flight from the civilisation that he detested and denounced. All this shows that Wittgenstein was basically an escapist. He had no guts to fight the Western civilisation, except making a few remarks here and there in his works. Or rather, he had guts to fight only those battles in which there was a chance for him to win. His sister refers to the appointment of Wittgenstein as a professor in Cambridge after winning some battles. Since Wittgenstein

---

15. *Ludwig Wittgenstein: Personal Recollections,* p. 101.
16. *Ibid.,* Fania Pascal, p. 57.
17. *Ibid.*

> did not possess the usual qualifications, for example he had not graduated from university, a formal demand should have been satisfied, which in such a case requires a solemn examination before a board of professors; even the official dress of the candidates is exactly prescribed, in the custom of English universities. Ludwig absolutely refused to put on the costume and it was an honour for him that he was exempted from this, and his examination was reduced to having the professors ask Ludwig to explain passages from his book.[18]

Examiners in question were Russell and Moore, and the book was *Tractatus Logico-Philosophicus*. This book was prepared when he was serving in the Austrian army during 1916-18. He was captured by the Italians, but he succeeded in sending the copy of that book to Russell while he was in captivity. Russell was instrumental in getting the book published in 1921. The title was suggested by Moore. To become professor Wittgenstein had to win two battles, refusing to write examination and then refusing to wear the university costume. But battle against the whole modern Western civilisation was too big for him. So he preferred to flee from this civilisation.

Wittgenstein was a religious man. The Western civilisation appeared to him withdrawing man from God, from what is eternal. Not the issues concerning eternity, but frivolous issues concerning houses, cars, etc., are given importance. As he wrote in 1946

> It is very *remarkable* that we should be inclined to think of civilisation — houses, trees and cars, etc. — as separating man from his origins, from what is lofty and eternal, etc. Our civilised environment, along with its trees and plants, strikes us then as though it were cheaply wrapped in cellophane and isolated from everything great, from God.[19]

Science and industry that the civilisation uses can give only physical comfort, that too for a few. It fails to give any comfort to the *spiritual* being of man; it cannot give him peace of mind. As he further remarked,

---

18. *Ludwig Wittgenstein: Personal Recollections*, Hermine Wittgenstein, p. 11.
19. *Culture and Value*, p. 50.

> science and industry, having caused infinite misery in the process, will unite the world — I mean condense it into a single unit, though in which peace is the last thing that will find a home. Because science and industry do decide wars.[20]

Even misery is permissible in the process of development, but the development should not culminate in misery. The development of science and industry does not have any chance of bringing peace to humanity and removing its misery. Therefore, Wittgenstein thought of running away from the European science and industry.

As a matter of fact, Wittgenstein planned to run away from Europe, leaving everything about his past behind. He already gave away all his property to his sisters and brothers on the ground that a philosopher should not own any property. He belonged to a talented wealthy family of Austria. Lack of any property was compensated by his conquering the Anglo-American world of philosophy; many considered him as the First Philosopher of our age. There is no doubt that he was responsible for two powerful movements in philosophy. The movement of *Logical Empiricism* that he initiated, became popular through the instrumentality of Vienna-Circle philosophers. Later in England he gave birth to *language analysis* movement. But these movements he created, and the philosophy that he did, were products of the civilisation that he rejected. So there was no other alternative with Wittgenstein except giving up philosophy. He decided to take up some non-academic work in Russia, even the possibility of medical profession was contemplated. He had attraction for physical labour.

Wittgenstein succeeded in visiting Russia, his dream-land, in 1935. It seems that he succeeded in impressing the academicians of that country. It was reported that

> he had been offered a chair of philosophy at Kazan, the university where Tolstoy studied.[21]

At that time Wittgenstein had no job, yet he postponed the decision to take up the chair. After his coming back from Russia, he never threatened his friends that he would run away to Russia. It seems he returned to the Western civilisation, quite disillusioned about the

20. *Culture and Value*, p. 63.
21. *Personal Recollections*, Fania Pascal, p. 43.

civilisation of the past, which Russia represented for him. Once the fancy dress was removed, the civilisation of the past perhaps appeared more ugly than that of the present. Ultimately, he came back to England, and in due course became a professor in Cambridge.

Finally, it is worthwhile to point out that like Gandhi, Wittgenstein gave very high respect to manual labour. He might have imagined that Russia gave central place to manual labour. As Rush Rhees writes,

> He would have felt no sympathy with a regime whose aim was to do asway with manual labour or make it unnecessary. He would have found no joy in the thought that manual labour could be replaced by machines.[22]

Wittgenstein saw that manual labour became secondary in the Western world. Machine everywhere was taking the place of man. He imagined that Russia gave importance to man. It is only after reaching Russia that Wittgenstein realised that Stalin was trying to do away with manual labour. Gigantic machines were introduced, agricultural farms became mechanised. Manual labour was fastly losing its respect. Russia was trying to imitate the West, and wished to surpass it. The only difference between Russia and the Western world was that the profit generated by the machine in Russia was going to the state, whereas in the Western countries it went into the pockets of the capitalists. The labourer suffered under both, capitalism and communism.

Let us now consider Gandhi of the *Hind Swaraj*. Concerning the Western civilisation he remarked,

> If India copies England, it is my firm conviction that she will be ruined. — It is not due to any peculiar fault of the English people, but the condition is due to modern civilisation. It is a civilisation only in name. Under it the nations of Europe are becoming degraded and ruined day by day.[23]

Gandhi does not wish to give the status of civilisation to modern European civilisation. Wittgenstein comes closer to Gandhi by denying culture to such a civilisation, a civilisation deprived of culture is no civilisation. What kind of degradation has this civilisation brought to man or his society? What a modern man would describe as 'development and progress' Gandhi describes it as the fall of man

22. *Personal Recollections*, p. 228.
23. *Hind Swaraj*, p. 18.

and fall of his values. The so-called modern man is overloaded with all kinds of dresses, he uses guns and revolvers for his personal safety, travels by rail and aeroplanes uses motor-cars, uses heavy machines for farming, works in factories and so on. Consequently, suffers from all kinds of physical and mental illnesses. Machine has replaced man, his physical strength has gone and his mental strength is slowly dying out. Modern man is always at the mercy of doctors and hospitals. Factories, motors and the engines of all kinds have completely polluted the atmosphere and have brought into existence new kinds of diseases, beyond the reach of doctors to cure. Modern man is a sick man, both mentally and physically. The worst feature of this civilisation, according to Gandhi, is that it

> takes note neither of morality nor of religion. Its votaries calmly state that their business is not to teach religion. Some even consider it to be a superstitious growth.[24]

This was echoed by Wittgenstein as we have already seen. The modern civilisation has separated man from his origin, from God, from religion and morality. Fall of religion would lead to the fall of morality. It is religion that sustains moral values. And once the religious and moral values are gone, the cities would be converted into hell. As Gandhi observed,

> there would be gangs of thieves and robbers, prostitution and vice flourishing in them and that the poor men would be robbed by the rich men.[25]

Prior to the Industrial Revolution, prior to the civilisation that it brought into existence, according to Gandhi,

> Men worked in open air. . . . Now thousands of workmen meet together and for the sake of maintenance work in factories and mines. Their condition is worse than that of beasts. They are obliged to work — for the sake of millionaires.[26]

The moral degradation of man is complete once he is converted into a beast. Millions of these beasts work for a few millionaires. All this is

24. *Hind Swaraj*, p. 20.
25. *Ibid.*, p. 17
26. *Ibid.*, p. 20.

because of the Industrial Revolution. A villager migrated to the city in order to amass wealth, but he got only poverty, the poverty of a wage-earner. He was free, but was worse than a slave. Describing his slavery Gandhi writes,

> formerly, men were made slaves under physical compulsion. Now they are enslaved by temptation of money and of the luxuries that money can buy.[27]

It is the temptation of money that has converted a wage-earner into a slave.

Gandhi is unlike Wittgenstein in criticising the modern Western civilisation. A criticism has hardly any significance if one is unable to provide an alternative. Gandhi discovered the alternative in ancient Indian civilisation. He pleaded for the retention of this civilisation. This may lead one into thinking that Gandhi is some kind of Hindu revivalist. But revival is required of something which is dead, or at least half-dead. But the civilisation to which Gandhi refers is not a dead civilisation; it is the living civilisation of India. Indian civilisation is a rural civilisation. Only an insignificant part of India lives in cities. And we, in our villages, 'have managed', according to Gandhi,

> with the same kind of plough as existed thousands of years ago. We have retained the same kind of cottages that we had in former times and our indigenous education remains the same as before. . . . Each followed his own occupation or trade and charged a regulation fee.[28]

These self-dependent village communities are not some entities of the past. Gandhi saw them operating in his own time, and he became fascinated about them. Rejecting the city-oriented Western civilisation, Gandhi opted for the ancient Indian civilisation where the villages were given supreme importance. In its ancient times, according to Gandhi,

> this nation had courts, lawyers and doctors, but they were all within bounds . . . (they) did not rob people, they were considered people's dependents, not their masters.[29]

---

27. *Hind Swaraj.*
28. *Ibid.*, p. 37.
29. *Ibid.*

So Gandhi is certainly not an enemy of doctors, lawyers and courts, as is the general impression, he only wishes that they should not rob the people. A doctor or a lawyer should charge only a regulation fee like the fee given to a barber or a washerman. Though the teachers escaped Gandhi's attention, following him, they should be advised to behave like their ancient counterparts. They should not have a luxurious life. It is the desire for money and luxury that prohibits them to do any significant academic work. If they follow the life-style of Gandhi or Wittgenstein, India too can expect academic excellence.

Gandhi's nostalgia about the past was of a very different quality from Wittgenstein's nostalgia. Gandhi was directly in touch with reality, the past of which he romanticised. He observed the Indian villages and their communal life, and started praising the ancient India that led to their generation. But Wittgenstein was twice removed from the reality that he romanticised. Russia of his dreams was the Russia of stories written by Tolstoy and Dostoievasky. These Russians already romanticised Russia in their stories, and when they were read by Wittgenstein he added his own colour to them. Wittgenstein once remarked,

> The earlier culture will become a heap of rubble and finally a heap of ashes, but spirits will hover over the ashes.[30]

Gandhi got inspired by the spirit of the ancient Indian culture that has not yet become ashes. Wittgenstein was different, quite different. The spirit of the earlier culture of Austria did not inspire him, though he was born and brought up in Austria, and also served there, first as a school teacher, then as an army officer. So also the spirit of the earlier British culture did not inspire him, though he had university education in Britain and later became a university professor in one of the British universities. What inspired him was not the spirit of any dead culture, it was the living culture of Russia that inspired him. And the inspiration came not by any direct contact, but by contact through fictions on Russia.

Gandhi calls modern civilisation a disease. But, according to him, it is not 'an incurable disease'.[31] He discovered its cure in the *Swadeshi* movement of Bengal. He plunged into it whole-heartedly in order to convert it into an all-India movement. Of course, he was not wholly

30. *Culture and Value*, p. 3.

31. *Hind Swaraj*, p. 21.

satisfied with this movement, the movement required the extension of its boundaries. This movement encouraged 'the mill industry of Bombay' on the ground that the Bombay mills were *Swadeshi*, they were not in the bounded walls of Britain. Sharpening the edges of the *Swadeshi* movement, Gandhi suggested,

> If Bengal had proclaimed a boycott of *all* machine-made goods, it would have been much better.[32]

Some machine that has travelled from England to Bombay, does not mean that its product would be Indian, simply because Bombay is in India. The machines that were operating in Bombay mills were imported. It was as good, or as bad, as Manchester cloth made in India. Gandhi believed in original charisma, not in the charisma that is borrowed. Bombay mills were operating on borrowed charisma. The worst feature of this situation is that the misery associated with the machine was also borrowed.

To Gandhi Bombay mills presented a bad picture of Manchester in India. 'The workers in the mills of Bombay have become slaves'.[33] By multiplying mills in India we would be 'reproducing Manchester in India'.[34] Gandhi was not only against the cloth mills of Bombay, he was against all kinds of mills, against all kinds of heavy machines, against the machinery-craze. Once machinery-craze comes to India, the invasion of Industrial Revolution on India would not be avoided, which means that the invasion of capitalism on India would not be avoided. Gandhi disliked India turning into a capitalist country. As he remarked,

> It would be folly to assume that an Indian Rockefeller would be better than the American Rockefeller.[35]

But this does not mean that Gandhi had a favourable attitude towards socialism or communism. For machine played the same dominant role in socialism as in capitalism, so the wage-earners would continue to be exploited.

Gandhi was satisfied with the *Swadeshi* movement only when

32. *Hind Swaraj*, p. 58.
33. *Ibid*.
34. *Ibid*.
35. *Ibid*.

the *Charkha* was added to it. *Charkha* was Gandhi's national alternative to the Manchester cloth, alternative to the cloth-mills of Bombay, and above all, alternative to the Industrial Revolution. About the implications of *Charkha*, the present author has written elsewhere which may be quoted :

> Gandhi . . . wished the machine and industry to reach each and every house of an Indian village. He had the vision of a perfectly employed India. His vision was realised when his machine, the *Charkha*, reached the villages of India. Most of the villages of India became big industrial centres, and most of the householders of these villages became industrialists. This was Gandhi's Industrial Revolution, quite unlike the Industrial Revolution that occurred in Europe. Man was dwarfed by the big industries of Europe. But man kept his dignity with the small machine of Gandhi. Invention of big machine led to unemployment, and unemployment led to the underworld of criminals in the cities and hunger and famine in the countryside.[36]

Gandhi only discouraged the craze for the big power-run machines. He wished Indians to develop a craze for small, hand-operated machines, *Charkha* being one of them. Gandhi's machine did not do away with the manual labour or made it unnecessary. Gandhi satisfied the wishes of Wittgenstein long before Wittgenstein expressed those wishes. Gandhi was interested in the welfare of the masses, not the welfare of a few chosen ones. He wished the masses of India to have a comfortable life, rather than to have a super-comfortable life for a few people. Both capitalism and communism, history has already proved, are no good alternatives. To avoid suffering under capitalism, the people jumped into communism. Continuity of suffering under communism again brought them back to capitalism. They forgot their earlier suffering, and are preparing to suffer afresh. It does not occur to people that capitalist and communism are two different faces of the same coin. Gandhi made an attempt to provide a fresh alternative, but neither the capitalists nor the communists accept it. His voice is not allowed to be heard.

Gandhi attacked not only the goods produced by the European industry, he also attacked the goods produced by the academic industry

---

36. See 'Historiography of Indian Civilization', *JICPR*, June, 1996.

of Europe. Though not a professional historian, Gandhi was quite well aware of the kind of history that has been written in the West. Though the English were trying to bring the European civilisation to India, they were failing. Failing, because they were unable to uproot the hold of the ancient Indian civilisation. German scholars came out to help their blood-brothers the English. Max-Muller, like Karl Marx, started operating from England. He tried to show that the Aryans and their gods did not take their birth on the banks of the rivers Sindhu and Sarasvati, they took their birth in Central Asia. Later the British scholars further shifted their original home to East Europe. How could the Aryans be Asiatic? They had to be Europeans, for all good things are produced only in Europe. Asia only imports them. Gandhi attacked the German scholars without naming them. When pointed out that such ordinary items of our daily use as matches, pins and glassware are imported from Europe to India, Gandhi remarked,

> Indeed, our gods even are made in Germany. What need, then, to speak of matches, pins and glassware.[37]

Gandhi preferred the *Swadeshi* goods (gods included) to *Videshi* (foreign) goods. While attacking the academic industry of the West, Gandhi has not spared the Indian academicians who are functioning under the hypnotic influence of the West. Commenting on the historians of the West, Gandhi remarked,

> They have a habit of writing history; they pretend to study the manners and customs of all peoples. . . .They write about their researches in most laudatory terms and hypnotise us into believing them. We in our ignorance then fall at their feet.[38]

Long ago when the Germans started manufacturing the Indian gods, we fell at the feet of the European historiographers. Since then we have not left our hold over those feet, though India is celebrating its fiftieth year of freedom from the foreign rule. Our hypnotic state continues, perhaps because we do not wish to be dehypnotised. It is not only history, the West has captured almost all our academic

---

37. *Hind Swaraj*, p. 59.
38. *Ibid.*, p. 31.

disciplines. Our condition is not very unlike the condition of Bombay mills, producing the Manchester cloth in India.

If one studies some remarks of Wittgenstein collected in *Culture and Value* and Gandhi's *Hind Swaraj* one would feel that Wittgenstein was a child of Gandhian thinking — but only a child. (May be because he never read Gandhi.) Wittgenstein lacked the courage, either of Gandhi or of Marx to change the miserable world in which he lived. He could think only in terms of escaping from the world that he disliked. What else can be expected from a university professor of philosophy? Of course, he was much above the ordinary professors. He at least thought about some serious issues concerning public life. Most of them pass their whole life in writing and talking about such insignificant issues as the issues of 'sense-data' and the verb 'to be'. Most insignificant issues of life assume the form of serious philosophical issues. Wittgenstein was at least on some occasions free from these insignificant issues.

After Gandhi's murder India decided to bring the Industrial Revolution, not the kind of revolution that was contemplated by Gandhi but the kind of revolution that occurred in Europe and brought to it the modern age. (Of course, the Indian academicians of our time find no connection between the Industrial Revolution and the modern age. According to them, India was modern even when it was not in a position to produce such ordinary items of use as matches and pins.) The days when India became free, the world was divided into two diverse camps, the camp of the capitalists and the camp of the socialists. Capitalism and socialism are two diverse manifestations of the Industrial Revolution. The rulers of free India decided to bring both capitalism and social to India. Therefore, they divided the Indian economy into two sectors, private sector and public sector. Thus, Gandhi had also to suffer his ideological death. He rejected all the three, capitalism, socialism and their industry.

The failure of mixed economy has led us to invite multinational companies. The pre-independence scene is reviving. Are we heading towards another round of slavery? If another round of slavery, we may not feel so bad about it. Not because we had so many rounds of slavery, therefore, we got acclimatised to it, but because an idiomatic change may occur to 'slavery'. 'Capitalist economy' is now called 'market economy', so our reactions have changed. May be slavery also acquires a new name.

2

Speech and Silence in Western Philosophy

A Critique of Wittgenstein from an Indian Point of View

Srinivasa Rao

ONE characteristic feature of some schools of Indian philosophy that distinguishes it from all Western schools of philosophy is the recognition of both thought and the absence of thought, both language and the absence of language or, in short, both speech and silence as facts having their own distinct significance. Thought and speech and also silence can be viewed in two distinct ways. Thought and speech can be viewed as positive entities and silence as their mere absence. Or, silence may not be viewed as the mere absence of thought and speech but as a special entity of its own kind. These two views are quite different since they slice reality in radically different ways.

In Indian philosophy we come across both these types of views. The Nyaya school, for example, regards silence as mere absence of speech. Silence is neither itself an entity not does it reveal any other positive entity. But the Advaita school chooses to regard silence as the most eloquent revelation of reality. All Western schools of philosophy follow the Nyaya way of thinking. They do not attach any positive or metaphysical significance to silence. Since philosophers in general argue a great deal and the Naiyayikas are not an exception to this, it appears very natural on their part to regard silence as the inability to argue any further. Silence is, thus, the complete failure or absence of thought and speech.

In the schools that do not attach any fundamental or special significance to silence, it is assumed that all reality is revealed through thought and speech. Silence prevails only when there is nothing to be revealed. Such schools are usually very analytical and their analysis of thought and language is done with great care and finesse. I think that while their analysis is unquestionably rigorous, exhaustive and subtle, it is also uniformly and consistently quasi-phenomenological. I wish to point out here that it is for want of a better term that I have chosen the expression 'quasi-phenomenological'. By this term I do *not* at all mean an analysis that looks as though it is phenomenological, but is not really one. I mean by it an analysis that is phenomenological, but is not fully so. It stops at a particular point or level and does not go all the way up or down to wherever the analysis may take. 'Quasi' should not be taken to mean that there is something fake about the phenomenologicality of the analysis; it only means that the analysis is not thoroughgoing

I also do not mean here by the term 'phenomenological' anything typically Husserlian — an exercise aiming at the attainment of transcendental essences. For me, an analysis is phenomenological when it does not ignore anything that is there already. It is an analysis that does not ignore the totality of experience in order to arrive at rigorous clarity regarding some part or aspect of experience. Therefore, in a proper phenomenological analysis, the experiencing consciousness, whatever is experienced by that consciousness and whatever is the outcome of that experience or of any analysis of that experience all have equal weightage and value and no one of them has any primacy. In an analysis that is fully phenomenological, there is nothing that is left out; there is also nothing that is distinctly preferred and valued.

In contrast to the above, a quasi-phenomenological analysis is weighted in favour of some element or other of totality. An overriding primacy is accorded to some particular element in the totality and the whole analysis proceeds with this primacy intact throughout. For example, primacy may be accorded to thought as exhibited by linguistic expressions or to entities that are supposed to be revealed by those linguistic expressions. In that case it can be argued either that we know something about the nature of the world only by the analysis of the language employed by us in talking about it or that it is the nature of the things in the world that somehow determines the structures and patterns of our thoughts and linguistic expressions.

Although either of the above approaches in themselves would

yield valuable insights, yet neither of them is accurate to a degree. The first view, for example, ignores the fact that we can know something about the nature of the world from an analysis of language only because those linguistic expressions are of someone who *already* experiences the world. The second view, for instance, does not take into account the fact that there are no 'pure objects' out there in the universe that make sense independently of thought and language. In so far as the totality of experience is ignored by these types of analysis, they are not fully phenomenological in nature.

I wish to argue in the rest of this paper that the philosophical analysis adopted by Wittgenstein was more phenomenological than linguistic in character. But, this phenomenological character appears to be neither typically Husserlian nor distinctly Indian. It goes far from the Husserlian kind, but does not come close enough to the Indian kind of analysis that we find, for example, in the *Mandukya Upanishad* and the Advaitic *Karikas* thereon by Gaudapada or the Buddhist *Madhyanta Vibhaga Shastra* of Asanga.

The *Tractatus* is studied with quite a few startling phenomenological discoveries and the most prominent among them is the depiction of how

> a gramophone record, the musical idea, the written notes and the sound waves all stand to one another in the same internal relation of depicting that holds between language and the world (4.014).

No amount of pure linguistic analysis of statements concerning music, nor musical analysis of the written notes of music nor any amount of physical analysis of the nature of sound waves would lead to the idea of how a black gramophone disc, a series of marks made on paper and a series of sounds produced by musical instruments which are all as diverse in nature as anything in the universe can be, picture the very *same* music by virtue of a shared 'logical form'. It is a fascinating phenomenological discovery. The idea that this logical form can only be revealed by language but not literally expressed by it is yet another phenomenological discovery.

At the end of the *Tractatus* Wittgenstein observes that

> there are indeed things that cannot be put into words. They *make themselves manifest*. They are what is mystical

> (6.522, emphasis in the text).

Shortly afterwards, in making his concluding remark

> What we cannot speak about we must consign to silence (7)

he is consigning the 'mystical' into the realm of silence. He does not attempt, like in the Indian tradition, to speak about the mystical, to speak about the unspeakable. This is because he has all along believed that

> the correct method is . . . to say nothing except what can be said, i.e., propositions of natural science . . . (6.53)

and that

> the limits of my *language* mean the limits of *my* world (5.62, emphasis in the text).

It is also to be noted that though the English translation of the original German text of passage 7 of the *Tractatus* contains the substantive 'silence', the original German text contains only a verb form 'schweigen' which means 'to be silent' which is just a synonym for 'not speaking'. Thus, there is only speech or its absence. Here, speech is an entity but its absence is not an entity. Therefore, only what remains within the confines of speech comes within the realm of knowledge.

This position is strikingly similar to the Naiyayika who identities speakability with knowability. According to him, whatever can be known can also be put into words. There is nothing that can be known and is yet inexpressible in language. Therefore, silence is a negative condition indicative of the inability to think and to speak out. Silence has no real significance of its own. Like zero in arithmetic which stands for the absence of any quantity, silence stands for the absence of any speech or thought. There is no analysis of the notion of silence in Nyaya. Likewise, after noting that whatever cannot be spoken about should be consigned to silence, Wittgenstein does not ask the further question: 'What is this silence?' That is because silence is not a separate realm populated by its own peculiar objects but it is just the outermost limit or boundary of language. That is as far as language can go, and *there is no going any further*. There is no way of analysing what lies beyond language, even if there is any such thing at all. The speaker is reducible to what he speaks and the analysis of speech is, therefore, inclusive of an analysis of the speaker. When there is no speech, there is no speaker either. There is no speaker who does not speak. Therefore, with the analysis of speech, everything stands analysed and understood. This very claim to completeness of analysis makes it a case of quasi-phenomenological analysis.

The focus of the *Tractatus* is so much on language that while the concept of thinking or thought figures in it at quite a few places, the concept of consciousness never figures in it. It appears that when Wittgenstein realised that language is not just about what we can speak of or that it is not a mere tool for describing the world, he continued with the kind of phenomenological analysis he had already carried out in the *Tractatus* but the analysis still very much continued to be quasi-phenomenological.

The point that Wittgenstein's phenomenological analysis is not a Husserlian search for essences is borne out brilliantly in the *Investigations* when he proposes his famous analysis of 'game' (1.66-67). What Wittgenstein discovers here is that all those activities called 'games' have *no* common essence by virtue of which they all come to be called games. But still, his analysis remains distinctly quasi-phenomenological throughout his work. I wish to argue for this point on the basis of a very significant remark by him in the *Remarks on the Philosophy of Psychology* which runs as follows:

> A man can pretend to be unconscious. But *conscious?* (Volume I, Remark 931, page 165e, emphasis in the text).

The next two remarks go into the questions arising out of situations in which certain utterances that may be made while being awake, while dreaming and while being unconscious. The remark quoted above obviously suggests that while it is perfectly possible for a man to pretend to be unconscious, it is not possible for anyone to *pretend* to be *conscious*. This is no doubt a remarkable phenomenological discovery. But the interesting question that arises here is: why is it impossible *even to pretend* to be conscious?

If we examine the language-game of pretending, and also the largely pretentious world in which we live, we find that virtually anything can be pretended. It is possible for me to pretend to be what I am not and also pretend to be what I cannot even be. I am not, and also I cannot be, another person but still I can pretend to be another person. I cannot be anyone except myself but still under certain favourable circumstances I can pretend to be not myself. I can pretend to be thinking when I am not thinking, pretend to be loving when I am not in love and pretend to understand something when I am not really understanding anything. I can pretend to be asleep or unconscious when I am awake or conscious. But, whatever extensive varieties of pretensions I may be capable of, I cannot pretend to be *conscious*. Why? The only reason seems to be that a person cannot pretend to be what he *already and always is*. I am already, and in some sense, always conscious and, hence, I cannot pretend to be conscious.

Even when I am deeply asleep and am not conscious of anything around me in the usual way, it is only one form of consciousness I seem to lack in that state, viz., the consciousness of the objects around me and *not* consciousness as such. If deep sleep is truly a total and complete *absence* of any form of consciousness as such, the recollection after waking up that one had slept deeply should be impossible. *Who* is it that is now recollecting that he had slept deeply? Unless the *he* who recollects and the *he* who had slept deeply are one and the same, the recollection makes no sense. Nobody goes into deep sleep, wakes up later on and wonders *who* he is. When I move from the waking state to the state of deep sleep, if there is a true and complete break and all consciousness disappears completely, then how is it that my sense of self-identity is not affected at all by this complete break?

These questions do not arise if it is admitted that whatever any person may be or believe himself to be, he is in fact — always and everywhere — a manifestation of consciousness which is why it is not possible for anyone to *pretend* to be conscious. This becomes evident only upon a full phenomenological analysis of any form of human experience. *That* there is such consciousness is certain, but *what* it is, is beyond all speech and thought. All thought and speech issue forth only from this consciousness whose existence is the precondition for all speech and thought. No speech and thought can *express* what this consciousness is because they themselves are expressed through this consciousness. That is where we encounter silence.

3

Language-game, Grounding and the Metaphysics of Meaning

Ahmed Nizar

1

The idea of what a sentence communicates when a speaker utters and a hearer comprehends its sounds very familiar and, therefore, reasonable, but a bit confounding too. It is familiar because the 'meaning' of an utterance can, often, quite reasonably be mentioned in common parlance. It is confounding because it posits 'meaning' apart from the sentence. This problem of meaning kept philosophers who were not themselves friends of metaphysics busy with the putative work of representing 'meaning' theoretically. It is the contention of this paper that Wittgenstein's famous solution of considering, instead, the practice with which that specific utterance is linked has exposed the otioseness of such efforts. This linkage need not be the context in which the utterance is made, though it is true that context makes the utterance relevant or sensible. It is also true that the utterance, 'The earth is round', if properly understood, will be made only in appropriate contexts. But its making sense does not depend on any of these contexts. 'We are satisfied that the earth is round.'[1] '. . . . We have definitively ascertained that it is round.'[2] Making sense of this utterance in appropriate contexts implies that the language-game to which it belongs is familiar to the utterer or the hearer. This utterance is a knowledge claim — hence, its status as a statement or proposition — and normally will have a back-up of verification

1. Wittgenstein, *On Certainty* (299).

2. *Ibid.*, 291.

procedure or system of verification. Wittgenstein says,

> The *truth* of my statements is the test of *my understanding* of these statements.[3]

But where does this *truth* of . . . belong to? To 'our frame of reference'. That is, the propositional status of an utterance derives from its role in a specific language-game.[4]

2

> We are quite sure of it does not mean just that every single person is certain of it, but that we belong to a community which is bound together by science and education.[5]

That is, one's capacity to use this sentence in appropriate contexts derives from one's being familiarised with a language game in which a large number of utterances are to be understood in their interconnectedness. That is, again, to understand any one such utterance in isolation from the language-game to which it properly belongs is to understand nothing. This particular language-game, for instance, is governed by the logic of 'knowing' which, in turn, is based on a whole system of verification.

> . . . This system is something that a human being acquires by means of observation and instruction.[6]

Wittgenstein uses 'acquires' instead of 'learns' (though he was not quite consistent with this use). This is because the logic of a language-game is not learned, that is, it is not mastered, but gained by a person as she becomes a part of a specific form of life activities, in course of which she observes what was going on and also gets instructed by others as to how to go on with certain kinds of activities. Many things we acquire in life are not things we are taught, but things of the sort we are expected to do, asked to do, or of the habit of doing, and in which we get instructions.

---

3. *On Certainty*, 80.
4. "What counts as an adequate test of a statement belongs to logic. It belongs to our frame of reference" (82). "The truth of certain empirical propositional belongs to our frame of reference" (83).
5. *Ibid.*, 298.
6. *Ibid.*, 279.

3

The term 'instruction' is significant. Under instruction, one is not perfectly free to learn what was being given. This learning has to follow a path acceptable to the instructors who are experienced actors in the field. When one observes under, or guided by, instruction it is not always likely that one is bound to see things as they are given. Because things as they are given are partly as they are instructed to be. Therefore, observation is laden with instructions. The concept of learning is inadequate here because, it presupposes a subject who is detachable and detached from what is learned and who is predisposed to learn, i.e., an agent who is instrumentally related to learning and what is learned. Being acquainted with a system of procedure is not comparable to this. In place of a pre-constituted subject we find here a subject newly constituted or reconstituted. If we persist in using the word 'learning', we might also add that a subject is constituted as it learns. Thus, to be actively engaged in a language game is to become a subject of a certain sort.

4

Wittgenstein also speaks of a world-picture described in terms of propositions of the sort in question which might form part of a mythology.[7] Word-picture is the background against which we distinguish between true and false.[8] On the one hand, single proposition that forms part of this mythology cannot be held to be 'agreeing with reality', and, for that reason, cannot be one which we can hold fast to.[9] On the other hand, it is mythology because the question of its correctness or incorrectness cannot be raised.[10] These propositions behave like rules, not explicit ones, and are 'learned purely practically'.[11] If it is true that what we hold fast to 'is not one proposition but a nest of propositions', then the ground for any single empirical proposition does not lie in its correspondence with the world but in the ways in which their interconnectedness is established.

---

7. *On Certainty*, 95.
8. *Ibid*., 95. Wittgenstein says, "Really 'The proposition is either true or false' only means that it must be possible to decide for or against it. But this does not say what the ground for such a decision is like (200).
9. *Ibid*., 215, 225.
10. *Ibid*., 94.
11. *Ibid*., 95.

This is the point of the remark made in the following passage:

> 204. Giving grounds, however, justifying the evidence, comes to an end; — but the end is not certain proposition's striking us immediately true, i.e., it is not a kind of *seeing* on our part; it is our *acting*, which lies at the bottom of the language-game.[12]

At the *bottom* of a language-game is our acting, i.e., by means of which propositions get their interconnectedness. Why at the bottom? Because, the ground here is not something that normally comes to the surface. In other words, the utterances we make carry along with them a world-picture the whole of which cannot be brought to the su.face at once. What gives significance to our utterances is not what happens at the surface level whether or not we actually involve in some activities at that level. These activities or context can make the utterances relevant or irrelevant, but cannot provide them a ground. The ground is a way of acting, a *practice*, or a 'form of life'. (Wittgenstein tried his best to do away with the notion of form of life.) The way of acting itself is without foundation.[13] That is, the *bottom* of the language-game is not grounded, even when facts are 'fused into the foundations of our language-game'.[14]

> 559. You must bear in mind that the language-game is so to say something unpredictable. I mean: it is not based on grounds. It is not reasonable (or unreasonable). It is there-like our life.[15]

The diffuseness of the foundation, or the foundationlessness of the foundation, of human language-games is one among many ideas Wittgenstein tried to work out in his last major work. *Philosophical Investigations* (*PI*) seemed to have just provided a tool for identifying the ground for our speaking activity which misled many philosophers to apply 'ordinary language analysis' to get rid of philosophical problems. The idea of the groundlessness of the ground is an outcome

---

12. Ludwig Wittgenstein, *O.C*, Basil Blackwell, Oxford, 1977, p. 28.
13. "... But the end is not an ungrounded presupposition: it is an ungrounded way of acting" (110).
14. *Ibid.*, 558.
15. *Op.cit.*, p. 73.

of Wittgenstein's own attempt to apply the notion of langugage-game to the problem of (Moore's) proof of the external world. Though this idea underlay many of the observations in *PI*, the main thrust of the work did not permit a reading in terms of this.[16] In *On Certainty*, however, Wittgenstein brought himself up against the groundlessness of the ground he often relied upon.

5

More light could be cast on the ground by considering how the practice on which a language-game is grounded is learned or changes. Recall that Wittgenstein uses the word 'acquires' instead of 'learns'. (" . . . I intentionally do not say 'learns'. 279) and also that observation and instruction play crucial roles in acquisition. He suggests that there is a deep structure of convictions in which all our arguments find their life (103-5). But the strength of the system or structure lies in our being subjected to instructions as we intellectually grow. It may be imagined that it is experience which teaches us to judge correctly.[17] But Wittgenstein's following passage proves to be the last nail in such an imagination's coffin :

> . . . We may derive it from experience, but experience does not direct us to drive anything from experience. If it is the ground of our judging like this, and not just the cause, still we do not have a ground for seeing this in turn as a ground. (130)

---

16. " . . . For note: here grounds are not propositions which logically imply what is believed". (481) "482. We are misled by this way of putting it: "This is a good ground, for it makes the occurrence of the event probable". That is as if we had asserted something further about the ground, which justified it as a ground; whereas to say that this ground makes the occurrence probable is to say nothing except that this ground comes up to a particular standard of good grounds — but the standard has no grounds!" "483. Justification by experience comes to an end. If it did not it would not be justification." In *Philosophical Investigations*, Basil Blackwell, Oxford, 1976, p. 136.

17. "274. . . . Experience can be said to teach us these propositions. However, it does not teach us them in isolation: rather, it teaches us a host of interdependent propositions . . . " Again, 275, "If experience is the ground of our certainty, then naturally it is past experience.

    It is not for example just my experience, but other people's, that I get knowledge from . . . "*O.C*, pp. 34-5.

Experience is neither the ground for nor the outstanding success of our game of judging.[18] The case of the meaning of words runs parallel to this :

> 126. I am not more certain of the meaning of my words than I am of certain judgments. Can I doubt that this color is called "blue"? (My) doubts form a system.

The role of rules in this is also dubious. We learn to use words 'meaningfully' not through rules, but are taught, as children, to use them in their interconnection with other words. We are taught to make sense in such and such way ; the interconnectedness of these senses form a system : this is what we practice. Rules do not emerge as we practice in a given manner, i.e., learning the rules is not required; acting in conformity with a practice is sufficient and this may be according to a rule.[19]

Language-game changes with time.

> 617. Certain events would put me into a position in which I could not go on with the old language-game any further. In which I was torn away from the *sureness* of the game.

Does this suggest that the regularity or continuity of the events determines how we employ words and, therefore, their meaning? Given such a situation, Wittgenstein asks, with respect to judgements,

> why, would it be *unthinkable* that I should stay in the saddle however much the facts bucked?[20]

One might stay in the saddle, but that would be extraordinary. When language-games change, it implies a change in the practice to which they are bound. It brings about a change in the concepts and thereby a change in the employment of words.

Clearly, Wittgenstein speaks of 'natural events' and 'facts' (may

---

18. "131. No, experience is not the ground for our game of judging. Nor is its outstanding success". *O.C.*, p. 19.
19. " . . . A meaning of a word is a kind of employment of it. For It is what we learn when the word is incorporated into our language. "62. That is why there exists a correspondence between the concepts 'rule' and 'meaning'." See also 44, 45, 46, 47, 139, 140 and 144 in Wittgenstein's *On Certainty*.
20. *O.C.*, 616.

I add here, 'social events' and 'social facts'?) as if he confronts them without the mediation of a frame of reference, i.e., identification of events and facts unmediated by language-games, without reference to a system of verification, is possible.[21] But he never meant these 'events' or 'facts' to be constituting an outside of the world-picture we carry or inaccessible to the bottom of our language-game. He finds himself very much inside the language-game and admits to being brought up intellectually in a certain fashion. It is as an insider that he wants to say that the ground on which this language-game is supposed to be raised cannot be shown to be grounded. The following passages will seal off any doubt about his intention :

> 608. Is it wrong for me to be guided in my actions by propositions of physics? Am I to say I have no good ground for doing so? Isn't precisely this what we call a 'good ground'?
>
> 609. Supposing we met people who did not regard that as a telling reason. Now, how do we imagine this? Instead of the physicist, they consult an oracle. (And for that we consider them primitive.) Is it wrong for them to consult an oracle and be guided by it? — If we call this "wrong" aren't we using our language-game as a base from which to *combat* theirs?
>
> 610. And are we right or wrong to combat it? Of course there are all sorts of slogans which will be used to support our proceedings.
>
> 612. I said I would 'combat' the other man,— but wouldn't I give him *reasons*? Certainly; but how far do they go? At the end of reasons comes persuasion. (Think what happens when missionaries convert natives.)

6

A theory of meaning such as having the project of constructing for a given language a meaning-theory which claims to give the meaning

---

21. " 63. If we imagine the facts otherwise than as they are, certain language-games lose some of their importance, while others become important. And in this way there is an alteration — a gradual one — in the use of the vocabulary of a language." *O.C.*, p. 10. Also, "617. . . . Indeed, doesn't →

of each and every sentence of that language cannot be said to have engaged in a reasonable project. In this section and the next it will be argued that if we go by a Wittgensteinian approach to understanding the working of language such a project is misconceived. A question can be reasonably raised whether a theory of meaning can be constructed as a set of propositions, which a native speaker is represented to have been guided by in understanding utterances in her language.[22] A propositional knowledge of any kind will fall short of representing the native speaker's ability. What philosophers expect from such a theory of meaning is a device to interpret any sentence of a given language. Such an interpretation in terms of a propositional knowledge will be inadequate because a native speaker still would have understood it in a way characteristically different from its theoretical representation. That is, there might be some aspects of her language mastery which escaped a representation of them in propositional terms. As section 4 of this paper shows, an utterance made in a given context is normally bound to a language-game in making sense. It is bound to a language-game along with a number of others in conjunction with which it describes the language-game. Since it is a way of acting, a practice, which binds and make them significant together as a group, any difficulty in determining the character of the practice in question will be carried over to the description of the language-game. A description of a language-game will not be adequate until one makes this description thoroughly phenomenological which is physically unattainable. A full account of the language-game is ideally retrievable but not practically. Since any single utterance's sense is practically — not deductively — linked to the sense of other utterances — that is, through a way of acting — whereby it takes part in the description of the language-game, any loophole in the exact reconstruction of this practice will render the sense of the utterance indetermiante. In fact, a language-game is a

→ it seem obvious that the possibility of a language-game is conditioned by certain facts?", *Ibid*., p. 82.

22. The ambition of such a theory is most vividly expressed by Dummett. He says, "A theory of meaning will, then, represent the practical ability possessed by a speaker as consisting in his grasp of a set of propositions; Since the speaker derives his understanding of a sentence from the meanings of its component words, these propositions will most naturally from a deductively connected system.û Dummett, *What is a Theory of Meaning (II)*, p.70, in G. Evans and McDowell, J., ed., *Truth and Meaning,* Clarendon, Oxford, 1976.

projection of a specific practice of which speaking activity is a proper part. Language-game, so to say, speaks of the 'logic' of this practice as a whole, but which is unpredictable and non-reasonable and, therefore, not reducible to propositional terms. The statements or propositions which we come to understand through observation and instruction proceed *en bloc* as a world-picture and behave like rules of the game. As the practice that is at the bottom of the language-game is distanced from us by the manner in which we inherit it, our relation to these statements are mythological.[23] This is the point at which judgments become principles of judgements and empirical propositions turn out to be methodological propositions.[24] Now, to give the meaning of such propositions, should we elicit them as 'rules' in which case to understand any one of them is to understand them as part of this mythology? Or should we 'explain their meaning' by describing the language-game to which they are bound and which is "learned purely practically, without learning any explicit rules."[25]? The second alternative will not end up in a theory of meaning with the ambition mentioned above. Moreover, why should one say that describing a language-game — if at all one succeeds in it is a theoretical representation of any proposition in question? The logic of language-game also exposes certain weakness in the imagining of the task of a theory of meaning. It is supposed in some versions of the theory of meaning that

> . . . since the speaker derives his understanding of a sentence from the meanings of its component words, these propositions will most naturally form a deductively connected system.[26]

Here, the weakness lies in assuming the *understanding* of sentences to be somehow related to the meanings of its component words. If a theory of meaning is to be a theory of understanding its propositions cannot be conceived of as forming a deductively connected system. Though the language-games bind uses of both words and sentences to a practice or a set of practices, the criteria for their uses are not

---

23. *O.C*, 94-9.
24. *Ibid.*, 124.
25. *Ibid.*, 95.
26. Michael Dummett, *op. cit.*, p. 70. Read this in continuation with the earlier quote from Dummett. By propositions here is meant those make up theoretical representation.

identical. What is minimally required of words for them to be used to make sense is their functioning in linguistic acts. But this is not what is minimally required of a sentence to make sense. For that we should know what point there is in acting linguistically. This is to ask question, to command, to assert, to plead, etc. This must be identified as the reason why a theory of meaning is not the same as a theory of understanding. In other words, the question is what it is to act linguistically (in the specified way). What guides a speaker in activities in which speaking is embedded is not a knowledge of sense of the sentences but a knowledge which is linked with the practices of stating facts, commanding, obeying, asking, etc. If the native speaker is capable of generating sentences and making sense of sentences heard without any expectation of the situation that is meant to be obtained, then the notion of meaning that may be applicable to such contexts has to be separated from that of understanding. For understanding, a notion of criterial satisfaction would be central. Understanding, then, lies in the knowledge of the satisfaction of the criteria accepted by the members of the community of speakers. This knowledge is, among other things, a knowledge about how to go about in a social world to which the native speaker and the language belong. This points to the socio-historical dependency of criteria. If criteria differ sharply among a community of speakers in a given period then there will be a set of sentences which are undetermined with respect to the question what it is to understand those sentences. Therefore, while it is true that

> The ascription to him (i.e., to the native speaker) of a grasp of the axioms governing the words is a means of representing his derivation of the meaning of each sentence from the meanings of its component words[27],

the same will not represent his understanding. In fact, the notions of

---

27. M. Dummett, *op. cit*. But when he adds, " . . . but his knowledge of the axioms need not be manifested in anything but the employment of the sentences" it appears like a rider and confuses his view. It is a sufficient condition for the employment of the sentence that one understands it. Therefore, if one employs a sentence, then according to the earlier quote, it must be by deriving its meaning from the meaning of its component words. Yet to understand that sentence this derivation of meaning is not sufficient! This is because, you can employ a sentence even when you do not understand that sentence. Despite this the meaning of that sentence in the derivative sense can be given!

meaning of words and meaning of sentences look unproblematic only when we operate with concept like referring and *signifying.*[28] To say that a word signifies something is to say nothing.[29]

As for the supposed meaning of a sentence it will be difficult to determine what is required for grasping it as sharply distinct from what is required for the grasp of the form of the sentence. Let us say there is specific set of procedures to determine the meaning of the utterances. If so, one should ask how this is applied before a language is mastered and after it is mastered. Both presuppose a knowledge of a certain act as a precondition of interpreting these utterances. One such act is making statements, others are asking questions, giving orders, etc. It is this knowledge that orders the linguistic data for interpretation in the first place. Let us imagine this interpretation method as taking place before the mastery of language. A portion of a language-game proceeds in this way: *S* utters *U* in the presence of *H*, upon which *H* is to do *j* to *a*. For this portion of language-game to proceed *H* is required to know that (1) *U* is addressed to her. But to know this she has to know (2) what it is to address. Then she should know that (3) doing *j* to *a* will satisfy *U*. That is, in learning this portion of a language-game H must look for the ways of satisfying *U*. Now, the criterion of satisfaction of *U* for *H* is the assent or dissent of *S*. But the conditions *H* should recognise for such satisfaction are not dependent on *S*, but a set of conditions involving activities of H concurrent with that of S and the physical environment. For learning the 'meaning' of *U*, *H* should know how to decompose *U* into parts by applying his newly earned knowledge of the distinctness of *j* and *a*. This knowledge is a formal one, i.e., based on logical features of the utterance, a case also of distinguishing various features of experience for applying labels to them. If Wittgenstein is correct the last mentioned is also a language-game at times. Now, what is proper to learning language as a system of 'meaning' is obtained through an act of severing, rather inventing, the concepts from the conditions of satisfaction and criteria (in the sense above) of utterances, which

28. " . . . Of course, what confuses us is the uniform appearance of words when we hear them spoken or meet them in script and print. For their application is not presented to us so clearly. Especially when we are doing philosophy". Wittgenstein in *PI*, p. 6.

29. "The word "to signify" is perhaps used in the most straightforward way when the object signified is marked with the sign". Wittgenstein, *Ibid.*, p. 7.

provide principles for ordering words. It is doubtful whether even in *Tractatus* Wittgenstein ever addressed questions concerning 'meaning' in this sense. Compare this with Saussure's concern with sign and what it signifies and his observation that elements of sounds and thought combine to produce a form not a substance.[30] Consider again the example of *H*'s understanding of utterance *U*. *H* has to understand *U* as it is actually meant in the language-that is, *j* -ing a is not a case of *y*-ing *b*. For, *S* might as well get *H j a* by uttering *U* while instructing her to *y b*. Thus, out of so many variables of satisfaction conditions *H* must choose the correct one, the one meant by *S*. This is done by applying a combination of rules of addition and elimination to more and more instances of utterances and more and more satisfaction conditions as and when *H* encounters them. This logical ability manifests as the application of a set of decomposition rules which categorise words by ordering them into a system. Mastery of words is partly an instance of the acquisition of this system. The same decomposition rules have to serve, once fully developed, as rules of composition. Now, the system, i.e., of meaning, is acquired through the procedures of understanding. But understanding itself is not explained in terms of this system. The role similar to that of context-principle in Frege is the logic of the language-game in Wittgenstein. To that extent Dummett's observation

> . . . but his (native speaker's) knowledge of the axioms (governing words) need not be manifested in anything but the employment of the sentences[31]

is Wittgensteinian in spirit. But by treating the 'meaning' of sentence as deriving from the meaning of its component words he is moving away from a Wittgensteinian problematique. Because the question of the principle of composition cannot be raised relevantly with respect to the *understanding* of a sentence as it could be in the case of the *meaning* of a sentence, i.e., as a formal feature of it. The 'meaning' as something present in the sentence and which a theory is claimed to be re-presenting is a relic of metaphysics. Once decomposition rules are found to apply in acquiring word-meanings, the same, as suggested earlier, would suffice to provide rules of

---

30. Saussure in Easthope, A. and McGowan, K. (eds), *A Critical and Cultural Theory Reader*, Open University Press, Milton, Keynes, 1992, p. 7.

31. Dummett, *op. cit*.

composition also.[32] Therefore, the questions raised by a theory of meaning might be simply pointless, namely, 'what is the fundamental notion we have to rely on in constructing a theory of meaning which purports to give meaning of all the sentences in a language? The question is pointless because, by hypothesis 'meaning' is already implicated in internal relations of a system and is of no interest to philosophers in this sense. It also confuses questions which linguists like Saussure ask and those which philosopher like Wittgenstein try to answer. Obviously, Wittgenstein was not answering questions which gives rise to a Derrida-like phenomenon.

7

When written or spoken texts are removed from the contexts of activities to which they could be seen as bound, or when such texts are not accompanied by any visible change in the speakers' or readers' actions, understanding is said to be a case of interpreting those texts correctly. Without the intention of the speaker or the specificity of the context to help the interpreter, how can she interpret correctly?

32. Supposing that a native speaker possesses the knowledge of individual words, the question is how does he, given such knowledge, understand any sentence of his language, (a) Will some compositional rules — some very formal, syntactic ones — be sufficient for him to interpret or produce any sentence with an understanding? (b) or does he need some explicit semantic rules to enable him to understand the utterances? If the answer to the question (a) is in the affirmative then our representation of the native speakers' knowledge of words should assume that it is very rich. If the answer to the (b) is in the affirmative, then this knowledge can be minimal or formal. This situation explains the differences in concern of the linguistically oriented semanticists and philosophically oriented semanticists. Whether a philosophically oriented theory takes truth or assertibility conditions as its central idea, it should hold a holistic view about the knowledge about words, in the sense that knowledge of any single word is linked to a knowledge of a large number of other words in that language. This is because if words derive their meanings from their characteristic roles in the employment of sentences then each of them gets involved in a vector of relations with other words. Linguistically oriented semantics seeks to find how meaning is encoded, rather than what ground would be necessary or sufficient or both for such encoding to take place. Philosophers would find it highly inadequate the generative semanticists' idea of assigning semantic markers to the terminals — lexical items — of syntactic tree for representing the structure of meaning. But this is how linguistic semanticists apologise for their lack of interest in background knowledge just as the philosophers do for their negligence of formal features of meaning.

What is supposed to be present here is 'meaning' which is not necessarily bound to the intention or context. Correct interpretation will enable one to grasp the meaning of the text. To put the problem in clear light, let us imagine what it is to encounter a text in normal circumstances. In normal circumstances a text is encountered as an aspect of face-to-face interaction, understanding will proceed partly by seeking the 'absent' context and intention. But where will one seek these, except in the text itself? If it is the text which shows, by itself, the context and intention, they are no longer external to the text. Let us call this circumstance a non-normal one in which context and intention are not external to the text. In non-normal circumstance a text is left to itself, and depends exclusively on its internal relations, to make sense. Such texts are not addressed to any one, and do not necessarily proceed from the intention of an author. Yet they are said to have a characteristic function of language, namely that of projecting meaning. When language finds a use in this sense, then meaning, and not understanding, is the more appropriate concept to be used in connection with it. Interpreting a text, then, will imply placing this meaning in the appropriate context and intention. In this sense, we understand a text when we interpret it correctly. Since the text-internal contexts and intentions are just like any other component of the text, any interpretation whatsoever may not yield an understanding. But the fact that it lends some interpretation irrespective of its being understood testifies its projection of meaning; in the sense that the interpretation tends to fall in a systematic, coherent pattern.[33] We may also recall that, for Wittgenstein, understanding a linguistic act is not necessarily linked to the intention of the actor or its context defined spatio-temporally, but proceeds from the recognition of it as being carried out as part of the language-game which is its acknowledged field.[34] Now, the question of the meaning of a text as distinct from a correct interpretation of it or the understanding of it is legitimately raised. There are both conceptual and historical aspects to this legitimisation. Historically considered the chances of language being used in non-face-to-face-interaction contexts increased exponentially in the modern period. Conceptual

---

33. This would mean that language is always, already disposed to bewitch us, and is always in a holiday mood. Understanding then will be a responsibility and Wittgenstein has his one foot in the Enlightenment.

34. For some classes of utterance or texts this field might include their contexts and intentions.

aspects of this legitimisation as explicated above is embedded in historical context. It is meaning in this sense the linguists like Saussure have conceived of as belonging to *langue*, and thinkers like Derrida have taken to be a function of the play of *difference* and, therefore, indeterminate.

8

Wittgenstein's account of language-games is non-essentialist. If it is supposed that there are rules governing uses of words or sentences then they are indefinite. If it is said of a proposition that it has a logical structure, then it does not approximate to a sentence's use as proposition, but can be seen as a requirement only of logical analysis.[35] There is no fit between exactness of logic and the inexactness of what is called language. This renders logic an inadequate tool for representing the working of language. 'Theoretical' efforts also suffer from similar problem. *Language* is a concept comparable to Saussure's *langue*, suggesting something of a totalising, systemic character. If language has a great deal of fuzziness about it and 'language-games' is appropriately used to talk about it, then 'sentences of a language' is a dubious notion. A theory which attempts to represent meanings of 'sentences' of a given 'language', projecting an ontolgoy consisting of these entities, therefore, is a misdirected endeavour. Language-game is employed to highlight the fuzziness of language-world with greater accuracy, where 'language' is only a limiting case. 'Sentence' is, similarly, a projection by simplifying the welter of differences that is the linguistic acts. 'Sentence' and 'language' are like 'individual' and 'society', and the debate in philosophy of language centering on atomism and holism is similar to the one in social sciences over methodological individualism and methodological holism. A reading of Wittgenstein for seeing how he overcame the dualism between structure and act, sentence and language, name and the object, etc., will be highly rewarding.

---

35. "102. The strict and clear rules of the logical structure of propositions appear to us as something in the background-hidden in the medium of the understanding. I already see them (even though through a medium): for I understand the propositional sign, I use it to say something". And also "107, The more narrowly we examine actual language, the sharper becomes the conflict between it and our requirement. (For the crystalline purity of logic was, of course, not a result of investigation: it was a requirement) . . . " *PI*, p. 46.

9

Structuralism is not merely the name of an school of thought having representatives in linguistics, literary theory and social theory. It is a viewpoint that informed several great achievements of twentieth-century thinking-positivism and non-positivism alike. Wittgenstein of the *Tractatus* working in the early decades of this century was also a structuralist and *Philosophical Investigations* is a self-criticism.[36] In the latter he tried to develop a style of thinking by which he could explicate the working of 'language' without presupposing an underlying structure that determines linguistic acts. By treating determinateness of sense as a limiting case of a general indeterminacy of language-games, Wittgenstein not only distanced himself from a structural explanation but brought the inquiry round to the particularities and details of linguistic activities. Though language-games are generally indeterminate and their ground, the way of life, is always uncertain, human beings none the less achieve an order in their linguistic activities. While both evolving-rather changing and uncertain, the language-games, therefore, also ensure a determinate way of proceeding with linguistic acts. Rules are implicated in every language-game, but a linguistic act is not always bounded by rules.[37] While a linguistic act has an uncertain foundation, in normal circumstances, one is certain of its sense.[38] In such a circumstance, doubting will be the limiting case.[39] This suggests a fluidity in the

---

36. Thus, Wittgenstein says in *Philosophical Investigations*, — "It is interesting to compare the multiplicity of the tools in language and of the ways they are used, the multiplicity of kinds of word and sentence, with what logicians have said about the structure of language. (Including the author of the *Tractatus Logico-Philosophicus*)", p. 12.

37. "And is there not also the case where we play and — make up the rules as we go along? And there is even one where we alter them — as we go along. "*P.I.*, p.39,, "85. A rule stands there like a sing-post. — Does the sign-post leave no doubt open about the way I have to go? . . . " *PI*, p. 39. . . . " The sign-post is in order — if, under normal circumstances, it fulfils its purpose." *Ibid*., p. 41.

38. "375. Here one must realise that complete absence of doubt at some point, even where we would say that 'legitimate' doubt exist, need not falsify a language-game". *O.C.*, p. 48.

39. "509. I really want to say that a language-game is only possible if one trusts something (I did not say "can trust something"). *Ibid*., p. 66. " . . . But since a language-game is something that consists in the recurrent procedures of the game in time, it seems impossible to say in any *individual*

→

relation between structure and act. That is, in *every* rule there is an non-rule, and in *every* act there is a non-act. It becomes, again, fuzzy.

In his later writing we find Wittgenstein encountering the most powerful urge of the modernity, i.e., of totalising rationality. Groundlessness of the ground discussed in section 4 of this paper can be seen as an argument amounts to showing groundedness as a subset of groundlessness. 608, 609, 610 and 612 quoted in section 5, also bear evidence to the fact that he has regarded rationality as a special case of irrationality. Attending to the nuances with readiness to become a *prey* to them rather than assimilating them into a scheme of comprehension is a persisting trait of Wittgenstein's later writing which is also a hallmark of what is today known as post-modern thinking. Yet, to call Wittgenstein post-structuralist or post-modernist is like saying of that platinum rod kept in Paris that it is one meter long.

→ case that such-and-such must be beyond doubt if there is to be a language-game — though it is right enough to say that *as a rule* some empirical judgement or other must be beyond doubt". *Ibid.*, p. 68. "126. I am not more certain of the meaning of my words than I am of certain judgements. Can I doubt that this colour is called "blue"? (My) doubts from a system." *Ibid.*, p. 19.

4

Criteria and the Conceptual Structure

Amitabha Dasgupta

CERTAINLY, the notion of criterion is one among the several notions with which Wittgenstein was highly preoccupied in his later writings. This is a notion which supports a particular view of language and meaning which in turn justifies a view of mind that upholds a particular form of relationship existing between language and mind. This, indeed, forms a coherent philosophical position which indicates that there is a relation existing between philosophical psychology on the one hand and philosophy of language and epistemology on the other. The central to this position is the theme that confirms operationalistic analysis of language and meaning. The nature of operationalistic analysis of language is not devoid of psychological implication. On the contrary, it is closely related to a type of philosophical psychology which may be described as logical behaviourism.

This paper does not intend to have an elaborate discussion on Wittgenstein's notion of criterion and the textual interpretation of it. We are, on the other hand, more interested in the implications that follow from his notion of criterion. Our major focus lies on the relationship between language and mind that Wittgenstein seeks to establish through his notion of criterion. Keeping this in view the main line of argument advanced in this paper may be stated in the following three propositions. First, Wittgenstein's formulation of the notion of criterion leads to an unsatisfactory view of the nature of language and mind. Second, the arguments that he has provided to defend his view may not be tenable. And, third, an attempt will be made to suggest an alternative framework that will be able to remove many of the difficulties encountered by Wittgenstein's method of analysis. Finally, as a part of the introductory note, it may be stated in this connection that this paper assumes the mentalistic standpoint as upheld by Chomsky and Fodor.[1]

1

THE NOTION OF CRITERION : TOWARDS AN OPERATIONALISTIC ANALYSIS OF LANGUAGE AND MEANING

One of the most significant problems with which later Wittgenstein was preoccupied was the problem of other mind. As we know, Wittgenstein's treatment of the problem of other mind has many aspects and becomes the principal source of giving rise to a set of wide ranging implications such as, semantic, psychological, epistemological, etc. Wittgenstein's analysis shows that the problem of other mind has a multifaceted nature.

Among the several aspects, one aspect of the problem of other mind is concerned with the justification of ascribing mental states to a person on the basis of his behaviour. The difficulty raised here is with the position which puts forward the claim that it is possible to tell on the basis of someone's behaviour that he is in certain mental states. If this is accepted the question that comes most naturally is : What justification could be offered when such a claim or ascription is made? In this respect, the position taken by the sceptics is historically well known. Their answer is that no good justification can be given when such ascriptions are made purely on the basis of behavioural characteristics. The celebrated position of Wittgenstein, on the other hand, is to show that the argument of the sceptics rests on a misconception and is also logically incoherent.

The basic tenet of the sceptical argument is that there are no logical /conceptual connections existing between prepositions about mental states and propositions about behaviour. To say this is to

---

1. Chomsky, N., *Reflection on Language*, Fontana Collins, 1976.

   Chomsky, N., *Knowledge of Language: Its Nature, Origin and Use*, Praegar Special Studies, New York, 1986.

   Chihara, S. and J. Fodor, 'Operationalism and Ordinary Language: A Critique of Wittgenstein, in *Wittgenstein* ed. G. Pitcher, Anchor Books, New York, 1966.

   Das Gupta, A., *The Second Linguistic Turn. Chomsky and the Philosophy of Language*, *PETER LANG*, Frankfortam Main, 1996.

imply that propositions which describe a person's behaviour in a certain way may not be the adequate ground for the ascription of mental states to that person. This standpoint led the sceptics to further argue that there is no way one can reasonably assume that a person other than himself can be truly said to feel pain or to have motives or to have any other mental states. The reason is that a person has a first hand knowledge about his own mental events. Since this knowledge is necessarily confined to one's own case it is difficult to talk about the mental states of other persons. The ascription of mental predicates to others, thus, looses its certainty since these ascriptions by nature necessarily depend on logically fallible inferences. These inferences are largely based on analogies and correlations which do not constitute the adequate ground for convincing justification. This is, in summary, the position held by the sceptics regarding the possibility of the knowledge of other minds.

Wittgenstein challenges the very premise of the sceptic's position. It is a challenge based on a crucial argument showing that there exists a conceptual relation between statements about behaviour and statements about mental events, processes and states. The upshot of this argument, as Wittgenstein claims, establishes that there are plenty of cases where our knowledge of the mental states of some person may not be necessarily based either on empirical correlations or on analogical argument. It is, on the other hand, based on, what Wittgenstein calls, a conceptual/linguistic connection.

The argument used by Wittgenstein against the sceptics has a broader implication. First of all, this argument involves taking a certain view of language and of meaning. Second, using this argument implies accepting a particular relation between language and mind. These two together constitute a unified thesis where the latter follows from the former. This is a thesis which shows that Wittgenstein's philosophical psychology is essentially dependent on his philosophy of language. It may not be inappropriate to say that Wittgenstein upholds a form of mentalism which is understood, defined and characterised in the light of views about language. It may be, thus, called linguistic mentalism where the notion of the *mental* don't have any independent status. It is a notion which is subsumed under the category of language. Wittgenstein's solution to the problem of other mind is, thus, a linguistic solution. We shall now take up the first thesis for discussion.

Language as activity

As mentioned earlier, Wittgenstein's solution to the problem of other mind involves taking a certain view of language and of meaning. But what is this definite view of language implied? It is the view which defines language as activity, or to put in Wittgenstein's words "speaking of language is part of an activity" (*PI*, Sec.23). But it will be wrong if it is thought that speaking involves any one kind of activity. On the contrary, Wittgenstein argues that there are countless kinds of language using activities or language-games. Speaking of language involves participating in these games (*BB*, pp. 67-8). If language is a matter of game then the meaning of expressions cannot be decided in any other term except only in relation to various language-games in which these expressions occur. Wittgenstein argues that words do not get their meaning in isolation from language games but only within the context of language games. According to Wittgenstein, thus, the analysis of the meaning of a word consists in showing the role or use that a word has in the language-game in which it occurs. In this connection, quite interestingly, Wittgenstein compared words with instruments and, just like, instruments are characterised by their functions words too can be characterised by their use or functions. As he remarks, we "think of words as instruments characterised by their use" (*BB*, p.67). This, indeed, is a highly significant remark pointing out a particular line of thinking and a new direction towards a philosophical analysis of meaning.

The Wittgenstenian view of words 'as instruments characterised by their use' suggests in an important sense a method of analysis. It is a method of analysis which inevitably leads to an operationlistic view of meaning. This is particularly evident in the context of the meaning of certain class of predicates. How do we determine the meaning of these predicates. We determine the meaning by reporting their application. Take the example of the language game played with the word *length*. To know the meaning of the word *length* implies the ability of reporting the dimension of physical objects. This involves knowing the procedures adopted in measuring length. Thus, for a person learning this game implies necessarily mastering these procedures, because procedures are vital to the formulation of this game. As Wittgenstein very aptly points out: "The meaning of the word *length* is learnt among other things, by learning what it is to determine length." (*PI*, p. 225) Notice that language here plays a specific role and while commenting on this, Wittgenstein states "Here the teaching of language is not explanation but training" (*PI*, Sec. 5). For Wittgenstein, language becomes a matter of training because, for him, "To understand a language means to be master of a technique" (*PI*, Sec. 199).

In view of this position, linguistic competence or the knowledge of language may be, thus, understood as a matter of mere ability. It is the ability to formulate a correct statement on basis of performing certain relevant operations associated with it. Thus, for example, for a person to be competent in the language-game played with length will mean acquiring the ability to form a statement like *X is three feet long* on the basis of performing certain operations associated with measuring the length of X. It may not be incorrect if it is said that the statement *X is three feet long* is the outcome of certain operations which we perform with tools like rulers, range-finders, etc. Considering this aspect associated with the expression *length*, a conceptual analysis of the word *length* cannot ignore in its account the operations that determine the applicability of length predicates. Accordingly, the rules of language-games governing the meaning of words cannot be conceived in isolation from those operations. As pointed-out earlier, taking account of these operations is essential to characterise the meaning of a predicate like. " . . . *three feet long*". The claim that is made here is conceptual. It is not on any practical ground but essentially on a conceptual ground that we are justifying the indispensability of taking those operations into account while characterising the meaning of a word. The crucial to this claim is that since these operations determine the applicability of a predicate they are conceptually connected with the predicate itself. Operations are, thus, conceptually important for understanding the meaning of certain words.

Logical behaviour of mental words

It has been mentioned at the beginning of this discussion that the operationalistic analysis of language subscribes to a particular form of relationship between language and mind. Accordingly, the notion of the mental assumes a different formulation. It is a formulation which suggests that understanding of mental words, such as, pain or dream my not be procedurally different from the understanding of such physical words as length. Determination of the meaning of these mental words may have the same operationalistic considerations as that of physical words. That means, taking account of relevant operations is essential for the analysis of mental words, because mental words are necessarily associated with certain operations or observations. It is on the basis of these operations or observations that we can determine the applicability of mental predicates. To put it in concrete terms, the analysis of words like *pain* or *dreams* will imply articulating the operations or observations by which we can determine that someone is in pain or he had dreamed (*PI*, p. 224). It is behaviour taken in a broad sense which includes verbal report that constitutes the basis for determining such predicates as *is in pain* or *has dreamed*, etc. As Wittgenstein argues, it is those typical features, of pain behaviour that enable me to say that someone is in pain. It, thus, evidently follows that pain and pain behaviour are conceptually connected and on this ground one can assert that a philosophical analysis of pain necessarily requires taking pain behaviour into account. One cannot fail to notice the unmistakable similarity existing between the logical behaviour of these two classes of words — physical and mental. The scenario associated with the word pain is same as the scenario associated with the word length. In the context of pain, we determine that someone is in pain on the basis of his pain behaviour and in the context of length we determine the applicability of a predicate, such as, *three feet long* on the basis of performing the relevant operations. In both cases reference to operations (in its extended sense) is essential for the conceptual analysis of words, namely, length and pain. The reason is the connection between the two is conceptual.

Towards a notion of criterion

The above discussion on the operationalistic analysis of language directly leads to Wittgenstein's view on criterion. It has been said that there is a logical/conceptual connection existing between pain and pain behaviour. But to leave this matter at this level without specifying the exact nature of this connection does not seem to be correct. Hence, very pertinently, the questions arises: What is the precise nature of this logical connection found between pain and pain behaviour? It cannot be a matter of simple entailment which allows us to say the fact that someone is screaming entails the proposition that he is in pain. It is here that Wittgenstein introduced the notion of criterion to bring out the exact nature of this logical connection. As he introduced the notion:

> It is part of the grammar of the word *Chair* that this is what we call *to sit on a chair*, and it part of the grammar of the word *meaning* that this is what we call *explanation of a meaning,* in the same way to explain my criterion for another person's having toothache is to give a grammatical explanation about the word *toothache* and in this an explanation concerning of the meaning of the word *toothache*. (*BB*, p. 24)

To give a grammatical explanation of the word *toothache* consists in spelling out the criterion in terms of which one can say that someone is having *toothache.* Wittgenstein made explicit the nature of this criterion when he said:

> When we learnt the use of the phrase 'so-and-so has toothache', we were pointed out certain kinds of behaviour of those who were said to have toothache. (*BB*, p.24)

As we can see, toothache is necessarily connected with certain kinds of behaviour and leaning the meaning of the word *toothache* will, thus, imply learning the connection holding between *toothache* and the behavioural characteristics of it. The connection existing here is a criterial connection where the behavioural characteristics constitute the criterion for the meaning of the word *toothache*. The meaning of a word cannot be, thus, conceived without the criterion associated with it. However, at this stage, as Wittgenstein made it clear, sceptics can always raise a question regarding the deceptive nature of behaviour. As Wittgenstein puts it:

> Now one may go on and ask: How do you know that he has got toothache when he holds his check? The answer to this might be. "I say he has toothache when he holds his cheek because I hold my cheek when I have toothache". (*BB,* p. 24)

As we can see, my ascription of toothache to someone on the basis of his behaviour is purely based on my first person account of what happens when I have toothache. It is on the ground of my own experience that I infer on the basis of my observation that so-and-so has a similar experience. But does this analogy necessarily hold in all cases? This is the question of sceptics and Wittgenstein is well aware of it. Keeping this in mind, he has this unique solution to offer:

> "And why do you suppose that toothache corresponds to holding his cheek just because your toothache corresponds to your holding your cheeks"? You will be at a loss to answer this question, and find that here we strike rook bottom, that is we have come down to conventions. (*BB*, p. 24)

Thus, to sum up, Wittgenstein's use of the notion of criterion signifies a special connection. The ultimate justification of this connection is based on the convention of language. The general picture of this connection may be expressed in the following terms. *X* is the criterion of *Y* in a situation *S* signifies an invariable relationship where the very meaning of the concept *Y* includes in its claim that the applicability or the presence of *Y* can be determined on the basis of *X* or coincides with *X*. This constitutes what Wittgenstein calls the grammatical use of *Y*. It is grammatical because normally the contrary does not happen. However, one may always deny this relationship where *X* may be accepted but *Y* is denied. Wittgenstein's answer to this will be simple. According to him, the man who is denying the relationship has to show only that there is something abnormal in the situation. The reason is that no evidence is required to make the claim of *Y* on the basis of *X*. Thus, to learn the rules for the use of *Y* requires to learn the criterion for *Y*. It is because of this centrality of criteria in the context of meaning that a change in the criterion implies a change in the meaning of a corresponding concept.

It has been stated at the beginning of this paper that to have an elaborate discussion on Wittgenstein's notion of criterion is not the major focus of this paper. It is, on the other hand, more interested in the conception of language and meaning that follow from his notion of criterion. In this respect we are specially interested in Wittgenstein's treatment of criterion in relation to mind and mental words. In the present section we have mainly dealt with these issues. Now the question arises: How far the Wittgenstenian analysis of mental words in terms of his criterion is adequate and valid? We shall now turn to the second section which will try to provide a critique of Wittgenstein's analysis of mental words offered in terms of his notion of criterion.

2

CRITERION : A CRITIQUE

We have said in our earlier discussion that mental words, like any other words, are understood in terms of language-game. The word *dream*, for example, would be understood in terms of the corresponding language-game in which the word dream plays its role and also in terms of the language-game of dream-telling. For Wittgenstein, it is the dream report which is extremely important since it is the waking testimony which constitutes the criterion which helps us to find out whether someone had dreams. The sceptics think of dream reports as a mere symptom, whereas for Wittgenstein, a criterial relationship exists between dream reporting and dreaming. This way the possibility of the sceptic's doubt that the dreamer's memory may deceive him when he reports the dream after waking may be removed on a logical ground. Thus, the rules which formulate the criterion for the application of the word dream determine the logical relationship existing between dreaming and dream reporting. The whole Wittgensteinian analysis, we will now show, is the outcome of a certain misleading conception of the relation between language and reality and thus we will point out the incoherent nature of Wittgenstein's doctrine and will then try to present an alternative method of analysis.

According to Wittgenstein, there is no sense in making a statement such as *He had a dream last night but he has forgotten it*, since there is no criterion by which to establish the truth of the sentence. This involves a counter-intuitive analysis of the concept of dream. In the first place, we point out that this conception of dreaming is not acceptable from the point of view of ordinary language itself. In ordinary language, it is perfectly sensible to say that I had a dream last night but I have forgotten it. If Wittgenstein is so faithful to ordinary language, then he must recognise what is considered as meaningful and what is considered as counter-intuitive in ordinary language. Secondly, researches in neurophysiology disprove Wittgenstein's conception of dreaming. Through a study of the brain waves (EEG) it is possible to empirically verify the statement whether or not someone had a dream the previous night. In this connection we may refer to Malcolm's view[2] which on the basis of Wittgenstein's analysis challenged the recent experimental evidence in physiology that tried to measure the time span of a dream. Malcolm's argument was that in the language-game played with *dream* there is no criterion other than waking testimony by which one could determine how long dreams last. The scientists' attempt to answer *How long do dreams*

2. Malcolm, N., *Dreaming*, Routledge and Kegan Paul, London, 1962.

last? is a result of conceptual confusion. In order to answer it one needs to adopt a criterion which ascribes some relevant properties to dreams. But to adopt a new criterion, according to Wittgenstein, means to change the concept, viz., the concept of dream. The scientists' concept, strictly speaking, is not a concept of dream. The whole analysis goes altogether against the well-accepted definition of neuropsychological research.

Malcolm accepts that on the basis of the behavioural features expressed by the person during his sleep it is possible to say that the person concerned had a dream though he may not remember the dream after he wakes. But in such a situation, Malcolm holds, "our words have no clear sense". A question that can be immediately raised here is: what does it mean to say that these words do not have a clear sense? Malcolm does not provide any satisfactory answer to this. As a matter of fact, he later contradicts his own stand. In his treatment of the concept of nightmare, he changes his earlier stand and holds that there is a sense of the term *nightmare* where behaviour during sleep is the criterion. Malcolm thinks that there are different concepts of dreaming just as he maintains that there are different concepts of sleep, e.g., one based upon report and another upon non-verbal behaviour. But this is definitely a most unnatural way of characterising the concepts of ordinary language.

Following Wittgenstein's and Malcolm's position that a dream report is the only criterion for dreaming, it is impossible to talk of children having dreams before they have learnt to speak. If, for them, words can be used only when their application can be strictly verified, then not only many of the ordinary uses would be left out but the non-linguistic thought will be ruled out too. They have overlooked the point that it is not impossible that a particular concept of mental activity may be modified and extended on the basis of further experience. The primary use of the word, *dreaming*, depends on the notion of dream-telling but this does not prevent us from extending the use of the word to include other criteria.

The reason for the counter-intuitive nature of the analysis is that it starts with a basic assumption that there must be criterion. As we have seen in our discussion on criteria, according to Wittgenstein, *X* is the criterion of *Y* only in the situation where the application of *Y* can be justified on the basis of the presence of *X*. Wittgenstein first of all has not given sufficient justification for his position. What we would like to argue is that the Wittgensteinian premise is not a self-evident one. There are plenty of instances particularly in the sciences, where *Y* exists independent of *X*. In other words, the meaning of *Y* can be taught without teaching that *X* is the basis of *Y*. If this is so, then *X* is not the criterion of *Y*. One such instance is Chihara and Fodor's example of Wilson Cloud Chamber in physics used for the detection of high speed charged particles. What is discovered through this instrument is that the formation of tiny bands of fog on the glass surface of the instrument indicates the existence of charged particles. But the formation of these streaks, as Chihara and Fodor comment:

> . . . is not a Wittgensteinian criterion of the presence and motion of these particles in the apparatus. That one can detect these charged particles and determine their paths by means of such devices is surely not, by any stretch of the imagination, a *conceptual* truth. C.T.R. Wilson did not learn what "path of a charged particle" means by having the cloud-chamber explained to him: he *discovered* the method, and the discovery was contingent upon recognizing the empirical fact that ions could act as centers of condensation in a supersaturated vapor.[3]

In other words, the physicists explain the formation of the streaks on the basis of the hypothesis that "high velocity charged particle were passing through the chamber". This example is by no means a special case. It is a generally accepted stand in the philosophy of science that scientists always approach the data with a set of hypotheses. Philosophers of science, such as Popper, Hempel, Hanson and others have shown that there cannot be any pure observation. Observation is always theory-laden. The theory at the initial stage might not necessarily enter in the form of a finished product. The problem, the terms of classification of data and the notation form the theoretical network within which only observation or knowledge of a fact can take place. Hempel[4] convincingly shows that observation statements are preceded by a hypothesis and that the former is logically dependent on the latter. The hypothesis is not generated by any observation but is only offered as a suggestion in solving a problem.

---

3. Chihara, S. and J. Fordor 'Operationalism and Ordinary Language : A Critique of Wittgenstein', in *Wittgenstein*, ed. G. Pitcher, p. 193.
4. Hampel, C., *Philosophy of Natural Science*, Prentice-Hall, Inc., Englewood Cliffs, New York, 1966.

The evidence of this, i.e., how observation is determined by a theory can be found if one looks into the way in which different inquiries proceed by theorising. This brings out the importance of a theoretical or conceptual framework in a knowing situation. We know the phenomena not in terms of criteria and symptoms but in terms of a theory.

This shows that the Wittgensteinian premise that *X* is the criterion of *Y* when the application of *Y* can be justified on the basis of the presence of *X* does not hold true in all cases. In other words, for such cases like the above, where *Y* 'is the path of high velocity particle', *X* does not constitute the criterion. The Wittgensteinian belief that there must be a criterion originates from a wrong philosophical theory of justification. Strawson also saw the inadequacy of Wittgenstein's position and denied the existence of necessary criterial relationship in human communication. 'Wittgenstein here', as he said,

> seems to me to be in a muddle. . . . What he has committed himself to is the view that one cannot sensibly be said to recognise or identify anything, unless one uses *criteria*; and, as a consequence of this, that one cannot recognise or identify sensations. But of course this is untrue.[5]

If we deny the necessary criterial relationship existing between concept and behaviour, then there are two major questions involved here. How do we explain the ordinary language mental terms? How do children learn these terms? This takes us to the notion of conceptual structure.

3

THE CONCEPTUAL STRUCTURE

In learning the various mental terms we do not learn the criterial connection holding between the mental terms and the corresponding behavioural pattern. Instead we form complex conceptual connections by which we are able to make an interrelationship between various mental states. It is this conceptual system to which we appeal when we attempt to explain the behaviour of others by referring to belief, desire, motive, sensation, etc. In other words, learning a language

5. Strawson, P., 'Review of Wittgenstein's Philosophical Investigation', in *Wittgenstein*, ed. G. Pitcher, p. 25.

means developing a system of interrelated concepts which we use in order to understand and explain the behaviour of others as well as our own. It is through the process of acquiring mental concepts that we develop a variety of beliefs involving them. These beliefs result in various expectations concerning how people are likely to behave. In other words, a common human understanding is presupposed in linguistic communication.

Language, if understood in the above sense, provides the clue to the understanding of human nature. It provides an insight into the structure of human nature. It shows that human nature is not an empty concept. The meaning of human nature implies certain distinctive capacities, faculties and activities. It is not only on the basis of this common human attribute that human beings act and communicate with each other, but they also share certain fundamental beliefs and deep-rooted human concerns. It is these beliefs and concerns that men must realise in order to achieve a truly human communication.

Apart from Strawson, who concedes the point about common human nature, analytic philosophers in general did not see that language has an essential relationship with human reality or *Dasein*. The inadequacy of analytic philosophers' analysis of mental words is largely due to their failure to see this essential relationship. The mental predicates which we use to account for behaviour can be looked upon as supplying evidence for the mental processes which we postulate. These mental processes are understood in terms of the conceptual system on the basis of the common human understanding. Human behaviour is like the cloud-chamber streaks in physics and the postulated conceptual system is like the physical theory where the properties of the particles are formulated and defined. Such a conceptual system is validated by the explanation it offers for the phenomena in question and may in fact lead to the discovery of other interesting phenomena hitherto concealed from observation.

In this connection we should mention that recent investigations in cognitive psychology show the important role that theory construction plays in everyday conceptualisation and concept formation. Much of our everyday conceptualisation involves manipulation of theories and explanatory models in terms of which experience is integrated and understood. We may, e.g., mention the works of Jean Piaget whose theory of the development of language and cognition is considered a landmark in this new area of research. Piaget shares the Gestalt conviction that humans structure the universe according to their innate perceptions and that the functional activity of reason is obviously connected with the general heredity of the organism. This is what he calls 'hereditary psychological reality' which is of primary importance for the development of the mental processes.

On the basis of his elaborate study of the development of physical concepts, e.g., the concepts of object, time, space and causality in the child, Piaget[6] has shown how knowledge is constructed by the individual. It is constructed both from the data of experience and from the data provided by the biological characteristics of the organism. This construction is done by the individual through the use of self-regulating mental mechanisms. The task of these mechanisms is to control the two basic functions: assimilation, which involves incorporation of experience into the existing mental structure, and accommodation, which involves the application of the existing structure to new experience.

Piaget's investigation indeed conforms to the rationalistic epistemology of Kant. Knowledge occurs through combining sense experience with the organising activity of the mind. The role of experience is to activate the intellectual process. In this connection we may refer to Chomsky's discussion[7] of the act of naming. In naming situation there is always an interaction between the cognitive structure of language and the system of common sense understanding, a name is always drawn from the system of language and the thing to which it is associated is chosen by the category of common sense understanding. Language includes various categories like personal names, place names, colour names and so on. Chomsky refers to Moravcsik's article on the Aristotelian theory of language where he says that

> there are no expressions that perform solely the task of referring. Individuals are given by certain privileged terms that specify domains of discourse.

The domain of discourse are necessarily related with the categories

---

6. Piaget, J., *The Construction of Reality in the Child*, Basic Books, New York, 1954.

7. Chomsky, N., *Reflections on Language*.

of common sense understanding. The act of naming is an interplay of the structures of the two systems which the mind may not be consciously aware of. In such a view names are not associated in an arbitrary way, nor are they the 'cluster terms' of Wittgenstein. Each name is placed in a definite linguistic category which enters in the system of grammar. Whenever an object is named, says Chomsky:

> . . . the hearer brings to bear a system of linguistic structure to place the names and the system of conceptual relations and conditions, along with factual beliefs, to place the thing named. To understand "naming" we would have to understand these systems and the faculties of mind through which they arise.[8]

This establishes the *prima facie* importance of the notion of structure in human communication.

We now address ourselves to the second question, viz., how do children learn concepts, e.g., mental predicates? It is possible for a child to learn the various means other than learning the criterial relationship. For example, if the concept of dreaming is defined as the inner event whose occurrence always causes some involuntary behaviour in our sleep and which is remembered when one correctly reports a dream, then definitely there are number of ways other than criterial relationship by which a child could learn the word 'dream'. One of the most simple ways is that a child could learn the word by being told that what he has experienced is a dream. Another way may be that a child, because of his prior understanding of the meaning of works like imagining and sleep, could learn what the word 'dream' means only when he is told that dreaming is like imagining in sleep.

It is not necessary that a child learns the meaning of the mental concepts only from his own case. A child with a fair amount of intelligence who does not have any experience of dreams can form an idea of a dream just on the basis of a set of theoretical inferences described above. If these characteristics constitute the concept of dreaming, then it is not impossible for a child to arrive at the notion without having any experience of dreaming. The same is true in the learning of sensation terms such as 'pain' and quasi-dispositional terms such as 'having a motive'. The child could learn those concepts

8. Chomsky, N., *Reflections on Language.*

by employing the inference pattern that is described to him.

The above position may be questioned on the ground that the suggested alternative does not seem to be a very plausible one. The children, in order to understand and use the various mental concepts, must acquire a complex conceptual system and for that they need to be taught about this system. But such a teaching will be so complicated and difficult that it will be virtually impossible to gain much success.

If such a system cannot be taught, it follows there is something which is unlearned in the very structure of our conceptual system. These unlearned structural properties can be characterised as innate. In the recent discussion in philosophy of science, one will notice that philosophers have started questioning the empiricist foundation of knowledge. Charles Pierce,[9] while answering the question 'How was it that man was ever led to entertain a true theory?', accepts the existence of certain innate capacities of mind as the precondition for successful theory construction. According to Pierce, man's mind is endowed with an innate capacity to imagine a correct theory of some kind and this is a necessary prerequisite for the attainment of any knowledge on the part of any human being. Popper,[10] despite his positivistic attitude, has admitted some sort of theory of 'expectations' which inevitably precedes any observation making. As Popper said:

> At every instant of our pre-scientific or scientific development we are living in the centre of what I usually call a *horizon of expectations*. By this I mean the sum total of our expectations, whether these are subconscious or conscious, or perhaps even explicitly stated in some language. Animals and babies have also their various and different horizons of expectations though no doubt on a lower level of consciousness than, say, a scientist whose horizon of expectations consists to a considerable extent of linguistically formulated theories or hypotheses. . . . In all these cases the horizon of expectations plays the part of a frame of reference: only their setting in this frame confers meaning or significance on our experiences, actions and observations.[11]

---

9. Pierce, C., 'The Logic of Abduction', in *Pierce's Essays in the Philosophy of Science*, Liberal Arts Press, New York, 1957.
10. Popper, K., *Objective Knowledge*, Oxford : At the Clarendon Press, 1972.
11. *Ibid*., p. 345.

We hold that, in order to understand the conceptual system, children do not need to have any teaching of the sort the ordinary language philosophers regard as necessary. As evidence, we cite the child's acquisition of language. Chomsky and his associates have shown that humans are born with an inner device of language acquisition, which predisposes a child to the rapid learning of any natural language. It is a remarkable fact in language learning that in a very short period of time and, on the basis of a relatively few utterances that he has heard, a child becomes a master of his language. He acquires the ability to produce and understand novel sentences. Such a linguistic ability or competence involves the use of a system of a highly abstract linguistic rules of considerable complexity and generality. The child is not taught any such rules. He intuitively knows these rules. A grammar, on this view, is a theory about the speaker's intuitive knowledge of the linguistic rules. The knowledge of these linguistic rules is intuitively given. The native speaker necessarily knows which is a correct move in his language. To sum up, all these findings from recent linguistics, cognitive psychology and philosophy of science singularly point out the inadequacies of Wittgenstein's notion of criterion and the conception of language that follows from it.

5

On the Problem of Communication
Wittgenstein versus Habermas

S. Paneerselvam

> What raises us out of nature . . . *language*. Through its structure, autonomy and responsibility are posited for us. Our first sentence expresses unequivocally the intention of universal and unconstrained consensus.
> — Habermas in *Knowledge and Human Interests*, p. 314

FOR centuries, philosophers believed that meaning, understanding and language were either phenomena of consciousness or to be explained by reference to it. In the analytical tradition, it was Wittgenstein who rejected this. Frege, for example, thought that meaning is an aspect of a word grasped by the mind, but Wittgenstein claimed that meaning of a word is its use. While many analytical philosophers conceived the notion of understanding as an act of the mind, Wittgenstein maintains that understanding something is to be able to do it, use it, or react coherently to it. For him, meaning is determined by the role a word plays in linguistic actions. Not only linguistic expressions, but also a variety of items like, gestures, mutual notes, blue prints and parts of picture puzzles, etc., have meaning. Anything that can play a role in our activities has meaning and the determinants of meaning are whatever determines the roles that these linguistic and non-linguistic items play. There are variety of items which Wittgenstein includes in the above list like, custom, the way people are brought up, culture, activities, people's interest, past experiences, natural reactions, and familiarity with language. What Wittgenstein conveys by this is that the determinants of meaning are primarily social and in order to understand the meaning of something, we must uncover the social factors determinative of its role in our activities. He was more concerned about the social determination of meaning and understanding than the philosophy of consciousness which has been a dominating factor from Descartes to Husserl and the Logical Positivists. It was believed that it is through consciousness a person controls his behaviour and takes cognisance of his surroundings. Wittgenstein argues that human beings and their activities are not to be understood in terms of consciousness. For him, an action in an unreflective reaction to the meaningfulness of the situation in which one is engrossed. Action is not scrutinised by consciousness. In the *Philosophical Investigations*, he says:

> When one thinks something, it is oneself thinking; so one is oneself in motion. One is rushing ahead and so cannot observe oneself rushing ahead. Indeed not.[1]

Wittgenstein thought that between being in a certain situation and acting in a certain way, no intermediate step is needed. He argues that between being ordered to do X and obeying the order, no intermediate conscious event of any kind need occur.[2]

Wittgenstein's language-game extensively deals with unreflective action. He explains how children, for example, interact with the environment and pick up language before they are able to reflect. By doing this, they learn the ability to speak without reflection as the situation warrants or demands. They, in other words, learn forms of unreflective behaviour, ways of 'spontaneously responding with words'. Wittgenstein says

> A language-game does not have its origin in reflection. Reflection is part of the language-game.[3]

Wittgenstein is keen on emphasising the fact that meaning and understanding are socially determined. The significance of his writings for social theory consists in the association of language with definite social practices. Language is intrinsically involved with that which has to be done. The constitution of language as meaningful is inseparable from the constitution of forms of social life as continuing practice. Language and social convention are shown in the

---

1. *Philosophical Investigations*, Part I, 456.
2. *Zettel*, 283-9.
3. *Zettle*, 391.

Philosophical Investigations, to be inextricably intertwined, so that to explicate one is to explicate the other. But the drawback is that Wittgenstein failed to relate the action theory to problems of institutional transformation. No doubt, Wittgenstein had to be complimented for the transition from the ideas of earlier thought to the later, where language and social convention play a primary role. But this theory has not concerned itself with social change or with power relations or with conflict in society. That view that language is primarily a medium of description has been replaced by the view that it is as a medium of social practice, no doubt, cannot be underestimated. Language is a medium of social practice, and as such is implicated in all the variegated activities in which social actors engage. Austin's example explains this. The words uttered in a marriage ceremonial do not constitute description of that ceremonial: they *are* part of that ceremonial. Wittgenstein's example of tool box also explains this.

Attempt to correct above shortcomings was made by some post-Wittgenstenian philosophers like Habermas. Habermas's *On the Logic of the Social Sciences*[4] challenges the existing division between the sciences and the humanities. McCarthy argues that while the natural sciences and the humanities are able to live side by side, in mutual indifference if not in mutual admiration, the social sciences must resolve the tension between the two approaches and bring them under one roof. Habermas's primary aim was to challenge the hegemony of 'empirical-analytical' conceptions of social science, to show that access to the symbolically structured object domain of social inquiry called for procedures similar in important respects to those developed in the text-interpreting humanities. In this attempt, he was influenced by the phenomenological tradition developed by Schutz, the linguistic tradition developed by Wittgenstein and Winch and the hermeneutical tradition developed by Gadamer, which really helped him to support interpretivism. For restructuring of social theory, Habermas makes use of the above three non-conventional approaches. Habermas says that hermeneutics and linguistic analysis convinced him that critical social theory had to break free from the conceptual apparatus of the philosophy of consciousness flowing from Kant and Hegel.

---

4. Habermas, *On the Logic of Social Sciences*., Shierry Weber Nicholsen and Jerry A.Stark, (tr.), UK: Polity Press, 1988.

According to Habermas, language and practice are linked in communicative action. This Wittgenstein calls 'the relationship between language-game and forms of life'. Habermas is aware of the fact that the problem of language has taken the place of the traditional problem of consciousness. The transcendental critique of language takes the place of consciousness. Wittgenstein's life forms which correspond to Husserl's lifeworlds follow not the rules of synthesis of a consciousness but the rules of the grammar of language-games. The linguistic approach, according to Habermas, leads to the grounding of an interpretive sociology that examines social action on the level of intersubjectivity. But the reciprocally interlocked and virtually interchangeable perspectives of a lifeworld don't produce intersubjectivity; but it is given with the grammatical rules of symbolically regulated interactions. Linguistic analysis could become very relevant for the methodology of an interpretive sociology only after logical positivism has passed through 'two stages of self-criticism', according to Habermas. He further says that both stages are evident in the works of Wittgenstein. For example, the *Tractatus* shows the transcendental status of the intended universal scientific language and the *Philosophical Investigations* exhibits this transcendental 'language as such' to be a fiction and discovers in the grammars of ordinary language communication the rules in accordance with which life forms are constituted. Thus, according to Habermas, we can distinguish between the *transcendental stage of reflection* and the *socio-linguistic stage*. He explains how linguistic transcendentalism of the early Wittgenstein's is in many respects similar to Kant's transcendental philosophy of consciousness. The Universal language depicts the world corresponding to transcendental consciousness as such. In *Tractatus*, Wittgenstein was convinced that the logical form of the understanding which provides the criterion for the correct working of language, should not be sought in the established grammars of ordinary language. In *Tractatus* he says:

> It is not humanly possible to gather immediately from it (ordinary language) what the logic of language is. Language disguises thought.[5]

Habermas explains how Wittgenstein had to give up the idea of a unitary language and a world of facts that would be represented in

5. *Tractatus*, 4.002.

that language. He says that in Wittgenstein's later philosophy there is a movement from the framework of a single world-view to different lifeworlds. The rules of these language-games are the grammars of both of languages and of life forms. To every life form, there corresponds its own logic, namely, the grammar of a particular and irreducible language-game. This stage Habrermas calls the second stage, the stage of *socio-linguistic self-reflection*. Thus, the critique of language completes the transition from the critique of pure reason to the critique of practical reason. This means, for Habermas, with the identification of language and life form, the practical reason becomes universal. Even the knowledge of the natural sciences is now constituted within the frame-work of life practice as *one* language-game among many. On this level, linguistic analysis loses the significance for the philosophy of science which was claimed in the *Tractatus*. Linguistic analysis no longer delimits the controversial area of the natural sciences. On the other hand, it acquires special meaning for the social sciences; it not only delimits the sphere of social action but also opens it up. Habermas explains how the grammar of life forms, i.e., the logical analysis of ordinary language touches the object domain of the social sciences themselves. He compares this with the earlier position of Wittgenstein where the logical clarification of the universal language could have only a propaedeutic function. In other words, the later position is concerned with *what is the world* and not with *the essence of the world*. By the rejection of the *Tractatus,* linguistic analysis includes many grammars, and the essence of the world is reflected in them. Linguistic analysis was once used to clarify the transcendental-logical presuppositions of the natural sciences, which were identified with science as such, but now it is equivalent in its structure to an interpretive sociology.

The connection between language-games and life forms is central to the grounding of interpretive sociology in terms of linguistic analysis. It conceives norms that guide action in terms of rules of communication in everyday language. Wittgenstein provides the clue for this and Winch develops this in detail. Winch explains how the linguistic communication logically points to social action. Wittgenstein has attempted the connection between language and praxis. He conceives language-games as a complex of language and praxis. He talks about the primitive use of language as one calling out the words and other acting immediately. In the *Philosophical Investigations*, he says:

> The children are brought up to perform *these* actions, to use *these* words as they do so, and to react in *this* way to the words of others.[6]

The language-game model puts language into relation with communicative action. It includes the use of symbols, the reaction to behavioural expectations, and an accompanying consensus about the fulfilment of expectations that, if it is disturbed, requires restoration of the agreement that is lacking. Otherwise interaction is interrupted and it disintegrates. The language-game, then, no longer functions. Thus, language-games put language into relation with communicative action. The internal connection between language and praxis can be demonstrated logically through an unusual implication of the understanding of meaning. In order to understand a language, we must have a command of it. Understanding, thus, means to be skilled in something, to be able to do or to have a command of something that one has practised and learned. Understanding a language and the ability to speak point that one has gained skills, has learned how to perform certain activities. In *Philosophical Investigations*, Wittgenstein explains how the word 'knows' is related to words 'can' and 'understanding'. Understanding is connected with the virtual anticipation of actions. The understanding of language indicates an ability to take certain actions, whereby this communicative action itself is linked to a symbolised expectation of behaviour. According to Habermas, *language* and *action* are moments of the same model of the language-game. Thus, the connection between *language* and *action* becomes understandable in the kind of learning processes that are linked to the understanding of meaning. To understand means, to have learned to be skilled at something in practical terms. Understanding language is the virtual recapitulation of a process of socialisation, according to Habrermas. Language and the activities are interwoven and 'to imagine a language is to imagine a form of life'.[7]

In this context, Habermas deals with the relation between language-game and linguistic analysis. If every statement is meaningful only in the context of its language-game and if linguistic analysis makes monadic language-games transparent, then the issue is, what

6. *Philosophical Investigations*, Part I, 6.
7. *Ibid.*, Part I, 19.

language-game this analysis is making use of. Habermas is of the view that Wittgenstein could not give a consistent answer to this question of the metalanguage-game of linguistic analysis. Though there is no answer to this question, Wittgenstein could have simply dismissed the question because, the above question arises only when we accord descriptive value to linguistic analysis. But, for Wittgenstein, it has only therapeutic value. It is not a theory, but an activity. But this is not sufficient, according to Habermas. A linguistic analyst must also play the role of an interpreter. He must always presuppose a concept of language-games as such and a concrete pre-understanding in which various languages converge. The interpreter mediates between different patterns of socialisation. In fact, linguistic analysis accomplishes a communication between different language-games. Habermas is of the opinion that Wittgenstein has not dealt this adequately and, hence, he moves towards Gadamer, who has made some attempt in this direction. According to Habermas, Wittgenstein analysed only one dimension of the language-game as a life form; for him, understanding was limited to the recapitulation of the training through which native speakers are socialised into their form of life. For Gadamer, this understanding of language is still not a real understanding, because the accompanying reflection on the application of linguistic rules becomes thematised only when a language-game becomes problematic. Only when the intersubjectivity of the validity of linguistic rules is disturbed, a process of interpretation comes into play to restore consensus. Wittgenstein explains how the rules of linguistic communication imply the conditions of the possibility of their own application. But at the same time, they are rules for the instructional practice through which they are internalised. But Wittgenstein failed to recognise that the same rules also include the conditions of the possibility of interpretation. To the grammar of a language-game belongs not only the fact that it defines a form of life but also that it defines a life form in relation to other life forms as one's own in contrast to those that are foreign. Tradition is the medium in which languages reproduce themselves. The process of socialisation through which the individual learns his language is the smallest unit in the process of tradition. Against this background, we see in Wittgenstein, the language-games of the young do not simply reproduce the practice of the old. With the first basic linguistic rules the child learns not only the conditions of possible consensus, but also the conditions of possible interpretation of the rules, which enables him to overcome and thereby also to express a distance. Hermeneutic understanding, which is only articulated in situations of disturbed consensus, is as fundamental to the understanding of language as in primary consensus.

Hermeneutic self-reflection goes beyond the socio-linguistic level of linguistic analysis suggested by the later Wittgenstein. It is true when the transcendental conception of language breaks down, language gains a new dimension in the pluralism of language-games. A grammar of language-games no longer governs only the linking of symbols but also their institutionalised application in interaction. But Wittgenstein still had too narrow conception of this dimension of application. He sees only the invariant contexts of symbols and activities and fails to appreciate that the application of rules includes their interpretation and further development. It is also true that Wittgenstein, in opposition to positivist bias, certainly first brought to awareness the fact that the application of grammatical rules is not in turn defined by general rules on the symbolic level but rather can only be learned as a connection between language and practice and internalised as part of a form of life. But he was positivistic enough to think of this process as the reproduction of a fixed pattern, as though socialised individuals were wholly subsumed under their language and activities.

Habermas contends that the grammar of language cannot contain a rigid pattern of application. One who has learned to apply its rules has learned not only to express himself in a language, but also to interpret expressions in this language. In other words, grammatical rules along with their possible application also imply the necessity of an interpretation. Habermas argues that Wittgenstein did not consider this aspect. And, hence, he was concerned with the practice of language-games ahistorically. Habermas further argues that with Gadamer, language acquires a third dimension. Grammar governs an application of rules that in turn gives further historical development to the system of rules. The unity of language, which disappeared in the pluralism of language-games, is dialectically restored in the context of tradition. Language exists only as something traditional, for tradition mirrors on a large scale the life-long socialisation of individuals in their language. According to Habermas, Gadamer transcends the monadic isolation of language-games and brings to consciousness the inherent reflectivity of ordinary language. For only when the intersubjective validity of linguistic rules is problematicised does an interpretation come into play which restores the consciousness, thereby overcoming a temporary distance and reproducing the system of rules. Thus, Habermas claims that the writings of Gadamer disclose a dimension of language neglected by Wittgenstein. The unity of language destroyed in the pluralism of language-games is dialectically restored in the contexts of tradition. Language *is* only as handed down. But Habermas attacks Gadamer's approach which converts this historical insight into an absolutisation of cultural tradition. Gadamar overlooks the fact that language itself is dependent upon social processes which are not wholly linguistic in nature. Habermas says:

> language is *also* a medium of domination and social force. It serves to legitimate relations of organised power. In so far as the legitimations of power relations, whose institutionalisation they make possible, are not articulated in so far as these only express themselves in the legitimations, language is *also* ideological.[8]

Habermas explains how in communicative action, language is used as a medium of proper communication. He says:

> only the communicative model of action presupposes language as a medium of uncurtailed communication whereby speakers and hearers, out of the context of their pre-interpreted lifeworld, refer simultaneously to things in the objective, social, and subjective world in order to negotiate common definition of the situation.[9]

Habermas argues that the dominant philosophical perspective of modernity is rooted in a subjectivistic 'philosophy of consciousness' against which he posits an intersubjective philosophy of 'communicative action'. Habermas calls for a 'paradigm shift' from the philosophy of consciousness to a philosophy of communication. Habermas's philosophy of communicative action is rooted in intersubjective communication and is grounded in social solidarity and the utopian potentials of languages: to engage in mutual

---

8. *On the Logic of Social Sciences, op. cit.*, p. 172.
9. Habermas, *The theory of Communicative Action,* Thomas McCarthy, (tr.), vol. I, UK: Polity Press, 1984, p. 95.

understanding, to forge uncoerced consensus, and so on. Habermas believed that the paradigm shift which he seeks begun in the transition from the philosophy of consciousness to a philosophy of language by Frege and Wittgenstein. But the philosophy of language is also too subjective. Hebermas claims basing its philosophical model on the same ego/object model rather than an ego/alter (self/other) model of communication. Some efforts toward this latter paradigm are also found in the social philosophy of Mead and Durkheim, but their work too is limited in that they failed to develop a theory of communicative action which specifies the conditions under which mutual understanding and consensus are reached. For developing a theory of communicative action, Habermas's argument will help to provide a reconstruction of the concept of reason in which rationality is transformed into 'communicative rationality. Instead of deriving the norms of critique from immanent historical forms, Habermas seeks the basis of a critical standpoint in the universally taken-for-granted features of language of communication.

Habermas's theory of communicative competence, which he calls a 'universal pragmatics', has the aim of systematically investigating

> the general structures which appear in every possible speech situation, which are themselves produced through the performance of specific types of linguistic expressions, and which serve to situate pragmaticaclly the expressions generated by the linguistically competent speaker.

Wittgenstein's understanding of language-games, and Austin's and Searles' analysis of speech acts — as well as Chomsky's analysis of linguistic competence — all these help Habermas to develop the theory that all linguistic communication presupposes a background consensus. This consensus can be analysed as involving four different non-reducible validity claims, of which the claim to truth is only one. They are: (1) the *comprehensibility* of the utterance, (2) the *truth* of its propositional content (when assertions are made), (3) the *legitimacy* or rightness of its performative content, and (4) the *veracity* of the speaker. In normal contexts of communicative action, these four claims are not questioned; but when a language-game is disturbed or the background consensus breaks down, then the appropriate form and level of discourse is required in order to assess the implicit claims to validity. Any of the four claims may be questioned.

By endorsing the paradigm shift to the philosophy of language according to the fashion in contemporary German thought, Habermas has been able to incorporate the retainable elements of the previous programme of critical thinking within the larger paradigm of the philosophy of language. Habermas attempts for a critique of what he calls 'subject-centered philosophy'. Analytic thought, following later Wittgenstein, follows a similar direction. Against this background, what appears questionable is the Habermasian critique of subject-centered philosophy. He argues in support of the theory that the reconstruction of a philosophy of language as a theory of rationality, based on the logic of speech acts which places the illocutionary as originary and then goes on to see, in the originary force of an utterance, the logical intersubjective primacy of speech over consciousness through a kind of argument which searches for the conditions for the possibility contained in every speech act, is supposed to reconstitute the transcendental in a linguistic sphere. The 'cognitive' reading of the modern philosophical tradition, with its attempt to incorporate aspects both of linguistic philosophy, particularly of Austin's and the later Wittgenstein's and pragmatism, particularly Mead's and Perire's, does not occur without risk.

For Habermas, linguistic intersubjectivity is the medium within which claims to truth, in the cognitive sense as well as claims to rightness and authenticity, can be raised and arbitrated. We cannot jump out of the language with which our subjectivity is interwoven. For Habermas, the intersubjective dimension of speech cannot be disconnected from the cognitive in this way. This is because it is a distinctive feature of articulated speech that even when an utterance takes the form of, say, a command or a question rather than of an assertion, it nevertheless possesses a content which can be put into propositional form. Even a request contains a reference to a state of affairs. Thus, Habermas argues against Wittgenstein that the meaning constitutive aspect of language cannot be examined in separation from its knowledge-constitutive aspect. Habermas views that Wittgenstein overlooks the fact that the cognitive use of language reveals the dimension which all speech acts must be related. He says that in every elementary utterance there appears a dependent proposition which depends upon the dominant proposition and which expresses the propositional content concerning which agreement is to be reached. This double structure of the speechact mirrors the structure of speech in general: an understanding cannot be reached wherı both partners do not simultaneously occupy both levels — (a) the level of intersubjectivity, which a speaker and hearer speak with each other and (b) the level of objects or state of affairs concerning which they reach agreement. This means that without the propositional content which is thematised in the cognitive use of speech, the interactive use of speech would also be impossible. Habermas suggests that it is precisely the one-sided emphasis upon the interactive use of speech in Wittgenstein which lent his later philosophy a predominantly therapeutic cast.

Habermas is aware of the 'dual structure of speech'. Every act of speech, communicates simultaneously on two levels; it conveys a content which, can, in principle, be cashed out in propositional form; but also establishes a metacommunication which specifies what he calls the 'sense of application' of the content. Metacommunication consists in a system of reciprocal expectations on the part of the participants in dialogue. Habermas is fully aware that metacommunication cannot be determined at the level of explicit knowledge. Metacommunication can be objectified in a further act of speech, but this act of speech will in turn possess its own metacommunicative level, so that dialogue is characterised by an intersubjective dimension which cannot be simultaneously established and objectified.

For Habermas, the relation of language, action and experience differ in principle in three forms of knowledge. In the *Knowledge of Human Interests* he says that

> empirical analysis disclosed reality from the viewpoint of possible technical control over objectified processes which hermeneutics maintains the intersubjectivity of possible action-oriented mutual understanding.[10]

In his *Theory of Communicative Action,* he talks of linguistic intersubjectivity. The idea here is to emphasise that validity claims are referred to intersubjective agreement. Communication oriented to reaching an understanding can be contained only to the degree to which participants credibly sustain the four types of validity claims, which are mentioned already. Communication depends upon the presupposition that each participant can justify the validity claims he raises. Although this presupposition may prove false, Habermas holds that it is unavoidable. For him, the goal of communication is coming

10. Habermas, *Knowledge of Human Interests,* Jeremy J.Shapiro, (tr.), London: Heinemann, 1972, p.191.

to an understanding in regard to each of the types of validity claims that culminates in reciprocal understanding, shared knowledge, mutual trust and accord with each other. This provides a foundation for social theory. It is vital to make the distinction between work and interaction and the latter according to him, is the basis of the communicative and symbolic activities through which social life is constituted. This allowed him to reformulate the three different types of knowledge-constitutive interests which govern all human activities. They are: (1) empirical-analytical interest in potential control (instrumental interest), (2) hermeneutic-historical interest in understanding (practical interest) and (3) critical interest in freedom and autonomy (emancipatory interest). The communicative action is system of reference that cannot be reduced to the framework of instrumental action because here language is monologic. Communicative action is a dialogue and has a system of reference which cannot be conceived in the behavioural system of instrumental action. Thus, all purely interpretative or humanistic approaches are guided by the hermeneutic-historical interests. It supports a model of communicative action where there is intersubjective action. But Habermas maintains that even this type of interest does not constitute an exhaustive approach to the study of social phenomena. They are restricted by the limits of medium of language which can be seen in the writings of Wittgenstein and Gadamer. In the empirical-analytic interests, there is a total denial of the critical approach and in the hermeneutic-historical interests, there is a pre-understanding of traditional heritage. Hence, there is a need for the third kind of interest, namely, critical-emancipatory interest which points towards an ideal space for free communication unmasking the hidden systematic distortions. The unity of knowledge and interest proves itself in a dialectic which takes the historical traces of suppressed dialogue and reconstructs what has been suppressed, says Habermas. This makes his position clear that only in the ideal speech situation, there is a genuine dialogue where there is no hierarchy between the speakers. By narrating the distinction between instrumental and practical interests which are concerned with control and survival, and mutual understanding respectively, Habermas proves how the emancipatory interest is concerned with the freedom from a dogmatic and controlling past. He admits that the form of social action here is communication which is made possible through ideal speech situation. The ideal speech situation is explicitly known by the basic distinction which Habermas makes between action and discourse. In any successful discourse, the speakers involved-in must have reciprocalicity. 'The competent speakers must reciprocally maintain with each of their speech-acts', says Habermas. If all the four conditions mentioned earlier are satisfied, then communication is not only complete but also unproblematic. The meaningful of language and its usage can become a complete process only in the form of discourse. Those who participate in the discourse no longer seek to exchange information of validity claims. All authentic discourse aims at a regulative ideal of universal, unrestricted communication.

Thus, the 'linguistic turn' of Wittgenstein has moved into another direction namely, 'social turn' in the hands of Habermas. Social practice, according to Habermas, is constituted both in labour and language. Language operates through social practice and it is not possible to neglect the social conditions, which play a role in all linguistic practices. This means that language and social practice always are inseparable.

6

Wittgenstein on Private Language

P.R. Bhat

1. Introduction

THERE are several versions of private language argument and each of which has different philosophical significance. A version of it makes it out to be the problem of philosophy of language and another makes it to be the problem of philosophy of mind.[1] Yet another version of private language argument makes it to be the problem of rule-following leading to a strong version of skepticism about knowledge.[2] The first version of the argument basically shows how the private language is not possible. The strategy adopted here is to show how language is impossible without ostensive definition by showing how ostensive definition is not possible with regard to sensations and feelings. Thus, a private language having significance only to oneself involving private vocabulary about one's own sensations, feelings and thoughts, is not possible. The second version forcefully argues that we have not knowledge of other minds. That is to say, we have no way of understanding the sensations, feelings, thoughts and intentions of others. In other words, finding meaning and significance to several cultural activities would be impossible without presupposing human mind. This version, thus, treats the private language argument to be a *reductio ad absurdum argument* designed by Wittgenstein to show how behaviourism without the assumption of human mind is inadequate. The third version of private language argument attributed to Wittgenstein by Kripke admits the merit in the argument of skeptic

1. O.R.Jones, (ed.), *The Private Language Argument* (*PLA*), MacMillan St. Martin's Press, 1971, p. 13.
2. Kripke, S., *Wittgenstein on Rules and Private Language* (*WRPL*), Basil Blackwell, 1982.

regarding rule-following. It is impossible for anyone to identify the rule that was followed in the past and the one that is being followed now. Thus, we cannot advance the *use theory of meaning* to explain our verbal behaviour. Moreover, there is no fact, mental or physical which could help us identify unique interpretation in a context where several competing interpretations fit the context in a suitable manner. Thus, even the *dispositional theory of meaning* is rendered incompetent to explain our rule governed behaviuour. We have no way of explaning to the skeptic how certain words acquire meaning. It is impossible to show how our past and present intentions are reflected in our actions. Thus, Kripke's version goes one step further by claiming that an adequate philosophy of language answering the skeptic is not possible and the option open is to grant the skeptic his point and yet find an alternative. This alternative is what is known as the *skeptical solution to the skeptical problem* where change in attitude is recommended as a way out of the problem. We ascribe intentions to others if the behaviour of an individual justifies such an ascription given the conventions of language, opines Kripke.

The word 'private' itself was debated over extensively. For instance, A.J. Ayer takes the term to mean something private as opposed to something public. Sense experience, feeling and thought are private as opposed to code language though contingently a code language is intelligible to only one individual. Diary noting of criminals in code language would not qualify to be called private since the notings in principle are translatable in several languages. In fact, such code languages are dependent on natural languages for effective functioning. Telegraphic language is one such language. A language, if in principle can be made public, would not qualify itself to be called private.[3] The second and a more important sense in which the term 'private' can be understood is the subjective experience of different individuals: their sensations, feelings and thoughts. However, there is no doubt that these experiences are private in a specific sense, that my experience of physical pain is exclusively mine, but the question remains whether these experiences qualify to be called language. The third sense in which one often interprets the term 'private' is the mode in which we think that we associate the inner experience with our external behaviour, including our verbal behaviour. Since the association between the word 'plain' and my experience of pain is known to me alone, the way other individuals can know

3. See A.J. Ayer in *PLA*, p. 51.

my pain is by inferring my pain from my verbal and non-verbal behaviour. Since human action is purposive, it is not possible to make sound inference about my perception, feeling and intention from my behaviour. This interpretation has eventually led to the problem of rule-following skepticism in the hands of Kripke where Kripke develops skepticism about knowledge presupposing rule-governed behaviour.

We want to address the issue of private language afresh from all the important perspectives. We must keep in mind the general framework within which Wittgenstein answers both the issues of language and knowledge satisfactorily. Having found merit in the *use* theory of meaning Wittgenstein had the project to show that the theory is adequate to explain the subjective terms like sensations, feelings and thoughts. He had to ensure that skeptic would not come in the way of such a project on philosophy of language, for if the skeptic has his way as demonstrated by Kripke subsequently, the skeptic would destroy in one stroke both the theory of meaning and the theory of knowledge.

What was evident to Wittgenstein, which is used in every form of the private language argument, is the two basic components required for satisfactory development of philosophy of language: referring expressions and predicate expressions. Wittgenstein systematically develops arguments to show how referring expressions themselves cannot constitute a language. While dealing with predicate expressions, i.e., expressions that involve rule-following, he again shows how there ought to be a link, which is generally in the form of conventions, between a predicate expression and its applications. Thus, the arguments advanced here would have the following strategy:

Even though Wittgenstein constructed *reductio ad absurdum argument* to show that the skeptic is wrong, i.e., we have to necessarily assume the existence of sensations, feelings and thoughts of others, he also gives clear examples where knowledge of intentions, understanding of others are known. If what is often called private is accessible to others, then the private language argument has lost its ground. We would like to argue, against the commonly held view, that Wittgenstein held the view that mental phenomena are accessible to others sometimes directly and sometimes using criteria in an indirect manner. What is important is to view a particular action in the context of a form of life, as a part of the totality and not in isolation in Wittgenstein. Note that we are capable of pretending and that makes it difficult to distinguish between a pretension from the genuine behaviour; but also note that we are capable of identifying pretensions as well. Skeptic conveniently assumes that we cannot identify pretensions and dismisses all knowledge.

2. Private language argument

There is a tendency in philosophers to think that proper names are relatively easier to analyse. A simplistic account of language learning begins with the learning of proper names using ostensive definitions. In *Investigations,* Wittgenstein extensively deals with ostensive definitions and proper names. He points out that naming is a fairly complex linguistic activity, which cannot be performed by the beginner of a language.[4] There are several ways that an ostensive definition can fail. One might mistake the direction of pointing; colour for the shape; background for the object; and so on. What makes an ostensive definition succeed is the familiarity of the context within which the ostensive definition is offered. One who does not know the institution of naming cannot understand ostensive definition at all. Moreover, naming is not possible without having prior familiarity of the use of language. For instance, if one points to the shape while defining a figure, one should not mistaknely think that the colour of the solid is being defined. Ostensive definition is a tool of language that can work only after the user has gained sufficient mastery of language. Wittgenstein is of the view that the use of proper names arises within the context of the use of language only after one knows how to make use of proper names. Naming is not performed for the sake of naming; it is a preparation for something else, say, the act of describing.

Language operates with two kinds of words, names and predicate terms. Even though Quine has made a serious attempt to show that names are redundant for logical purposes, the arguments are inconclusive with respect to the functions of names in language.[5]

---

4. Wittgenstein, L., *Philosophical Investigations* (*PI*), 2nd edn. Basil Blackwell, Oxford, 1974, § 257.

5. W.V. Quine *Pursuit of Truth,* revised edition, Harvard University Press, Cambridge, 1992, pp. 32-3. Quine finds no difficulty about proper names or their occurrence in the form of existential quantifiers in the context of translation. Also see his article 'On What There Is' in *Contemporary Readings in Logical Theory* (d.) by I.M.Copi and J.A. Gould, N.Y. The Macmillan Company, 1967.

The function of names is taken over by the existential quantifiers and, thus, making the proper names redundant only in the context of quantified logic. Natural language has proper names as essential component.

The first argument against private language attempts to show how words pertaining to sensations, feelings and thoughts cannot be defined ostensively. Reference theory of meaning takes naming to be the only linguistic activity that gives meaning to words, but naming itself is considered to be a preparation for further linguistic activity, according to Wittgenstein.[6] For instance, we use names to describe the things named. Ostensive definition to name a thing is possible only after gaining certain familiarity in the use of language. Sensations, feelings and thoughts cannot be named using ostensive definitions. We cannot point to anything using 'this', 'that' in defining sensations, feelings and thoughts. These words do not function like proper names to be demonstrative pronouns.[7] Hence, it is not possible to name any of the experiences, feelings and thoughts using ostensive definition. This failure to name experience would make it impossible for us to describe unique experiences of each individual. Definite descriptions too would fail, since definite descriptions do often make use of the demonstrative pronouns. The pain in my foot, although I succeed to refer to unique pain in my foot at a given time, others have no way of using this expression as a definite description. It might be the case that I had pain, not in the foot, but in the spinal cord which has resulted because of the brushing against the backbone resulting in the false sensation of pain in the foot. Moreover, after Kripke, it is amply clear that definite descriptions do not function like proper names.[8]

As is the case with sensations, which differ from person to person, we may also speak of meaning, which would differ from person to person. If we go by reference theory of meaning and if we admit the possibility of private language, the meaning of the term 'toothache' would be different to different individuals, since each individual would have experienced pain differently given the difference in the intensity and duration of their experiences. This argument is defective can be provided in the following way. Ask the question: How is it that the

---

6. *PI,* § 26.
7. *PI,* § 9 & § 30.
8. Kripke, S.A., *Naming and Necessity* (*NN*), Basil Blackwell, 1980, pp. 55 ff.

individual is able to identify the pain as toothache when it occurs second time? If the argument that my sensations are different from the sensations of others and, hence, my meaning of the term is different from the meaning others assign to the same term, then we will have to admit that the meaning of the term 'toothache'. when it occurred on a Monday is different from the meaning of the same term when the pain occurred on Saturday. Thus, we would require words to reprent every experience of ours everyday of the week and there would be no word representing common aspects of these experiences. Thus, the function of one word 'toothache' in our natural language would be performed, by innumerable words in this perspective. If this is the account of all words of sensations, feelings and thoughts, any operation in language is made impossible.

As we mentioned earlier, a language cannot consist of only proper names. We would require general terms too, to describe, to explain and to do lot many other things that we normally do with language. That is to say, one needs terms which have several applications. For instance, we need terms like 'pain', which can be used again and again, when we have the experiences in several occasions. We cannot even speak of 'experience' more than once unless we have a term that can be used in varied occasions. The terms such as 'pain', 'sensation', 'experience', 'feeling', etc., belong to public language. In developing a private language if one makes use of these terms, then the private language would be in the public domain since its intelligibility is derived from the public language. At best such a private language would not be anything different from a code language, a simplistic version of which would be telegraphic language or the language of traffic signals.

What is important to note is that Robinson Crusoe too cannot have a private language in the sense required. One can imagine that he names each and every important experience in his life. Yet, he cannot compare any two experiences in his life. That would be possible only if he abstracts sufficiently enough from these experiences and uses words that are general in nature. If he abstracts, to the level where he can speak of the 'same' or 'similar', he is already in the domain of public language. Others observing his behaviour sufficiently long could learn his signs and their usage.

Without the concept of generality, one cannot have rules, and, hence, Robinson Crusoe cannot have rules unless he abstracts from his experiences. And any meaning Crusoe or we assign to any sign would be at this general level of a rule having several applications. That is to say, it is quite clear that there cannot be a rule that has application only once, and consequently, there cannot be a predicate having only one possible object of predication. We said, one possible object of predication, which is different from a predicate having only one application. For instance, the present Queen of England has only one true application, and yet there could be several individuals to whom the expression applies in different possible worlds. Generality takes us beyond individuality and this is the reason why we are able to abstract and construct a general term by just observing one example. It is enough to observe one moon to form the concept of moon, because we can conceive of moons having known just one moon.

Robinson Crusoe may not have a language, but we being born in a community, it is impossible to develop a private language without interference by the natural language. A word in private language is understood in terms of its equivalent in the natural language. That is the way we explain a word in French by giving its equivalent in English.[9] If language is a form of life, it is just not possible to have two languages, which are not translatable, if both the languages cover the same domain of life. Translation of a private language into his mother tongue must be possible for an individual since both are forms of life being languages. Both the languages cover the same domain, private language of an individual being narrow; his mother tongue would cover the domain of private language. If private language is translatable into a natural language, then it does not remain private in any significant sense and if no translation of private language into a natural language possible, one wonders whether we have justfiably used the term 'language' to refer to perceptions, feelings and thoughts.

In this a real possiblity? Can it be the case that the subject has two criteria and the others have only one regarding the mental states? The answer ought to be in the negative. Rules by virtue of their generality are public; even the individual who obeys rules privately obeys the public rules. Otherwise, to think that one is obeying the rule would have been adequate example of obeying the rule.[10] It is misleading to claim that experience gives us the meaning. No doubt

9. *PI*, § 208.
10. *PI*, § 202.

that certain feelings accompany certain intentions. For instance, I change my decision to go away tomorrow. This feeling may be psychologically related to my taking certain decision, but the feeling does not constitute the meaning. This is the reason Wittgenstein claims that the exclusive experiences and feelings of individuals do not constitute part of the language.[11] And when we speak of criteria, we are in the domain of language. The person, who uses the public criteria, need not have to pay attention to the private feelings. For instance, the private feeling that would be aroused in perceiving a red rose need not be the same for all and yet red rose is red for all those who perceive it.[12] There is public meaning that is common to all. Criteria are necessarily public. Hence, no private meaning is possible.

3. Skeptic and the rule-following

Rule-following paradox was elaborated by Kripke to draw our attention to the philosophical difficulty about meaning and knowledge if the skeptic is right. The skepticism about meaning and knowledge is developed by the skeptic by refuting the very possibility of language both natural and private. The skeptical arguments that are valid against natural language are equally valid against private language. Wittgenstein and Kripke's formulation of the thesis of Wittgenstein, draw our attention to the rules governing the behaviour of predicate expressions rather than expressions themselves. There are subtle advantages in this, especially when our mindset is in favour of *reference theory of meaning*. The major advantage is that we can keep the distinction between the referring expression and predicate expression intact; and the private language argument in this formulation focuses on predicate expressions rather than referring expressions as names. In summary, the problem is as follows: Rules are said to be conventional in line with the *use theory of meaning*. That is to say, linguistic rules are invoked arbitrarily and followed thereafter to form a convention. If intention is subjective and if rules are arbitrary, then when we observe the behaviour of an individual, we invariably assign meaning to his behaviour invoking some rules. It may be incidentally true that the rule we invoke to understand the behaviour of the agent is identifical to the rule that he follows. Often it may not be the case. There is no way we can ensure that the rule

11. *PI*, § 269-72.
12. *PI*, § 272.

that he follows and the meaning he attaches to his behaviour are the same as we do. The agent might have specific significance to his behaviour following a certain rule and we might assign different motive and different purpose to his behaviour. This is very likely, since we have no fact or evidence that can give us some idea as to which rule the agent is following. If the above picture is gloomy, Kripke meakes us feel embarrassed by raising the question: would the agent at least know which rule he follows? One is tempted to say that he must know which rule he follows since under normal circumstances it makes no sense to say that I do not know my intentions. However, if there are no facts that indicate the rules the agent follows, a corollary of this is that the agent cannot be sure whether he has followed the rule 1 or 2 in the past. Even if he knows that he has followed rule 1 in the past, if rule 2 has identifical applications with respect to past instances of rule 1 and rule 2 differs from rule 1 only in unaccomplished cases, the agent cannot know whether he has followed rule 1 or rule 2 from all the facts about himself. It can happen that the first few observed days of two systems of calenders have the same days and months, yet one cannot conclude that the two individuals follow the same calendar; the year of new calendar might come to close earlier than the year of another calendar.

Kripke makes Wittgenstein the advocator of skepticism of rule-following. It is another matter that the issue is debatable. Our own reading of Wittgenstein is that he did not advocate such a view. We believe that he constructed rule-following skeptical argument only to refute skepticism in its best formulation. However, Kripke's formulation of rule-following skepticism has philosophical merit of its own. Kripke's skeptic poses the problem in the following manner. It might happen that all the observed cases and even the unobserved but expected cases could be in accordance with rule 1 while the rule might differ in the case of unobserved and not yet estimated behaviour of the agent. That is to say the rule 2 which the agent follows is different from rule 1 though both the observer and the agent think that they apply the same rule since the nomenclature of the rule is the same. Both the observer and the agent speak of the rule plus, but one has rule of addition in mind and the other has the rule of *quaddition* in mind though both speak of, let us say, the rule of summation.[13] The rule of *quaddition* is the same as rule of addition

13. We can make the skeptical argument of Kripke more powerful by claiming that the nomenclature remains the same though the rules followed are different.

till we reach the number 57 but differs from the rule of addition when the summation of 57 + 68 is to be performed. The total instead of being 125 when one performs *quaddition,* it would rather be 5.[14] Basically what the rule of *quaddition* demonstrates is that rules are arbitrary and any arbitratiness of rules cannot be questioned if conventionalised. Kripke's skeptic can now speak of several competing rules of addition that only differ in their unobserved cases. If this argument is accepted, then no observer would be able to conclude which rule the agent has being followed since several competing interpretations of his behaviour based on different rules which differ only in their unobserved cases equally fit the context.

The rule-following paradox raises the fundamental issue of the relation between rules and their extensions. On the one hand we say that when we learn the rule, we grasp the entire rule. Moreover, we consider that a rule can have infinite applications, and grasping the rule would mean grasping infinite applications of these rules.[15] This is the position of Baker and Hacker, for instance, which claims that a rule is internally related to its extension and, hence, a rule determines its attention.[16] Wittgenstein draws our attention to another obvious fact about ourselves. Since we have observed only a few cases of the application of a rule, i.e., we know only finite set of applications, whereas the rule has infinite applications; one cannot reasonably claim that one knows all the cases of applications. This is the position held by Malcom who claims that rules do not determine their extensions.[17] Those who say that a red rose is red and a white rose is white in the dark are the ones who believe the rule determines its extension and those who say that the colour of both the red rose and the white rose in the dark are indistinguishable since they are not perceived in the dark[18] are those who hold that rules do not determine their extension.

---

14. *WRPL*, pp. 21 ff.
15. The comparison of rules with rails is apt. Beginning of a series is one like the visible section of rails, and invisible part of them that are laid to infinity can be compared to unlimited application of a rule. See *PI,* § 218.
16. Baker, G.P. & Hacker, P.M.S, 'Malcom on Language and Rules', *Philosophy*, vol. 65, 1990, pp. 170 ff.
17. See Malcom, N., 'Wittgenstein on Language and rules' *Philosophy,* vol. 64, 1989, pp. 5-28.
18. See *PI,* § 514-15.

Wittgenstein admits that we are tempted to think that when we grasp the rule, we grasp the infinite applications of the rule, and yet we need to make new decisions when an actual context is encountered where we proposed to apply the rule.[19] There is no doubt that we understand the word and if we understand the word we know the use of the word, and obviously if we know the use of the word we know the contexts in which the word could be applied and, hence, the conclusion: rule determines its extension. And if this conclusion is valid, then it cannot be the case that we have doubts about the next number in a series given the rule and the first few numbers of the series.

Consider Wittgenstein's example of trying to figure out the rule that is being followed. *A* has written down the numbers, 1, 5, 11, 19, 29; at this point *B* says he knows how to go on.[20] *B* has discovered that the formulae $a_n = n^2 + n - 1$ is being followed. It is also possible that *B* does not think of formulae, he finds the series of differences and finds the series 4, 6, 8, 10 and says he can go on. Or *B* grasps the numbers 1, 5, 11, 19, 29 as series and says that he can go on exactly the way he would have done in the case of 1, 3, 5, 7, 9 and so on. Kripke's skeptic would have problems with all these. Each one of the methods adopted to find the next number in the series is considered to be possible, but Kripke's skeptic would not agree with this. Since the value of *n* in the formulae could be different in the every application. He could not be sure that the next number has to be 41, for instance. And when we follow the second method, Kripke's skeptic cannot be sure whether the next number in the series would be 12 after 10, it could be 13 ! And the subsequent numbers could be 16, 19 and so on. The grasping of the rule could be different to Kripke's skeptic and according to Wittgenstein it ought to be the same for all. This seems to be a crucial point of difference between Kripke and Wittgenstein since the latter says that when we grasp a rule, we grasp it at once; we know its infinite applications at once.

Since Wittgenstein admits the revisionary nature of rules, he would not hesitate to say that in some cases, our understanding might have to be revised. Yet what is important to note is that several individuals can grasp the rule that is being followed by an agent. He admits that doubts lead to modifications of our hypothesis and

19. *PI*, § 197.
20. *PI*, § 151.

expectation. We reassure ourselves of the rule that is being followed by predicting the next application and confirming it. Moreover, we cannot jump to the skeptical conclusion that we in fact doubt simply because we can imagine a doubt.[21] Kripke's skeptic exploits this ability to imagine a doubt to advance his argument. He builds his argument on the basis of the logical possibility that it is possible for the agent to follow the rule *quus*. If knowledge is a mental state, if fear is a mental state, doubt too is a mental state. It may be there; it may not be there at different time intervals. Kripke's skeptic needs to show that doubt is there as a mental state all the time in all the individuals to prove his point. Otherwise, he has to admit that there are cases of certainty and, hence, skepticism has a weak case. It would not be enough if Kripke's skeptic shows that there is a logical possibility that everyone doubts all behaviour of himself and that of others all the time. This is equally true of the experience of one's own sensations, feelings and thoughts.

Wittgenstein, on our reading, wants to reject any skeptical conclusion of the above sort. For him, the *use theory of meaning* has to establish the relationship between rules and their application. That is to say, the use of a word is its application. The application of a rule indicates that it is not simply thinking that is important; it is not the intention alone that is important; but the behaviour or the action that is what matters. In fact, intention is measured against action. Wittgenstein is trying to unearth this relationship. There would be no point of speaking about *use as meaning* without the application of rules. If this were the case, thinking that one is obeying the rule would have been following the rule.[22] And applying a rule would mean that it is not mere interpretation. That is the reason why Wittgenstein opposes the view that whatever one does is, on some interpretation, in accord with the rule by saying

> any interpretation still hangs in the air along with what it interprets, and cannot give it any support. Interpretations by themselves do not determine meaning.[23]

It is an active process of thinking or doing something that gives

21. *PI*, § 84.
22. *PI*, § 202.
23. *PI*, § 198.

meaning.[24] And if the rules are interpreted without any regularity in their use, then they cannot be conceived as rules of language.[25] Simply an interpretation without application is useless and, hence, has no practical consequences. The act of interpretation does not take place without a proper hypothesis. 'When we interpret we form hypotheses, which may prove false.'[26] Therefore, for Wittgenstein, a skeptic would be a genuine skeptic if and only if he practices skepticism; and we would have private language if and only if we use such a language.

4. Mental states and mental processes

What we want to show is that Wittgenstein has not denied the notion of mental states whereas he attempts to show that what is known as 'private language' is impossible. This he wants to show as a part of his larger project, namely, the reference theory of meaning is terribly inadequate. Secondly, he wants to prove the skeptic wrong. He uses the *reductio ad absurdum* argument to prove him wrong.[27] What is known as *rule-following* skepticism after Kripke, is the *reductio ad absurdum argument* developed by Wittgenstein with the sole purpose of rejecting it as absurd. The words like 'sensations', 'feelings', 'thoughts' belong to the language of public domain and, hence, they must have meaning in the ordinary language which, of course, follows from his conviction in the *use theory of meaning.*

The issue of private language became important partly because the philosophers have failed to note the distinction between mental states and mental processes which Wittgenstein discusses in great detail in *Philosophical Investigations*. Perception that has led to belief is a mental state, whereas perceiving is a mental process. Experiences, whether sensual or that of feelings, are classified as mental processes. Generally when we suffix 'ing' to a word of mental state, we obtain a mental process. But note that '*seeing as*' is a mental state to Wittgenstein since it involves a point of view, not a process. When we describe a physical state such as my room; we describe our state of mind. The word 'describe' is wrongly applied to sensation when we say that we describe our pain.[28] Several individuals,

---

24. *PI*, § 212.
25. *PI*, § 207-8.
26. *PI*, § 212.
27. See N. Malcolm in *PLA*, p. 41.
28. *PI*, § 290.

especially the ones who attribute behaviourism of one form or the other to Wittgenstein, take both mental processes and mental states to be something 'private'.

Often we fail to mark the difference between a mental state and a mental process resulting in the mystery of our mind. This distinction is a based on some other basic distinction in Wittgenstein: something that can be described and something that can only be expressed. He holds, as mentioned above, that a mental state can be described, whereas a mental process can only be expressed.[29] To describe a mental state, we do not have to use the demonstrative pronouns such as 'this', 'that'. For naming, we need to have some criteria to 'fix the reference' to use Kripke's terminology,[30] or we need ostensive definition, but describing would not require fixing of reference or ostensive definition. In contrast, mental processes cannot be described, but can only be expressed. Sensations, for instance, are indescribable. Speaking of them, Wittgenstein remarks:

> It is not a something, but not a nothing either! The conclusion was only that a nothing would serve just as well as a something about which nothing could be said.[31]

But mental states are not mental processes and, hence, they cannot be called private in the sense that others cannot understand them. So, mental states have duration, they have beginning and end. For instance, belief is a mental state. One can meaningfully say that I have begun to believe that globalisation has started yielding fruits. I can indicate that I have changed my belief by claiming that I no more believe that Newton's theory of motion is right.

The large part of the confusion arises because one cannot describe mental processes. These mental processes are said to be individualistic, only the individual concerned experiences them. Mental states are not such individualistic phenomena, though we tend to classify both mental processes and mental states under one type. For instance, several individuals can have the same mental state. Several of us believe that Ashoka fought Kalinga war. Or, for instance, several individuals can have the same intention, intention of building an educational institution for instance.

29. *PI*, § 290.
30. *NN* p. 55.
31. *PI*, § 290 & § 304.

A mental process is expressed in behaviour. There is an identity between mental process and human behaviour. For instance, the process of suffering and the expression of suffering such as avowals are enmeshed together. Thinking, believing, expecting, hoping, etc., are all processes which are expressed in one's behaviour and describing them would be describing the behaviour itself, In contrast, expectation, having some opinion, hoping for something, knowing something, and being able to do something, are all called mental states.[32] The sentence 'I am afraid' is a description of a state of mind.[33] Mental states have duration; one can speak of change of opinion for instance. Language does not enter the arena of mental processes, but certainly speaks of mental states. What Wittgenstein rejects is the possibility of private experiences as processes entering the language but not their counterparts, i.e., the mental states. Belief, attitude, expectation, hope, thought, memory, etc., one can have as mental states, but believing, feeling, expecting, hoping, thinking, remembering, etc., apart from these being expressions of corresponding mental states, there is nothing that is significant to language in these processes.

A note of caution here. 'Mental process' is an expression in language that all of us are familiar with. This expression is one like 'pain' having meaning in language. When we reject mental processes as not part of language, we reject the individualistic unintelligible processes and not the general term 'mental process'. Therefore, it is important to keep in mind that when we reject 'pain' having only individual significance, we reject ununderstandable specific individual experiences. We cannot speak of unspeakable and, hence, the mental process we speak is always in general terms and in the domain of public.

As noted earlier, mental states can be described; they can be expressed in words and in behaviour. Since these mental states are states of the mind, even introspection is not required to know them. We do not introspect and speak about our intentions. The mental states of individuals are known to others from their behaviour including their verbal behaviour. Hence, there is no mental state, for instance any fear, hope, expectation, belief, understanding, or knowledge that cannot be expressed in language. A proposition can be expression

---

32. *PI*, § 572 & 573.
33. *PI*, § p.191.

of belief, hope, expectation, etc., which are mental states.[34] Believing as a mental state has duration; it has some beginning. When I change my belief, it would have an end too. I can express my belief independently of its duration in a sentence.[35] That is to say, one can speak of truth conditions of these mental states. Since a proposition would take a truth value, descriptions of mental states[36] too can be true or false.

Since understanding is a mental state, anything that is a mental state does not require any further interpretation to grasp it. Therefore, a question about mental state, e.g., 'How do you know that you believe?' cannot be asked sensibly in most cases.[37] We are aware of our mental states and others can know about our mental states, through our expression of mental state either verbal or otherwise.

5. Intention and meaning

Having made the distinction between mental states and mental processes, we can now apply this distinction to our concept of intention. Intention is a mental state, not a process, holds Wittgenstein.. Therefore, intention can be described. An inner process cannot be described, but an inner state can be. There is nothing that corresponds to an intention in the physical or biological world. For instance, I had the intention to come to Hyderabad. Can we ask when did the intention begin and when did the intention got fulfilled? What was the case when I did nothing towards my goal? Did I still intend to achieve the end? Wittgenstein holds that intention is always in the present and, hence, I had the intention to reach Hyderabad all along till I reached Hyderabad.

Since rules are intentional, they too must share the attribute of mental state. The rule exists as a mental state all along even when we use or do not use the rule. The rule of plus exists as a mental state all along we perform the function of addition. A rule guides our behaviour so to speak. It guides us all along like a blind man is being

34. *PI*, § 574.

35. *PI*, pp. 188, 191-2.

36. *PI*, § 585. Description of mental states are possible " 'If I tell someone' I can't keep my mind on my work today; I keep on thinking of his coming '— this will be called a description of my state of mind'.

37. *PI*, § 587.

guided by his son holding his hand.[38] Following the rules is like obeying the order; we are trained to do so, says Wittgenstein.[39]

Wittgenstein is clear that we cannot speak of past intentions. The grammar of the expression 'I was then going to say . . . ' is misleading. It gives us the impression that we remember our past intentions. The expressions 'I could then have gone on' is closely related to the former expression.[40] It is misleading to believe that we remember our past intentions; however, it would not be wrong to claim that I have understood the possibility of my having such an intention. We speak of our present intention when we speak of our past intentions.[41] We interpret our past intention in our present mental state. While discussing the notion of 'seeing as' Wittgenstein makes it abundantly clear that we have the ability to perspectivise. The other expression 'a picture' too indicates this point. Wittgenstein uses duck-rabbit example to demonstrate this point.[42] Our past intentions are grasped exactly the way we would grasp the intention of others. We read off our past intentions on the basis of our present perspective.

Thus, to believe that one's intention is private is not to believe that it is subjective and personal the way sensations and feelings are. All mental states including intentions have duration. The same intention can last for several days, months and years. All along, the individual might do several things relevant to achieve his goal. His intentions can be known exactly the way we can know the rules that others follow. We can know the intention of a cat and a beast in a natural surrounding, says Wittgenstein.

> What is the natural expression of an intention? — Loot at a cat when it stalks a brid; or a beast when it wants to escape.[43]

Intention is expressed in our natural behaviour. Though intentions are mental sates, they can be known, if not instantaneously, by

---

38. *PI*, § 172-3.
39. *PI*, § 206.
40. *PI*, § 606.
41. This point has been discussed in detail in 'Intention in Wittgenstein', *Indian Philosophical Quarterly*, vol. XX, No.3, July 1993, pp. 279-308 by the author.
42. *PI*, pp.194 ff.
43. *PI*, § 647.

observing the behaviour of the concerned individual for considerable duration.

There is no mystery about mental states. I cannot know what is there is the box without opening the lid; similarly, I cannot know the intention of an individual without observing his behaviour. If my inability to know what is there in the box without opening the lid is not a mystery, why should my inability to know the intention of an individual without observing his behaviour be so mysterious?

It seems possible to speak of individual intentions and collective intentions. However, Wittgenstein seems to say that individual intentions are made possible because of the institutions such as language. For instance, it is possible for me to intend to play a game of chess, since the game exists as part of the social institution. Wittgenstein claims that intention is embedded in its situation, in human customs and institutions.[44] What is the super-connection between the intention and the object intended? He asks. Should we say that until one has not made the move, one does not know the intention of the player of chess? He finds the answer in the list of rules, in the teaching of it, in the day-to-day practice of playing it.[45]

Institutional rules are intentional; that is to say we have agreed to abide by the rules. In other words, we know the goals and functions of these rules and we know all the applications of the rules when we grasp the rules or invent them. We invent new games, and new language games as well. The tricky question is: How do we introduce these new institutions if institutions are needed to express our intentions? The answer seems to lie in the institution of language itself. We are born in an environment that spoke language. Language is a form of life.[46] We make use of this institution to build new institutions, and use these new institutions to build yet another institution and so on. It may be pointless to ask how did the first institution, say of language, came into existence, since we found human civilisation that always spoke one language or the other, tribal or developed.

---

44. *PI*, § 198 & 337.
45. *PI*, § 197.
46. *PI*, § 19, 23, 241.

6. Assertion and ascription

The above account, which institutionalises the intention, found justification in Kripke's reading of Wittgenstein. Wittgenstein on Kripke's reading speaks of assertibility condition instead of truth condition applicable to statements about mental states. Wittgenstein's skeptical solution concedes to the skeptic that no 'truth conditions' or 'corresponding facts' in the world exist that make a statement like 'Jones, like many of us, means addition by '+' 'true'.'[47] Granting the skeptic his argument, Kripke invokes the notion of 'skeptical solution to the skeptical problem', and speaks of ascribing intentions to the agents based on their behaviour.[48] This ascription of intention to the agents is made possible by the institution of language and society. According to Kripke, Wittgenstein gives up the attempt to prove the skeptic wrong, and offers a compromised solution to the problem of rule-following skepticism. Given the institution of language, certain assertions about the intentions of others could be made on the basis of their behaviour. When the criterion to ascribe belief to others is satisfied, the members of that community have the linguistic license to ascribe belief to the agent. For instance, if an individual behaves the way we do in following the rule of addition, on the basis of his behaviour, we could ascribe him the intention of following the rule of addition. Ascription of intention to behaviour of Robinson Crusoe is done by conceiving him to be a member of our community says Kripke.[49]

Kripke does not notice that this skeptical solution too is infested with problems. For instance, it is paradoxical to say that we are justified in ascribing an intention to an agent yet admit that one might be wrong. Kripke's vision of assertibility condition[50] only goes, thus, far: we are justified in making the ascription on the basis of the behavioural criteria. Our attitude towards the agent and our subsequent behaviour depends on what ascription we make about the agent. Quite true, yet the important point is overlooked here. For instance, we may ascribe motive of theft to an individual based on certain behaviour of the individual. However, this question might be very relevant: is he a thief? It can be the case that he suffers from certain

---

47. *WRPL*, pp. 86, 90.
48. *WRPL*, pp. 68 ff.
49. *WRPL*, p. 110.
50. *WRPL* pp. 73-9; 110-12.

psychological ailment. It is possible that there is a psychological need for him to pocket things when others do not notice. When looked at the agent from this psychological perspective, the agent has not committed any immoral act, but is a patient requiring psychiatric treatment when he pockets a thing quietly. We are now able to say that the members of the community wrongly ascribed intentions of theft to this agent. How is it that they are wrong, if they were linguistically justified in ascribing a certain motive to the agent?

Kripke mistakenly believes that assertibility and truth conditions are mutually exclusive and we cannot speak of truth conditions in the context of mental states. If assertibility condition is met, we make assertions whether it is about the physical state or whether it is about the mental state. For instance, we make hypotheses and predict certain behaviour of physical objects and of human beings. Hypothesis is something which takes the value of true or false.[51] The same is true of what is known as assertion or ascription. If we make assertion, the statement is true if known after verification; similarly, if we make ascription the statement is verified against the behaviour including verbal behaviour of the agent. If I claim that there is a beetle in the box when the lid is on, I made an assertion; similarly, when I claim that you intend to open the door, I made an assertion about your intention. Both the beetle in the box and your intention are not perceived, yet I have made assertions about both. Whether there are grounds for making any assertion applies equally to both statements about physical states and about mental states. Meticulous and careful individuals may not make assertions even about physical world without having adequate evidence as is the case with scientists; similarly meticulous and careful individuals may not make statements about the mental states of others without sufficient grounds as is the case with morally sensitive individuals. Thus, from a certain point of view, one can speak of truth conditions in both the cases. What constitutes the truth condition is the condition under which the proposition is true. The statement about the beetle is true if the beetle is there in the box; similarly, the statement about your intention is true if you have that intention. The method of verification in each case may be different. One may open the lid of the box and see in the former case, and one may watch the behaviour of you and test his hypothesis about your intention. Verification need not be direct all the time.

---

51. *PI*, p. 212.

Intention being a mental state and since Wittgenstein does not find the need of any method to acquire knowledge about one's own mental state including introspection, speaking of one's own intention does not seem to serve any purpose other than making statements about oneself. Telling about myself by speaking of my intentions goes beyond the statements about intentions.[52] However, even the most explicit expression of intention by itself is insufficient evidence of intention claims Wittgenstein. The most explicit expression of intention would be making explicit statement about one's own intention, as is the case when I say 'I am going to take two powders'.[53]

A lingering doubt would trouble everyone, especially when someone claims that we cannot know our past intentions. One remembers thoughts, feelings, movements, and also connections with earlier situations, but not past intentions claims Wittgenstein.[54] If intentions are mental states and if mental states can be described and expressed, why cannot we know our past intentions? Cannot we speak about our past mental states? For instance, we remember instances where we were afraid of certain animals. If fear is a mental state, one surely remembers several situations where one was scared of snake, fire, etc. Or, for instance, if a letter inviting a friend of mine to visit our institute is returned to me after a week since the addressee is not found, can I not read the letter again and know the intent of that letter? It may be said that if my past intention coincides with my present intention, there is no harm in treating it to be my present intention rather than speaking of it as my past intention. And if I claim that my past intention is different from my present intention, for instance, if I change my intention of inviting my friend to visit our institute, this would be a situation where I have two present intentions expressed in two different ways: one I call the past intention of inviting my friend, the other, the present intention of not inviting him. There is no absurdity if I have several intentions at a given moment, some of them conflicting with one another.

Yet Wittgenstein does not seem to face the above problem. If a new decision is to be taken after reviewing the situation, a new intention would be expressed. Since, intention is expressed in action,

---

52. *PI*, § 659.

53. *PI*, § 632.

54. *PI*, § 645.

I could not be writing letter to my friend inviting him and not having the intention to invite him.

It may look as though the account given above is unsatisfactory from yet another point of view. For instance, one might opine that the regularity in the use of words cannot be explained without reference to past intentions. Similarly, customs, rituals, etc., cannot be explained without the intentional component being attached to them.

Such a reservation seems to be unfounded. If rules are mental states, then one can view presently all the varied occasions where one has performed the function of addition as cases of following the rule of addition. To say that the same rule is being followed even today is to commit ourselves that the same intention is being expressed all along when we followed the rule in the past. All our past behaviours can be viewed as occasions where we applied the rule of addition; not only that we can construct hypothetical situations where we would follow the rule of addition. This is the import of saying rules have infinite applications including past and future applications.

7. Concluding remarks

We have advanced interconnected arguments above to show how private language is impossible in various senses. The version of private language that is problematic to philosophers is the one that rejects both the possibilities of language and knowledge. Private language argument rests on the mistaken base of individualistic feelings and experiences as the source of meaning. Even the individualistic feelings and experiences that are at a general plane are not inaccessible to other individuals is the contention of Wittgenstein. This is brought out well in his distinction between the mental processes and mental states discussed above.

The difficulty with the account of Wittgenstein is that we believe that there can be individual intentions and there could be collective intentions. Wittgenstein constantly draws our attention to the fact that both individual as well as collective intentions are expressed through social institutions. Individual intentions without social institutions seem to be impossible for Wittgenstein, whereas, the private language argument emphasises the individual intentions without social institutions.

If the logic of intention is such that it is always in the form of mental state, then there is no possibility of intention being embedded in anything else but in human subjects. The most troubling element in the whole private language argument is this: Can individuals have their intentions that are different from the intentions of others? Several of us tend to believe that the intention of an individual as against collective intentions have to be admitted; otherwise, the question of who invokes the convention for the use of new words? cannot be answered. It is one thing to claim that there are collective intentions and the rules are rules by virtue of collective intentions in the social contexts, and it is yet another thing to claim that these rules can be modified and new rules can be invoked. To overlook the possibility of individual intentions seems to deny the very possibility of human freedom and individual roles in a democratic set-up. But admitting the possibility of individual intentions apart from the collective intentions need not commit one to the possibility of private language. Individual intentions can be made public; they are accessible to others when we observe their action in real life situations.

7

Kripke-McGinn Controversy on Rule and Rule-following

Ganesh Prasad Das

In this paper, I propose to revisit the controversy between Saul A. Kripke and Colin McGinn on rule and rule following. The Kirpke-McGinn controversy is by now fifteen years old as Kripke published his work on *Wittgenstein on Rules and Private Language* (1982) and McGinn's work containing his rejoinder to Kripke was published two years after under the title, *Wittgenstein on Meaning* (1984). Norman Malcolm has already published his assessment of the contentions of Kripke and McGinn in his book entitled *Nothing is Hidden* in 1986. I propose to look back at the situation not in the hope of becoming a disputant or participant in the said controversy but to make a few humble points so that one could command a clear view of the dispute.

The general words which are used in sentences express concepts and Wittgenstein assimilates these concepts to games.[1] The use of concepts is a rule-governed activity very much as games like cricket and chess are. A general word is open-ended. The instances to which this could be applied are not finite. So the question arises as to how our finite minds can give rules that are supposed to apply to an infinite number of cases. It appears that each new application we make is a leap in the dark. This gives rise to a paradox which Wittgenstein formulates as follows:

> No course of action could be determined by a rule, because every course of action can be made out to accord with the

1. Wittgenstein, L., *Philosophical Investigations,* (tr.) G.E.M. Anscombe, Oxford, Basil Blackwell, 3rd edn., 1968, p.183 E.

> rule . . . if everything can be made out to accord with the rule, then it can also be made out to conflict with it. And so there would be neither accord not conflict here.[2]

In an inductive generalisation, there is said to be such a leap or hazard when there is passage from particular cases to a general case. This leap is sought to be warranted by some principles which are necessary *a priori* and are not a generalisations from particular cases. If it is so regarded, then there ensues a paradox which is called the 'paradox of induction'. Whatever that might be, the problem is different here in case of the rule for the use of general word. It is not a question as to how a given general word or concept has been abstracted from experience but how is it that the concept which is abstracted from experience is applied to further experience. Taking, for instance, the concept red, it can be said that the concept is abstracted from some tracks of experience like red sunset, red apple, red apparel, etc., and then applied to other tracks like red tullips and red lips. But the tension precisely lies here. Can it be made sure that the rule of application of concept red is available here? What right does one have to be sure that the present application is in conformity with the previous application and that both the applications are in accordance with a single unitary rule. If one does not have this right, then is it the case that the present application is different from the previous ones and so is in conflict with these? but never the less all the previous applications and the present one could be seen to be in conformity with a different rule. What is the logical guarantee that the concept red is not the concept *gred* and the concept table is not the concept *tabair*?

So far there has not arisen a conflict between *A* and *B* with regard to the application of the concept red. All the instances cited above are regarded as red by *A* and agreed to by *B*. But suppose, both of them enter into a regal reception hall. As they enter into the hall, *B* says. 'It is a nice red carpet'. When *A* reacts, 'this is not red'. In this context, if the sceptic draws the conclusion that *A* did not have the proper grasp of concept red which was granted to him but the concept which he had then grasped is the concept *gred*. Similarly, if there is any disagreement between *A* and *B* over the application of the concept table, can it not be due to the fact that *A* had the concept of *tabair* whereas *B* thought that he (*A*) had the concept table. To

2. *Op. cit.*, Sec. 201.

quote Kripke's words:

> . . . I think that I have learned the term 'table' in such a way that it will apply to indefinitely many future items. So I can apply the term to a new situation, say, when I enter the Eiffel tower for the first time and see a table at the base. Can I answer a sceptic who supposes that by 'table' in the past I meant 'tabair', where a 'tabair' is anything that is a table not found at the base of Eiffel Tower or a chair found there?[3]

What I have understood by table is different from that understood by another. In the past my application of the concept *tabair* and another's application of the concept table were co-incidental. But until the present instance, it could not be revealed that my concept is the concept of *tabair* whereas another's concept is the concept of table. Such an unbridgeable hiatus could be supposed to be there between the previous application of a rule and the present one.

'Now, I know how to go on', is the general form of expression of the grasp of a rule. It may be the rule for expansion of a mathematical series or for a mathematical addition or it may be for application of a general word. This sceptical problem as illustrated above is brought out smoothly with mathematical example. Suppose, I am asked to continue the series 2+4+6+8+10+. . . . Then I write 2+4+6+8+10+2+4. . . . Can it be gain-said that I have not followed the rule properly in expanding the series? Why it must be that the rule for the expansion of the series is 'Go on adding two to the previous number' and why can it not be 'Add two to the previous number, but when it becomes a set of five numbers repeat the set'? Or, to take a different example, I am asked to work out the sum 1000+75 and I write 1000+75=1005. Who can conclusively establish that the rule is not, 'When any number is added to 1000, it is 10005', that the concept is the concept quaddition rather than addition as Kripke puts it.

According to Wittgenstein, individuals are not classified as belonging to this concept or that on the basis of some essence underlying them. This is done on the basis of characteristics which crisscross and overlap with one another in varied ways. But this cannot

3. Kripke, Saul A., *Wittgenstein on Rules and Private Language*, Oxford, Basil Blackwell, 1985, p.19.

be the basis in case of the rules. It cannot be said that the rule which is applied is not unitary and the same. There is the self-same rule in a changing series which criss-cross and overlap with one another.

There cannot be rule as such or rule by itself apart from its application. Although there could be different applications of the same rule, the rule applied cannot be different on different occasions. There is no rule essence, yet the rule is unitary and there is no family resemblance between applications of a rule but applications belong to one ground. According to Quine, we learn the word 'Sepia' (or 'red' or 'table') by induction. He takes the behaviourist's and the non-behaviourist's theories of learning in his stride. David Pears would perhaps say that the learning is by intuitive generalisation.[4]

The sceptical challenge is not epistemological. It is not that there is something in the mental history or external behaviour as evidence such that although I could not know it because of my limitations and omniscient God who is bereft of all limitations could know it. This challenge is a logical one. In presenting the paradox the present uses of words as in the case of red, table, expansion and addition are taken for granted. But the logical point which is sought to be established is that there could be no such.

According to Kripke, Wittgenstein gives a sceptical solution to a sceptical problem. A sceptical solution of a sceptical philosophical problem consists in conceding that the sceptic's negative assertions cannot be answered. Wittgenstein does not give a non-sceptical solution, i.e., straight solution pointing out some hidden fact that he overlooked. There is no such superlative facts either in the internal or in the external world the perception and admission of which would solve the sceptical paradox. Perhaps Kripke takes cue from A.J. Ayer who in his *The Problem of Knowledge,* concedes to the sceptic that there cannot be refutation of sceptic's challenge to the effect that no course of action could be determined by a rule simply because no rule-following in the present could be identified as being the same as that followed previously.

It is not rejection of identify in the soft sense or in the relative sense but in the hard or absolute sense. As Wittgenstein puts it,

> Are two things the same when they are what one thing is?

4. Wittgenstein, L., *op. cit.,* Sec.106.

> And how am I to apply what the one thing shews me to the case of two things?[5]

He contends in the *Tractatus* in the similar vein,

> to say of two things that they are identical is nonsense, and to say of one thing that it is identical with itself is to say nothing at all.[6]

Hence, it cannot be said that two instances of following a rule are identical. There is a traditional solution to this sceptical paradox. Application of concept or invocation of a rule ultimately involves sensations, i.e., facts concerning the states and activities of mind. All identifications rest on the identification of sensation. This solution has the Kantian flavour. According to Kant, all appearances of the objective world are ultimately appearances to the mind. According to him, concepts are applied to particulars by schemata. A schema, according to Kant, is a rule for the production of images. Although Kant is conscious that he is not offering a psychological account of knowledge, yet his proceedings in this regard cannot alleviate the doubt that he is surreptitiously bringing in the psychological method to bear on logical issues. Whatever that might be, Wittgenstein does not accept such a straight solution but he does not contend, for that matter, that identification does not rest on the identification of sensations. Wittgenstein seeks to change the very orientation of the question at issue. The question is not, 'How can we show private language or some other special form of language to be impossible?' the question is instead, 'How can we show any language at all to be possible?'

Identification through sensation is sought to be adverted by behaviourism. Kripke makes a conjecture that Wittgenstein's *Philosophical Investigations* was influenced by Wattsonian behaviourism like Russell's *Analysis of Mind*. Wittgenstein rejects Russell's behavioural analysis because it makes the relation between thought and subject external. External relations are non-logical, causal relations. Ayer finds in his assessment of scepticism that the available ways of meeting it by naïve realism, reductive analysis and scientific generalisation do

5. *Op. cit.*, Sec.215.
6. Wittgenstein, L., *Tractatus Lagico-Philosophicas*, (tr.) D.F. Pears & B.F. McGuinness, London, Routledge & Kegan Paul, 1961, 5.5303.

not succeed. He finds out a surrogate defence of knowledge by the method of linguistic analysis. In almost the same way, he seeks to trace Wittgenstein's way of meeting the sceptical challenge. In the *Tractatus,* Wittgenstein's seeks to conceive meaning of proposition in terms of its truth-conditions. 'To understand a proposition means to know what is the case if it is true'?[7]

This has an advantage over the concept of meaning in terms of method as provided by the logical positivist, 'The meaning of a proposition is the method of its verification'. One can understand a proposition, therefore, without knowing whether it is true but the conception of meaning in terms of truth-conditions is not free from trouble. It involves the presupposition of possible worlds over and above the actual world in which we live, move, and communicate with one another by means of language. In the *Investigations*, Wittgenstein conceives meaning in terms of assertibility or justification conditions.[8] According to the crude version of the referential theory of meaning, a meaningful expression corresponds to an entity. Similarly, according to the *Tractarian* explanation of meaning, a meaningful proposition corresponds with a fact, although a possible fact. Conception of meaning in terms of assertibility or justification conditions eliminates this supposition and makes it simple.

> All that is needed to legitimatise assertions that some one means something there be roughly specifiable circumstances under which they are legitimately assertible and that the game of asserting them under such conditions has a role in our lives. No supposition that 'facts correspond' to those assertions is needed.[9]

Kripke understands that the replacement of truth conditions by justification conditions in the *Investigations* has two-fold achievement. Firstly, it finds a new approach to the problems of how language has meaning different from that of the *Tractatus*. Then, secondly, this approach can also account for assertions about meaning themselves, which are assertions within our language.[10]

---

7. *Op. cit.,* 4.024.
8. Kripke, Saul A., *op. cit.,* p. 74.
9. *Op. cit.,* pp. 77-8.
10. *Op. cit.,* p. 77.

McGinn does not agree with Kripke's illustration of Wittgenstein's views. According to him, Wittgenstein does not offer a positive view as Kripke makes out. Wittgenstein's aim is primarily negative and his intentions are therapeutic. We should not, therefore, expect him a positive theory of meaning especially when he is averse to it.

> If one tried to advance theses in philosophy, it would never be possible to debate them, because everyone would agree to them.[11]

Wittgenstein offers three negative theses. Firstly, to mean something by sign is not to be the subject of an inner state or process. This thesis has two aspects : (i) meaning does not consist in some experiential process, (ii) meaning or understanding is not a process of the mental apparatus. Secondly, to understand a sign is not to interpret it in a particular way. Thirdly, using a sign in accordance with a rule is not founded upon reasons. All the three theses are connected with one another and are inter-dependent. As per Kripke's reading, the positive thesis is, to understand a sign is to have a mastery of a technique or custom of using it. Wittgenstein does not offer this last-mentioned thesis according to McGinn. Wittgenstein urges that there should be an end to all explanations and description alone must be there. When he contends that doubting must have an end, he means to say that when there is description putting everything as it is, then there would be a termination of doubt. Wittgenstein is not an intellectualist.[12] He is rather a linguistic phenomenologist.[13] Rule following is quite unreflective and automatic.[14] Wittgenstein does not see a distinction between 'rule' and 'expression of a rule'. So

> he is concerned to give a theoretically un-prejudiced description of the actual phenomena of following a rule — to remind us what really goes on when a rule is being followed.[15]

Wittgenstein makes the points very clearly in the *Blue and Brown Books:*

---

11. *Philosophical Investigations, op. cit.*, Sec. 128.
12. McGinn, Colin, *Wittgenstein on Meaning*, Oxford, Basil Blackwell, 1984, p. 74.
13. *Op. cit.*, p.29.
14. *Op. cit.*, p.16.
15. *Op. cit.*, p.20 Footnote Emphasis added.

> Tables, ostensive definitions and similar instruments I shall call rules in accordance with ordinary usage. The use of a rule cannot be explained by a further rule.[16]

He has difficulties to understand the concept of a rule in terms of 'cause':

> How am I able to obey a rule?' — If this is not a question about causes, then it is about the justification for my following the rule in the way I do.
>
> If I have exhausted the justifications I have reached bedrock, and my spade is turned. Then I am inclined to say: this is simply what I do.[17]

He has difficulties too to understand it in terms of 'because',

> He must go on like this without a reason Not, however, because he cannot yet grasp the reason but because — in this system — there is no reason. (The chain of reasons comes to an end.)[18]

Of course, doubting has an end but the significance of this statement must be grasped properly. There is a termination of doubt when at long last there is a point which it cannot penetrate. As Descartes has it in 'I think, therefore I am'. There is a termination of doubt too at the very start, nipping in the bud, so to say, Wittgenstein embraces the second alternative, but not the first, as he perceives that reason and doubt are not correlative.[19] I obey the rule blindly', Wittgenstein says. Further, '. . . the end is not an ungrounded presupposition. It is an ungrounded way of acting'.[20] The termination is not a certain proposition.[21]

There is no rule apart from, beyond, and besides use. Only use can determine use. L.S. Stebbing quotes E.M. Foster's dictum, 'Only

---

16. Oxford, Basil Blackwell, 1958, p. 90.
17. *Philosophical Investigations, op. cit.,* Sec.217.
18. Wittgenstein, L., *Zettel,* Oxford, Basil Blackwell, 1967, Sec. 301.
19. McGinn, *op. cit., p.22.*
20. Wittgenstein, L., *On Certainity* (tr). Denis Paul and G.E.M., Anscombe, Oxford, Basie Blackwell, 1977, Sec.110.
21. *Op. cit.,* Sec.204.

connect' as a precise statement of the process of reasoning. We can put, if you please Wittgenstein's view precisely in Foster's style thus: 'Only see connections'. This is the kind of *weltanschauung* the philosopher is looking for. According to Wittgenstein

> The words, 'language', 'proposition', 'order', 'rule', 'calculation', 'explanation', 'following rule' relates to a technique, a uniform.[22]

There are three aspects of this view of Wittgenstein which might be labelled as epistemological naturalism. This is an antidote to the mythologising which results from an unduly rationalistic picture of the phenomena.[23] The three aspects are, (i) rule following in actual behaviour is not a hidden process, (ii) a rule is grasped if it is obeyed repeatedly, and (iii) using and reacting to the signs is habitual and unreflective.

Kripke insists on linguistic normativeness and says that there is no property of a word from which we can read off its correct use and so there is nothing for meaning to be.[24] According to McGinn, the basis of the normative is the natural. At some level, 'meaning is fixed by our nature'.[25] The sceptic is presupposing the *Tractarian* model of meaning in terms of stating facts. But the author of the *Investigations* is laying emphasis upon the role of criterion and the place of language in our lives. Wittgenstein does not have the sort of gap that Kripke's sceptic trades on between meaning and naturally determined use. Kripke's dialectic is a kind of non-cognitivism which does not appreciate that the notion of meaning is essentially a social one. Wittgenstein is putting forward the paradox in section 201 of the *Investigations* quoted above as a *reductio ad absurdum* of the interpretational conception. It is not that interpretations determine meaning and it is not that meaning does not consist in individualistic facts. Certain sorts of facts fail to determine meaning when there is substitution of one sign for another. But it is not that, no facts determine meaning. The *fact* that gives sign's life is a fact about use, not about a fact about inner states. McGinn alleges that Kripke

---

22. Wittgenstein, L., *Remarks on the Foundation of Mathematics,* Oxford, Basie Blackwell, 1956, Sec. 341.
23. McGinn, C., *op. cit., p.42.*
24. Kripke, Saul A., *op. cit., p.61.*
25. McGinn, C., *op. cit.,* p.86.

nowhere registers Wittgenstein's concern to connect understanding with the concept of *ability*. Wittgenstein insists:

> The grammar, of the word 'knows' is evidently closely related to that of 'can', 'is able to', but also closely related to that of 'understands'. (Mastery of a technique)[26]

The language which states facts shows the ability of the user of language, according to McGinn. Ability is not something *ab extra.*

Kripke appeals to 'community concordance' in use. That is, the community provides the guidance in applying a sign correctly. My present use of sign is correct because it agrees with the use of that sign by others. But, according to McGinn, Wittgenstein rejects such idea of guidance explicitly,

> It gives expression to the fact that we look to the rule for instruction and do something without appealing to anything else for guidance.

Agreement with regard to meaning shared by us is not in need of any intermediary notion like that of community. It is infructuous, because the idea of a supposed intermediary, something interpolated between the sign and its use comes in surreptitiously as a reason. Kripke's thesis becomes a constitutive or metaphysical one as he seeks to find out what it is to mean something and what it is for linguistic use to be correct. There is no fact about me either physical or psychical that constitutes my meaning something. What meaning rests on is the bedrock of our natural propensities.

There is, according to Wittgenstein, no paradox. The paradox is only apparent. The way out of the paradox is not to give alternative interpretations but to see that there is a way of grasping a rule which is not an interpretation, but which is exhibited in what we call 'following a rule' and 'going against it'. The given is the forms of a life that is the rock bottom, that is the paradigm.

The bone of contention between Kripke and McGinn is over the idea of community. Kripke thinks that the notion of community is necessarily connected with the notion of rule following. But McGinn thinks that it is dispensable. Only regularity of behaviour is what is

---

26. *Philosophical Investigations,* Sec.150.

needed. Following a rule is a practice but practice for him is not common practice but repeated practice. Norman Malcolm sides with Kripke with the comment that regularity of behaviour by itself does not exhibit rule following. Following a rule has an 'environment', he says. This is the environment of teaching, testing and correcting which are ongoing processes. 'To withdraw that environment is to withdraw the concept of following a rule.'

I am inclined to agree with Kripke and Malcom in this respect. '*Communis*' is the root for both the words 'community' and 'communication'. Language is the primary mode of communication. The primary sense of communication is communistic (not communal or communistic as these are much abused political terms). The sense of communication as individualistic (not subjective) is only derivative.

In conclusion, it may be pointed out that Wittgenstein is a dialectician-*par-excellence*. He explores the alternative answers that could possibly be offered to a question which is fundamental and disquieting. He then seeks to show the tensions which each of the alternatives generates as well as the tensions which they release. Therefore, it is a characteristic of his procedure that leaves most of such questions unanswered. It is not safe to conclude from this that they imply a positive thesis. In his previous work, the *Tractatus,* Wittgenstein has admirably shown a distinction between saying and showing. Philosophers at different times attempt to say what cannot be said. Following a rule is shown by our practice of using language. The notion of rule and the notion of rule-following do not have status apart from language. This also shows that Wittgenstein is intent to demolish illegitimate dualistic notions like this.

Very often it is said that Wittgenstein belongs to twentieth century and twentieth century belongs to Wittgenstein. The excellence of his contribution to philosophy will continue to be refreshing and enlightening even in the twenty-first century.

8

Wittgenstein on Necessity and Objectivity in Mathematics and Logic

Sadhan Chakraborti

WITTGENSTEIN'S philosophy of mathematics and logic haunts every researcher in this area although a very few succeed eventually, the history shows, to enter into this majestic castle. The present paper is an attempt to have a clear view of this castle, though it may turn out to be an usual failure, through the deep fog surrounding it.

Much of the dispute among commentators *vis-à-vis* the nature of mathematics and logic concerns whether Wittgenstein was realist or an anti-realist. Although Wittgenstein is normally read as an anti-realist concerning mathematics and logic there are oppositions to this reading, e.g., Cora Diamond's *Realism and the Realistic Spirit*[1] is devoted to argue against anti-realist readings of Wittgenstein's philosophy of Mathematics. Before entering into this prolonged debate let me put it very clearly the sense in which the issue of realism is understood throughout this paper.

The word 'realism' is no more used as a blanket term. The talk of realism *simpliciter* is now replaced by talk of realism concerning a specific subject-matter. So the concept of realism is a relativised to a certain class of entities. Michael Dummett has given a new formulation of realism by relativising it to a class of statements instead of a class of entities.[2] This turn from entity to language marks the

1. Cora Diamond, *Realism and the Realistic Spirit : Wittgenstein, Philosophy and the Mind,* MIT Press, Cambridge, Mass., 1991.
2. Michael Dummet, 'Realism' in *Truth and Other Enigmas,* Duckworth, 1978.

present-day discussion on realism. The peculiarity of a realism concerning a class of statements consists, says Dummett, in maintaining the objectivity of the statements of this class. The word 'realism' is used in this paper in this Dummettian sense. So, when it is asked 'Is Wittgenstein a realist or an anti-realist concerning mathematics and logic?', what is intended is whether Wittgenstein maintains the objectivity of mathematical and logical statements or not.

Using a coinage of John McDowell, Putnam characterises the debate on objectivity in his Dewey Lectures[3] published in 1994 as the *recoil* phenomenon : an oscillation between two extreme positions, with each camp reacting to the untenable part of the other, resulting, finally, in two untenable positions. On one side of the divide are those who deny objectivity in all fields. They hold that there are only incommensurable narratives. On the other side of the divide are those who attempt to secure objectivity, but do so at the cost of clothing it in metaphysical mystery.

> The first side points out the illusions in the second's metaphysics and then recoils to anarchy. The second shows the inherent contradictions in the anarchist position, and then recoils to building more epicycles in its metaphysical castle.[4]

Wittgenstein's philosophy of mathematics and logic should be understood in the background of this recoil phenomenon of objectivity.

Philosophers belong to the objectivity camp picture mathematics as transcendent : a mathematical proposition has truth and meaning regardless of human rules and use. There is an underlying mathematical reality which is independent of our mathematical practice and language and which adjudicates the correctness of that practice and language. One of the most influential personalities in this camp is the famous mathematician G.H. Hardy who says in *A*

3. See Putnam's Dewey Lectures, "Science, Non-sense, and the Senses : An Enquiry into the Powers of the Human Mind", *The Journal of Philosophy,* vol. 91, No. 9, 1994, pp. 445-517.

4. Steve Gerrard, 'A philosophy of mathematics between two camps' in *The Cambridge Companion to Wittgenstein,* ed. Hans Stuga and David G. Stern, Cambridge University Press, 1996, p. 171.

Mathematician's Apology[5]:

> I believe that mathematical reality lies outside us, that our function is to discover or observe it, and that the theorems that we prove, and which we describe grandiloquently as our "creations", are simply our notes of our observations'.

Another renowned personality belonging to this camp is Gottlob Frege a Platonist, who holds that logical and mathematical truths like '¬(P & ¬P)', '2+2=4' are necessary and objective and that this objectivity can only be secured by assuming that their subject-matters are not private ideas in the minds of individuals, but abstract entities inhabiting, a third realm beyond space and time.

Bertrand Russell too says that logical propositions are completely general truths about the most pervasive traits of reality.

All of the positions mentioned so far assume that mathematics and logic are sciences which make statements about entities of some kind, just as empirical sciences make statements about physical objects.

At the beginning of Wittgenstein's career the anarchist camp would have been exemplified by a view called *psychologism*. Mathematicians and Logicians like George Boole belonging to this camp hold that the laws of logic describe how human beings (by and large) think, their basic mental operations, and these laws are determined by the nature of the human mind.

The exemplars of the objectivity camp combated psychologism, ". . . 317 is a prime" Hardy asserted, "not because we think so, or because our minds are shaped in one way rather than another, but because it is so, because mathematical reality is built that way".[6] Frege and Russell believed that identifying the laws of logic with the laws of psychology would necessarily lead to a complete loss of objectivity. Frege's *Grundgesetze*[7] contains a typical argument for the route from psychologism to anarchy:

> If we could not grasp anything but what was within our own selves, then a conflict of opinions [based on] a mutual

5. G.H. Hardy, *A Mathematician's Apology*, Cambridge University Press, 1967.
6. *A Mathematician's Apology*, p. 130.
7. Gottlob Frege, *The Basic Laws of Arithmetic*, tr., and ed. M. Furth, Berkeley and Los Angeles : The University of California Press, 1964, p. xix.

> understanding would be impossible, because a common ground would be lacking, and no idea in the psychological sense can afford us such a ground. There would be no logic to be appointed arbiter in the conflict of opinions.

Wittgenstein has criticised vehemently the assumption of the objectivity camp that mathematical and logical propositions describe a sophisticated reality of which we can have special experience. The fundamental thought of the *Tractatus Logico Philosophicus* (*TLP*) is that this assumption is false.[8] Wittgenstein attacks Frege's and Russell's idea that the logical particles occurring in a logical statement are name of entities (functions inhabiting a Platonic realm in the former case and 'logical objects' with which we are acquainted through logical experience in the latter). The role of logical particles, he says, is not to name objects of any kind. In *TLP* he says,

> My fundamental idea is that the "logical constants" are not representatives; . . . (4.0312).

He also says,

> At this point it becomes manifest that there are no "logical objects" or "logical constants" (in Frege's and Russell's sense) *TLP* (5.4).

Since there is no logical object, logical statements cannot be about entities. The role of logical statements is not to describe reality lying out there. "The propositions of mathematics", says Wittgenstein, "are equations, and therefore pseudo-propositions" (*TLP*, 6.2). Mathematical propositions being pseudo-propositions are not descriptions of anything at all. Wittgenstein never wavered from rejecting the metaphysical picture of the objectivity camp.

Wittgenstein's rejection of the underlying assumption of the

---

8. See Ludwig Wittgenstein, *Tractatus Logico Philosophicus,* tr. D.F. Pears & B.F. McGuinness, Routledge & Kegan Paul, London and Henley, 1961, 5.552-5.5571.

   Also see Somnath Chakraborti, "Tractatus-e- Maulobakya Prasanga' ["*Tractatus* on Elementary Propositions'] in *Wittgensteiner Darshan,* ed. Prahlad Kumar Sarkar and Somnath Chakraborti, Dasrshan O Samaj Trust, 1998. Sri Chakraborti has reformulated Wittgenstein's argument against this assumption.

objectivity camp in the historical background sketched above may naturally suggest that he was a philosopher of the anarchist camp. But this suggestion is palpably wrong. Wittgenstein never rejected his predecessors' anti-psychologism. Frege linked his context principle with his fight against psychologism. In the *Foundations of Arithmetic*[9] Frege has explained how psychologism arises out of the violation of the context principle throughout his philosophical career. He says, 'An expression has meaning only in a proposition' (*TLP*, 3.314). So he emphasised his opposition to psychologism as did Hardy, Frege and Russell. He believed that Frege had satisfactorily smashed the anarchist camp in its psychologistic form.

Thus, we see that since Wittgenstein opposes psychologism, he would say that mathematical and logical statements do not possess subjectivity : the Law of Noncontradiction ¬,(P & ¬,p), for example, is not a statement about the way people actually think. He also opposes, as we have seen, the Hardyan objectivity of mathematical and logical statements. So the question naturally arises : Did Wittgenstein deny the necessity and objectivity of mathematical and logical statements altogether? The answer is straightforwardly no. Wittgenstein had no doubt about the necessity and objectivity of mathematical and logical statements. His problem was how to account for it. The Hardy-Frege-Russell way of explaining the necessity and objectivity of mathematical and logical statements was not acceptable to Wittgenstein.

So he raises the question in *Remarks on the Foundations of Mathematics*[10] (*RFM*) :

> But then what does the peculiar inexorability of mathematics consist in?

Wittgenstein gives an account of the necessity and objectivity of mathematical and logical statements by relating them to linguistic rules. According to him, these statements do not describe a special kind of reality, but reflect linguistic rules. These statements are not

9. Gottlob Frege, *The Foundations of Arithmetic*, tr. J.L. Austin, Basil Blackwell, Oxford, 1953, section 60, p. 71.

10. Ludwig Wittgenstein, *Remarks on the Foundations of Mathematics*, tr. Anscombe, The MIT Press Cambridge, Massachusetts and London, 1956, Section 4.

descriptive, they are normative. The necessity and objectivity of these statements are, says Wittgenstein, due to their normativity.

The development of Wittgenstein's philosophy of mathematics and logic is found through certain stages. Steve Gerrard has distinguished, in his 1996 article[11] three stages of the development: early, middle and later. The early stage is found in *Notebooks* 1914-1916[12] and *TLP*. The middle period view dominated Wittgenstein's thought from 1929 through the early 1930s. Wittgenstein's view at this stage is called by Gerrard 'the calculus conception' and it is mostly found in *Philosophical Grammar* (*PG*).[13] The later stage starts from the middle of 1930s. *Philosophical Investigations* (*PI*),[14] *Lectures on the Foundations of Mathematics* (*LFM*),[15] *Remarks on the Foundations of Mathematics* (*RFM*)[16] contain Wittgenstein's thought of the later stage.

One common thread of Wittgenstein's account of necessity and objectivity of mathematical and logical statements is that the special status of these statements is not due to the peculiar character of what they represent, but due to the fact that they are linked to rules which provide the pre-empirical frame-work of representation. They reflect the necessary preconditions of this representation. Wittgenstein argues that mathematical and logical propositions look like experiential propositions which are descriptive in nature, but actually the relations of mathematical and logical statements to reality is entirely different from that of experiential propositions. The similarities of grammatical appearance of these two kinds of proposition seriously misled philosophers like Hardy, Frege and Russell of the objectivity camp as

---

11. Steve Gerrard, 'A Philosophy of Mathematics Between two Camps', *The Cambridge Companion to Wittgenstein,* ed. Hans Sluga and David G. Stern, Cambridge University Press, 1996.
12. Ludwig Wittgenstein, *Notebooks 1914-16*, tr. G.Anscombe, Blackwell, Oxford, 1961.
13. Ludwig Wittgenstein, *Philosophical Grammar*, ed. by R. Rhees, tr. A. Kenny, Blackwell, Oxford, 1974.
14. Ludwig Wittgenstein, *Philosophical Investigations,* ed. G.E.M. Anscombe and G.H. von Wright, tr. G.E.M. Anscombe, Blackwell, Oxford, 1973.
15. C. Diamond (ed.) : *Wittgenstein's Lectures on the Foundations of Mathematics,* Cambridge 1993, Cornell University Press, Ithaca, 1976.
16. Ludwig Wittgenstein : *Remarks on the Foundation of Mathematics*, ed. H.G. von Wright, R. Rhees and G.E.M. Anscombe, trans. G.E.M. Anscombe, Blackwell, Oxford, 1978.

well as the exemplars of the anarchist camp to treat mathematical and logical statements as descriptive.

It is unfortunate that Lovibond associates homogeneity of language with Wittgenstein's philosophy. In *Realism and Imagination in Ethics*[17] she says :

> What Wittgenstein offers us . . . is a homogeneous or "seamless" conception of language. It is a conception free from invidious comparisons between different regions of discourse . . . just as the early Wittgenstein considers all propositions to be of equal value . . . , so the later Wittgenstein . . . regards all *language games* as being of "equal value" . . .

Wittgenstein did say 'all propositions are of equal value' in *TLP* (6.4). But this should be read in conjunction with his other remarks in *TLP* like. 'The propositions of mathematics are . . . pseudo propositions' (*TLP* 6.2), The propositions of logic are tautologies. Therefore, the propositions of logic say nothing' (*TLP* 6.1, 6.11).

All that Wittgenstein intends to say is that all genuine propositions are of equal value and their equality consists in the depiction of reality. Mathematical and logical propositions are not genuine propositions, they do not depict or describe reality at all. Wittgenstein holds that the special status of these necessary propositions is due to the fact that they reflect the necessary preconditions for depicting reality.

The position of Wittgenstein has a striking similarity with that of Kant who holds that mathematical judgements are possible in so far as they express necessary preconditions for experiencing objects. But there are differences between these two positions. In contrast to Kant, Wittgenstein would say that these preconditions no longer reside in a mental machinery. Again, unlike Kant, Wittgenstein is of the opinion that mathematical propositions are analytic.

One may try to find an analogy of Wittgenstein's position with logical positivism. The goal of logical positivists was to account for logical and mathematical necessity without reducing it to empirical generality, lapsing into Platonism or admitting synthetic *a priori* truth. According to the logical positivists, necessary propositions are analytic, i.e., true solely in virtue of the meanings of their constituent words.

---

17. Sabina Lovibond, *Realism and Imagination* in Ethics, Blackwell, Oxford, 1983.

Wittgenstein's position cannot be identified with that of logical positivists. In fact, these two positions are, in one respect, diametrically opposite. The contrast between Wittgenstein's position and that of logical positivists has been explained by Amitabha Dasgupta in terms of compositionality and growth.[18] Dasgupta argues that in the positivist theory meaning is compositional whereas in Wittgenstein's theory it is not so. Again, the positivist conception of mathematics fails to explain the growth of mathematics, whereas Wittgenstein's conception succeeds to explain it. But I think that this way of showing the contrast between Wittgenstein's position and that of logical positivists concerning logico-mathematical necessity cannot show the real contrast between the two positions. The real contrast can be shown in the following way. Unlike logical positivists, Wittgenstein would not say that the meanings of the constituents determine the necessity of logico-mathematical statements. Rather these statements give meaning to the constituents. The key to understanding the status of necessary propositions is the concept of a grammatical rule. Grammatical rules are standards for the correct use of a word which determine its meaning.[19] The linguistic appearance of logico-mathematical statements is that of statements of fact, but their actual role is that of grammatical rules. It is the normative character of these statements, says Wittgenstein, which determine their necessity. By making the rules do all the work, Wittgenstein was trying to avoid both psychologism and Hardy's underlying mathematical reality. This also helps to exhibit the differences between his position and those of Kant and logical positivists.

Wittgenstein's grammatical perspective concerning logico-mathematical necessity has been misinterpreted by Dummett as a full-blooded conventionalism, a variety of anarchism.[20] According to

18. Amitabha Dasgupta, 'Wittgenstein on Mathematical Necessity', *Journal of Indian Council of Philosophical Research,* vol. IX, Number 3, 1992.

    (a) Ludwig Wittgenstein, *Philosophical Occasions,* ed. J.Klagge and A. Nordmann, Hackett, Indianapolis, 1993, p. 51.

    (b) Ludwig Wittgenstein, *On Certainty,* G.E.M. Anscombe, and G.H.Von Wright, tr., G.E.M. Anscombe, and D.Paul, Basil Blackwell, Oxford, 1969, pp. 61-2.

    (c) Ludwig Wittgenstein, *Philosophical Grammar,* ed., R., Rhees, tr. A Kenny, Blackwell, Oxford, 1974, p. 337.

19. Michael Dummett : 'Wittgenstein's Philosophy of Mathematics' in *Truth and Other Enigmas,* Duckworth, London, 1978.

20. L.Wittgenstein, *RFM,* Vi-49A.

Dummett, Wittgenstein believes that the logico-mathematical necessity of any statement is always the direct expression of a linguistic convention. It is not that our calculations and proofs follow from an antecedent set of agreed upon conventions, but that at every step a new decision is required. So the misinterpretation goes like this. By denying the picture of an underlying mathematical reality, through his anthropological method, by stressing the contingent factors that yield our logico-mathematical language and by claiming that at each step the calculations or proofs could have been otherwise Wittgenstein reduced logico-mathematical necessity to the level of the conventional. It is as if Frege saved us from psychologism only to have Wittgenstein deliver us to sociologism.

Wittgenstein foresaw this possible misinterpretation. 'What you say', writes Wittgenstein in *RFM*, assuming the voice of someone who has misinterpreted what has gone before,

> seems to amount to this, that logic belongs to the natural history of man. And that is not combinable with the hardness of the logical 'must'.[21]

That Wittgenstein did not assimilate, unlike Locke, the logico-mathematical propositions to the proposition of natural history escaped the notice of Dummett. In *RFM* Wittgenstein says,

> But the logical "must" is a component part of the propositions of logic, and these are not propositions of human natural history. If what a proposition of logic said was : Human beings agree with one another in such and such ways (and that would be the form of the natural historical proposition), then its contradictory would say that there is here a lack of agreement. Not, that there is an agreement of another kind.[22]

It should be noted here that in *TLP* and other earlier writings Wittgenstein treated mathematical and logical statements as pseudo-

---

21. L.Wittgenstein, *RFM*,, VI-49.
22. (a) A Quinton, *the Nature of Things*, Routledge and Kegan Paul, London, 1973, pp. 216-17.

    (b)M. Dummett, *Frege* : Philosophy of Language, Duckworth, London, 1973, pp. 596-601.

    (c) C. Wright, *Wittgenstein on the Foundations of Mathematics*, Duckworth, London, 1980, pp. 329-30.

propositions in the sense that they do not describe reality, rather they reflect the necessary preconditions for depicting reality. At this earlier stage he did not clearly explain what determines the necessity and objectivity of mathematical and logical statements. It is in the middle period that he clearly stated that the necessity and objectivity under consideration is determined by the normativity of the statements concerned.

But what exactly does Wittgenstein intend to say when he says that mathematical and logical statements give meaning to the components of these statements? Let us explain it with an example. '$P \rightarrow \neg\neg p$' is regarded as a logical statement which is necessary indeed. One may hold, like a logical positivist, that the necessity of the statement depends upon the meaning given to '$\neg$' by the following truth table :

p	¬P
T	F
F	T1

If this is the meaning of '$\neg$' then when 'p' is true '$\neg p$' will be false and in that case '$\neg\neg p$', will be true. So, if 'p' is true then '$\neg\neg p$' must be true [$P \rightarrow \neg\neg p$]. Wittgenstein does not admit this way of explaining the necessity of logical statement. He wants to say that '$p \rightarrow \neg\neg p$' gives meaning to the logical constant '$\neg$'; it is a rule giving meaning to '$\neg$'. It prescribes how to use '$\neg$'. In all experimental situations we simply follow this rule. The logical statements are viewed by Wittgenstein as rules which license transformations of experiential statements. Similarly, mathematical statements prescribe the use of mathematical operations which we simply follow in experiential situations. As logical and mathematical statements antecede experience in an innocuous sense, they can neither be confirmed nor be confuted by experience. This peculiar kind of antecedence, which is different from Kant's, as pointed out earlier, renders intelligible the apparently mysterious 'hardness' of necessary propositions. So, according to Wittgenstein, mathematics and logic as such are always measure, not things measured. We follow them to judge experience, not experience to judge them.

Wittgenstein's rejection of the logical positivistic account of logico-mathematical statements as analytic in the sense that they are necessarily true by virtue of the meaning of their components brings him very close to Quine. Quine questions the very notion of analyticity as advocated by the logical positivists. He shows that this notion belongs to a cluster of intentional concepts including 'synonymy', 'self-contradiction', 'necessity', definition' and 'semantic rule'. These concepts cannot be defined without using other members of this family. Quine thinks that this amounts to a vicious circularity.

Despite this similarity Wittgenstein's position must be contrasted with that of Quine. For Quine, logic and mathematics are meaningful by virtue of their being connected with experience and the truth or falsity of logical and mathematical statements is determined by the success or failure of predictions, made on the basis of them, from scientific theories. According to Quine, there is no qualitative difference between logico-mathematical statements and empirical statements. The only difference between them admitted by Quine is that in the holistic web of beliefs the logico-mathematical beliefs occupy the central position and the empirical ones occupy its periphery. This only means that we are more reluctant to abandon the former beliefs. Wittgenstein by contrast, advocates necessity of logico-mathematical statements which empirical propositions are lacking. And, to repeat, the necessity of them is determined by their normativity. So Wittgenstein is opposed to Quine's reductionism.

Quinton, Dummett and Crispin Wright argue that Quine's assimilation of logico-mathematical statements to the empirical ones sits uneasily with his own holistic picture of a web of beliefs.[23] Recently Hans-Johann Glock observes in 'Necessity and Normativity'[24] that a collection of beliefs can only be woven into a web if certain propositions are not merely abandoned with greater reluctance, but play a different role, viz., that of establishing logical connections between different beliefs.

Thus, we see that Wittgenstein gives a kind of autonomy to logic and mathematics. Experiential statements are descriptive and are answerable to or justified by logico-mathematical statements which look like descriptive ones but actually they are rules. These rules do not need further justification. They are self-justifying. They are self-

---

23. Hans-Johann Glock, 'Necessity and Normativity,' in Hans Sluga and David. G. Stern (eds.), *The Cambridge Companion to Wittgenstein*, Cambridge University Press, 1996.
24. Arthur Prior, "The Run About Inference Ticket", *Analysis*, vol. 21, 1960.
25. N. Belnap, "Tonk, Plonk and Plink', *Analysis*, vol. 22, 1962.

justifying because they are meaning-giving. This was Wittgenstein's position in the middle period of his philosophical career. Such a position is known as formalism.

Arthur Prior has raised a serious objection, in his article 'The Run About Inference Ticket',[25] to the unrestricted licence for whatever logical laws one chooses. He argues that this may render the entire language inconsistent. His example is a binary connective '*' having its introduction rules in common with 'or' and its elimination rules in common with 'and'. From 'P' we may derive 'P*Q' by the help of the introduction rule for '*'; then we can derive 'Q' from 'P*Q' by the help of the elimination rule for '*'. Similarly, we can derive '¬ Q' from 'p'. So we can derive 'Q&¬ Q' from 'P' by the help of the introduction rule for '&'. Thus, the rules for '*' yield a contradiction. Hence, if logic is given absolute autonomy then our language will be full of contradictions.

Belnap, Dummett and others who share the view with Wittgenstein that logical rules are self-justifying, have imposed certain most general restrictions on logical rules. Belnap has mentioned in his article 'Tonk, Plonk and Plink'[26] two restrictions, viz., conservative extension and uniqueness. Dummett has imposed a further condition, viz., stability.[27] They have explained how by the imposition of these restrictions the above kind of inconsistency can be avoided.

Wittgenstein, being a genius, anticipated this kind of undesirable consequence of his formalism advocated in the middle period of his philosophical career. But he did not follow the line of thought as found in Belnap and Dummett for avoiding the consequence. In the later period he revised his position. In this period he feels that the logical and mathematical rules require some kind of justification. In *LFM* he says:

> If we allow contradictions in such a way that we accept that anything follows, then we would no longer get a calculus, or we'd get a useless thing resembling a calculus.[28]

For the justification of logico-mathematical rules Wittgenstein relates logico-mathematical language, in his later period, to *language-games*

26. Michael Dummett, *The Logical Basis of Metaphysics,* Harvard University Press, Cambridge, Massachusetts, 1991.
27. L. Wittgenstein, *Lectures on the Foundations of Mathematics,* p. 243.
28. L. Wittgenstein, *Remarks on the Foundations of Mathematics,* vol. 28.

and ultimately to our form of life.

In *RFM* says :

> The rules of logical inference are rules of the language-game[29].

In *PI* Wittgenstein has given a detailed account of language-game which is presupposed here. It should be kept in mind that even in the later period Wittgenstein has retained the normative character of logic and mathematics. Even in *RFM* we find him to say:

> We can conceive the rules of inference — I want to say — as giving the signs their meaning, because they are rules for the use of these signs. So that the rules of inference are involved in the determination of the meaning of the signs. In this sense rules of inference cannot be right or wrong.[30]

In *RFM* he also remarks :

> What I am saying comes to this, that mathematics is normative.[31]

So the necessity and objectivity are retained even in Wittgenstein's later period. And here also he says that the necessity and objectivity of logic and mathematics are due to their normativity. But what is new in this period is that the logical and mathematical rules are tied down to the language-game. He holds that logic and mathematics form networks of norms and they are parts of a family of language-games. The logico-mathematical rules which we follow in this family of language games cannot be altered once these rules are laid down and practised.[32] No new rule can be introduced which conflict with this family. Herein lies the necessity and objectivity of mathematics and logic. Given the background of a family of language-game, mathematical and logical statements are not revisable. By contrast, experimental statements are revisable even within this family of language-game.

This feature of non-revisability distinguishes Wittgenstein's position concerning logic and mathematics from that of intuitionism.

29. L. Wittgenstein, *Remarks on the Foundations of Mathematics,* V.23.
30. *Ibid.*, V.40.
31. *Ibid.*, V.31.
32. *Ibid.*, V.23.

It should also be noticed that although Wittgenstein related the legitimacy of logico-mathematical rules to our practice, hisS position should not be identified with pragmatism, because in pragmatism logico-mathematical propositions are revisable, but it is not admitted by Wittgenstein. Thus, Wittgenstein's position concerning logic and mathematics should be distinguished from descriptivism as advocated by Hardy-Frege-Russell camp as well as from psychologism. It should also be distinguished from the position of Kant and that of logical positivists. It is also illegitimate to identify his position with Quinean reductionism or Dummettian verificationism. Neither is it legitimate to identify his position with intuitionism or pragmatism.

A further question arises here. The question is : 'Are logico-mathematical statements revisable outside a family of language-game?' One interpretation of Wittgenstein's philosophy is that there can be alternative different families of language-game in which logic and mathematics form different networks of norms. So although logico-mathematical statements are necessary within a family of language-games, they are contingent from the externalist point of view. Perhaps this kind of interpretation led W.W. Tait to observe that 'necessity rides on the back of contingency'.

Another interpretation is that the necessity of logico-mathematical statements is ultimately tied down to the constitution of human mind and under the present constitution of it no change of logico-mathematical rules is possible. Philosophers who give this interpretation, take to distinguish a fourth and last period of Wittgenstein's philosophy which was dominated by his philosophy of psychology. Here I do not like to enter into this debate.

So, what I see throughout the three stages of the development of Wittgenstein's philosophy of logic and mathematics is that according to him, logico-mathematical statements are necessary and objective. Since Wittgenstein advocates necessity and objectivity of logic and mathematics he should be regarded as a realist so far as logic and mathematics are concerned. But the distinctive feature of his realism consists in the belief that the necessity and objectivity of logico-mathematical statements are due to their normativity. He says in *RFM*. :

> Not empiricism and yet realism in philosophy, that is the hardest thing.[33]

33. L. Wittgenstein, *Remarks on the Foundations of Mathematics*, V.23.

9

Logical Necessity, Conventionalism and Forms of Life

Wittgenstein's Philosophy Revisited

R.C. Pradhan

WITTGENSTEIN'S account of logical necessity needs a fresh appraisal in view of the controversy it has raised in the recent discussions on the subject. There have been conflicting opinions as to whether Wittgenstein accepted anything as logically necessary, this is, whether there are necessary truths in logic and mathematics. One of the dominant views in recent discussions is that of Dummett's,[1] according to whom Wittgenstein has offered an extremely anarchic view of logic and mathematics resulting in the virtual denial of logical necessity *per se*. On the other side of the debate are those like Barry Stroud[2] who oppose the anarchic interpretation of Wittgenstein and offer a modest defence of logical necessity as a matter of form of life. There is, however, a third opinion like that of Putnam's[3] which is that, on both Dummett's and Stroud's accounts, there is no escape from conventionalism which denies logical necessity as an irreducible normative fact.

My aim in this paper is to show that Wittgenstein's concept of

---

1. See Michael Dummett, 'Wittgenstein's Philosophy of Mathematics' in *Ludwig Wittgenstein : Critical Assessments,* vol. 3, ed. Stuart Shanker, Croom Helm, London, 1986, pp. 121-37.
2. See Barry Stroud, 'Wittgenstein and Logical Necessity' in *Ludwig Wittgenstein: Critical Assessments,* vol.3, pp. 289-301.
3. See Hilary Putnam, 'Analyticity and A priority : Beyond Wittgenstein and Quine' in *Realism and Reason* (*Philosophical Papers, Vol.3*), Cambridge University Press, Cambridge, 1983, pp. 115-38.

logical necessity does not lapse into conventionalism and that there is a grammatical account of logical necessity that avoids the disastrous consequences of conventionalism. I shall argue that the necessary propositions of logic and mathematics are part of the framework of our thought and language and so they determine the necessary conditions of our understanding of the world. In that sense, the logical necessity of such propositions is bound up with the logical structure of language and the world.

I agree with Putnam that logical necessity is irreducibly normative and that necessary truths constitute the conceptual connections through which we understand the world. However, I do not find convincing his view that Wittgenstein, by appealing to the forms of life, has given up the normative character of logic and mathematics. I agree with Stroud that, according to Wittgenstein, the concept of logical necessity must be located in our forms of life without inviting the possibility of conventionalism. Logical necessity has to be located in the framework of human thought and forms of life since the necessary propositions constitute the limits of our thought and language. This I would like to call a transcendental account of logical necessity which is committed neither to conventionalism nor to anthropologism.

1. Necessity and contingency: Wittgenstein's tryst with logical necessity

Wittgenstein follows the logical tradition established by Frege in his recognition of the fact that there are necessary propositions in logic and mathematics as distinguished from the contingent propositions of the empirical sciences. He admits that there are propositions which cannot but be true and so are necessary in our language such as the propositions of logic and mathematics, and there are other propositions, especially in empirical sciences, which are factually true, but could be false under different circumstances. The latter are called contingent propositions which are different from the necessary propositions in that their truth-value shifts according as the situations in the world change. Thus, there is a clear-cut distinction between the necessary and contingent, and also the *a priori* and the *a posteriori* in Wittgenstein's philosophy which is responsible for his adherence to the notion of logic that distinguishes between what is logically true and what is not. The notion of logical truth dominates his philosophy from the *Tractatus Logico-Philosophicus* to the

Philosophical Investigations and the *Remarks on the Foundations of Mathematics.*

Wittgenstein pursues the idea of logical necessity as a matter of serious logical concern in his *Tractatus* where he is busy surveying the domain of logic as distinguished from the domain of the empirical sciences. According to this project, the domain of logic is the domain of necessity, and outside it everything is accidental. He writes:

> The exploration of logic means the exploration of *everything that is subject to law.* And outside logic everything is accidental. (*TLP* 6.3) (italics original)

This is a reiteration of the statement already made at *TLP* 2.012: 'In logic nothing is accidental'. This suggests that logic alone deals with necessity as everything that is not within logic is accidental, that is, contingent. Further on, Wittgenstein makes a very decisive claim that

> there is no compulsion making one thing happen because another has happened. The only necessity that exists is the logical necessity. *(TLP* 6.37)

This again is followed by a stronger claim:

> Just as the only necessity that exists is *logical* necessity, so too the only impossibility that exists is *logical* impossibility. (*TLP* 6.375) (italics original).

Thus, Wittgenstein's statement on logical necessity as revealed in the above passages contains his strong message that logic is concerned with necessity not in any trivial sense but in the sense in which it can show the logical structure of language and the world. Logically necessary propositions, therefore, are not the formal symbols to be played with, but are those that play a significant role in the mirroring of the essence of language and the world. That is to say, the necessary propositions of logic and mathematics do have a substantial role to play in language, that is, they show 'the formal-logical-properties of language and the world' (*TLP* 6.1-6.11) because it does not militate against his claim that logical propositions show the logical form of language and the world.

Wittgenstein has not got rid of this logical strategy in his post-*Tractatus* writings in spite of the fact that he has given up much of the metaphysical baggage[4] while exploring the domain of logical necessity. He has, for example, given up the claim that logic is something sublime and that it is hidden in the structure of language (*PI* Sec. 89). And also he has given up the claim that logic can reveal the *a priori* structure of reality independently of our actual use of language (*PI* Secs. 89, 97). The metaphysical sublimity of logic which follows from the Fregean legacy is given up precisely to make logic more concerned with the natural language and our actual logical practices. This, however, does not deny the fact that logical propositions are necessary and that they show the formal properties of language and the world. Logic is not a science of the logical truths in the Fregean sense, but it has all the responsibility of a normative science to fix the limits of language and the world. In this limited sense, logic is not empirical but transcendental[5] (*TLP* 6.113). That is, logic can still claim to represent the scaffolding of language and the world.

Wittgenstein's opponents in philosophy of logic and mathematics are not only the metaphysicians who make logic sublime and non-empirical as he seems to claim in the *Investigations* (Sec.97), but also the logical positivists who have made it conventional and trivial in the sense that they have made logic and mathematics irrelevant to our understanding of reality. His disagreement with Frege is not on the fact that logic is a normative science and that it has much to reveal about our understanding of the world, but on the fact that the logical truths are independent of our language and thought. Frege's uncompromising Platonism makes Wittgenstein turn away from the Fregean legacy, not, however, to embark on the positivist course of reducing logical necessity to mere linguistic conventions, but to search for new grounds of the necessary propositions in logic and mathematics. The logical positivists have wrongly taken the *Tractatus* as the source-book of their conventionalistic[6] interpretation of logic and mathematics.

---

4. See Wittgenstein, *Philosophical Investigations*, tr. G.E.M. Anscombe Basil Blackwell, Oxford, 1953, sections 90-7.
5. See D.S. Shwayder, 'Wittgenstein on Mathematics' in *Studies in the Philosophy of Wittgenstein*, ed. Peter Winch Routledge and Kegan Paul, London, 1969, pp. 66-116 for a transcendental interpretation of Wittgenstein's later philosophy of logic and mathematics.
6. Cf. G. Baker, *Wittgenstein, Frege and the Vienna Circle* Basil Blackwell, Oxford, 1988, Part II.

The logical positivists, especially Carnap[7] and Ayer,[8] have been of the view that the logical propositions are tautologies and are true by virtue of their meaning alone. That is to say, according to them, such propositions are linguistic conventions such that they are meaningful by virtue of their syntactic structure or from alone. In this way, conventionalism as a theory of logical necessity has gained currency in analytic philosophy. The major achievement of this school of thought is that it takes logic and mathematics as consisting of linguistic conventions which constitute the main body of the necessary truths. Thereby, it refutes the Kantian view that there are synthetic *a priori* truths in arithmetic and geometry. Besides, it seeks to develop the formalistic view of logic without any metaphysical commitments to the reality of the necessary truths independently of the grammatical conventions.

Wittgenstein was never sympathetic to the positivist view of logic and mathematics precisely because he did not accept their radical empiricism, He has shown antipathy not only towards the positivist theory of language as a formal system, but also for their view that logic and mathematics are part of a formal language developed for formal calculations. If logic and mathematics are formal devices, they are as good as any system of symbols, and so do not carry any deep significance. But Wittgenstein considered both logic and mathematics as the domain of necessary truths which occupy a central place in our language. He is one with Frege so far as the centrality of the truths of logic is concerned, but rejects the Fregean demand for an independent domain of logical truths. In this regard he agrees with the positivists that logic and mathematics cannot be independent of our language. But he does not go all the way with the positivists to demand a reduction of logical truths to linguistic conventions.

Wittgenstein's later view of logic and mathematics has been a matter of controversy because he seems to have made mathematics and logic conventional and anthropological[9] phenomena. The interpretation of Wittgenstein's *Lectures* and *Remarks* as holding

---

7. See. R. Carnap, *The Logical Syntax of Language*, Routledge and Kegan Paul, London, 1937.
8. See A.J. Ayer, *Language, Turth and Logic*, Gollanez, London, 1936; Penguin Books, 1946, Chapter 4.
9. See D.F. Pears, *Wittgenstein,* Fontana/Collins, 1971, Chapter 7 for his interpretation of Wittgenstein's concept of logical necessity as anthropocentric.

conventionalism and anthropologism has been one of the dominant views of the recent times, But this is a matter of opinion only in the sense that the real Wittgenstein is neither a conventionalist, not even in the moderate sense, nor is he an anthropocentrist. For him, the biggest challenge is to refute such 'isms' in the philosophy of logic and mathematics. He is interested in destroying such fanciful edifices constructed by philosophers for a better and clearer view of how logic and mathematics work.

Wittgenstein is of the opinion that logic and mathematics are autonomous in the sense that they function as they do under their own laws, and not because they are conventions and contrivances made by a community of language-users. They are human to the extent they are found to be used by human beings. But that does not make them anthropocentric. Similarly, they are part of language, but for that matter they are not linguistic in nature. All that Wittgenstein is searching for is the way logic and mathematics are central to human concern. That makes him accept logic as transcendental in the sense that it must reveal the necessary conceptual connections which underlie human language and thought.

In this sense, Wittgenstein could be considered a champion of logical necessity because he thought it central to human thought. Logical necessity is not a mere human creation because in that case it cannot be necessity at all; besides, it cannot be based on a community decision, because it is likely to lose its necessary character. It is ultimately what it is, that is, how it is located in the conceptual system and the language that we have, without the possibility of lapsing into human conventions.

2. Deflating Platonism

Wittgenstein's concept of logical necessity goes contrary to what is known as Platonism in view of the fact that he rejects the Platonist picture of logic and mathematics. For him, the idea of logical truths being independent of the human mind and language is a metaphysical idea that has no justification except for the fact that it suits the temperament of some philosophers who postulate logical and mathematical objects beyond the world of experience. The Platonists among mathematicians do postulate such abstract entities. G.H. Hardy has the following to say in defence of Platonism:

> . . . mathematical reality lies outside us, that our function is to discover or to observe it, and that the theorems which we prove and which we describe grandiloquently as our 'creations' are simply our notes of our observation.[10]

This point of view which is also known as metaphysical realism commits itself to the reality of mathematical objects which is a matter of discovery rather than of creation by the mathematicians. This also has the added consequence that the mathematical objects are real independently of our recognition of them.

The realist makes it clear that the truth of mathematical and logical propositions does not depend on us, that is, it is not of our own making. Such propositions are necessary in the sense that they are true eternally and objectively without being dependent on us. As Frege puts it:

> . . . the laws of nature, and likewise those of mathematics, have held good at all times and not just since they were discovered. This shows us that these thoughts, if true, are not only true independently of our recognising them to be so, but that they are independent of our thinking as such.[11]

That is to say that the truths in mathematics and logic as in other sciences are a matter to be discovered which remain true even if we fail to cognise them. They are, therefore, cognition-transcendent and investigation-independent.

The fact of the matter, according to the realist, is that there are not only objective logical and mathematical facts, but also that the truths corresponding to them are objective and necessary. This constitutes the main thrust of the Platonist programme in logic and mathematics. As Dummett puts it,

> for the Platonist, the meaning of a mathematical statement is to be explained in terms of its truth-conditions, for each statement, there is something in mathematical reality in virtue of which it is either true or false.[12]

10. Thomas Hardy, *A Mathematician's Apology*, Cambridge University Press, Cambridge, 1941, pp. 63-4.
11. Frege, *Pasthumous Writings*, ed. Hans Harmes *et al.*, Basil Blackwell, Oxford, 1979, p.133.
12. Dummett, 'Wittgenstein's Philosophy of Mathematics', p. 121.

It is because of this commitment that the Platonist holds that the truths of logic and mathematics must hold necessarily. They are a matter of discovery rather than of invention because we can come to recognise them in course of our logico-mathematical investigation.

Wittgenstein is decisively against the Platonist programme because he finds in it the metaphysical picture of a domain of necessary truths that has no connection with what human beings do and how they act. The Platonic realm of truths seals the truths off human language and thought. Therefore, these truths have no necessity for human thought and action. It is our of this conviction that Wittgenstein makes a radical revision in the Platonist framework which makes the necessary truths of logic and mathematics binding on human thought and language. These truths are supposed to be the bedrock of human thought in the sense that they determine how human beings think and use language. That is the reason Wittgenstein writes in the *Tractatus:*

> The propositions of logic describe the scaffolding of the world, or rather they represent it. They have no 'subject-matter'. (*TLP* 6.124).

Further, he adds:

> Logic is not a body doctrine, but a mirror-image of the world. Logic is transcendental. (*TLP* 6.13)

Here obviously Wittgenstein is not making logic committed to a metaphysical realm of truths; that is why, it has no 'subject-matter'. But yet, there is a very significant function for it in terms of its representing the logical from of the world, i.e., the way the world could be made available in human language. This is the reason why logic is transcendental in that it reveals the necessary structure of human thought and language.

Wittgenstein's later philosophy of logic and mathematics pursues the Tractarian model of logical necessity in a much radical fashion only to emphasise that Platonism does not work and that we must get a way from the extravagant claims of it regarding the status of the necessary truths. The *Remarks* and the *Investigations* repudiate the fact that logic and mathematics need a metaphysical grounding in the hidden essences which have no location in the necessary structure of human thinking. The *Remarks* makes the following claims against Platonism:

> The mathematician is an inventor, not a discoverer, (*RFM*, I.168).

Further, it adds:

> The propositions of logic are indeed the expressions of 'thinking habits' but also of the habits of thinking. That is to say they can be said to show how human beings think, and also what human beings call 'thinking'. (*RFM*, 1.131)

Thus, logic now takes care of what human beings think and how they think without being psychological and anthropological in its investigation. Logic does not lose its rigour, as Wittgenstein points out in the *Investigations* (Sec. 108). The significant point is that the task of logic is still to demarcate the limits or boundary of thought which is rather a transcendental task rather than a mere psychological and anthropological one.

Wittgenstein is concerned with the limits of language precisely to determine the sense of the linguistic expressions. He is assured of the fact that there is nothing that logic can do if it is not the demarcation of sense from nonsense, of what can be grammatically correct from what is not. Thus the goal of logic is the same as that of grammar in the sense that both aim at showing what are the necessary conditions of something making sense. The later Wittgenstein does not discard the basic transcendental nature of the task of logic:

> for logical investigation explores the nature of all things. It seeks to see to the bottom of things and is not meant to concern itself, whether what actually happens is this or that. — It takes its rise, not from an interest in the facts of nature, nor from a need to grasp the causal connexions: but from an urge to understand the basis, or essence, of everything empirical. (*PI* Sec. 89)

Though the motto of logic is not to search for the hidden essences, yet it is concerned with the logical truths underlying language and thought. There are truths which are necessary logically and mathematically for human thought and are not empirical. Hence, the effort to make logic turn towards the necessary and *a priori* structures of human thought and language.

3. Dispelling the shadow of anthropologism

This way of relating logic and mathematics to human thought and language, i.e., human forms of life has invited the charge of anthropologism in Wittgenstein's theory of necessity. It has been claimed by Putnam that Wittgenstein in fact has made logic and mathematics anthropological phenomena by locating them in our forms of life.[13] This is due mostly to Wittgenstein's interest in the application of logic and mathematics to human life. In fact, Wittgenstein claims: 'mathematics is after all an anthropological phenomenon' (*RFM*, V, 26). Besides, he openly advertises for the human interests in the practices of logic and mathematics. This has the effect of creating the impression that Wittgenstein is more interested in human forms of life than in logic and mathematics themselves. His interest in the natural history of man may create this impression. Consider the following passage:

> What we are supplying are really remarks on the natural history of man: not curiosities, however, but rather observations on facts which no one has doubted, and which have only gone unremarked because they are always before our eyes. (*RFM*. I, 142)

Here the intention is to suggest that the remarks on logic and mathematics are really remarks on the natural history of man, that is, on how man has been practising these disciplines in course of the development of the human intellectual history. The emphasis on the 'natural history' has an anthropological ring about it since the study of the natural history of man is generally an anthropological study.

Hilary Putnam suggests that Wittgenstein did involve himself in the anthropological study of mathematics, and, of course, of logic and language in general. According to him, the reference to forms of life while studying mathematics is the sign of there being anthropologism, as

> Wittgenstein is claiming that mathematical truth and necessity *arise in us,* that it is human nature and forms of life that *explain* mathematical truth and necessity.[14] (italics original)

---

13. Cf. Putnam, 'Analyticity and A Priority', pp. 115-17.
14. *Ibid.*, p. 117.

What is of interest here is that Putnam attributes anthropologism to Wittgenstein in the belief that the latter sought to uncover the anthropological elements in logic and mathematics, not the logical elements whatsoever. Now it is a matter of debate whether Wittgenstein is interested only in the empirical aspects of the natural history of man or in the logical aspects of the so-called forms of life. Putnam takes the forms of life as the empirical phenomena, and for him anybody who talks of the natural history of man must be a naturalist and an anthropologist. Putnam believes that both Dummett and Stroud, who have commented on Wittgenstein's notion of mathematical and logical necessity, have accepted an underlying anthropocentric element in it.[15]

Now the question is: Is Wittgenstein really doing anthropology of mathematics while he is talking about the forms of life involved in inference and proof in logical and mathematical calculations? That is, is he making mathematics and logic empirical phenomena only? To say that logic and mathematics have only a human significance need not be construed as a statement about the empirical character of these disciplines. In fact, every truth in logic can be given a human relevance, but that does not mean that logic has no other significance. Those who believe that logic and mathematics are empirical have something more to say since they reduce the truths of logic and mathematics to empirical generalisations in the way J.S.Mill[16] did. Wittgenstein, however, has never been inclined towards such a conclusion as he agrees with Frege and Russell that logical truths are non-empirical and formal in nature. In fact, he goes to the extent of saying that logical truths are tautologies which say nothing factual about the world. This makes him assert that logic and mathematics have nothing to do with the world in the sense that they are not derived from our experience of the world. They retain a strong sense of non-empiricality about them, according to him.

Wittgenstein is of the opinion that logical and mathematical propositions, though not derived from experience, none the less take for granted that there are certain empirical facts already available when we make judgements in logic and mathematics. The fact that

---

15. "Analyticity and A Priority".

16. J.S. Mill, *A System of Logic*, Longman, 1873. For the criticism of Mill's view, see Frege, *The Foundations of Arithmetic*, tr. J.L. Austin, Basil Blackwell, Oxford, 1950; Reprinted 1989, sections 7-9, pp. 9-17.

there must be a flat surface to draw geometrical figures and that there must be paper and ink to make mathematical calculations is an empirical fact, but it has nothing to do with the truth of the mathematical propositions (*PI* IIxi, p.226). For example, the truth of the statement that the three angles of a triangle make 180 degrees has nothing to do with the flat surface of the blackboard. Thus, the whole of logic and mathematics could be demonstrated even if we have no regular blackboards. But it cannot be the case that we can carry on mathematics if there were no physical world at all or if in the physical world everything changed frequently: 'this would make our normal language-games lose their point' (*PI*, Sec. 142). But from this nothing follows regarding the nature of the truth of logic and mathematics.

The distinction between the logical and the empirical propositions is very much intact in Wittgenstein's thought for the reason that it is this distinction that speaks for the importance of the propositions of logic and mathematics. These propositions differ from the empirical ones not only in the fact that they express rules but also in the fact that they represent the logical features of the world of experience itself. As Wittgenstein would say, the logical and mathematical propositions are grammatical in nature such that they represent the grammatical connections in language:

> The connexion which is not supposed to be causal, experiential one, but much stricter and harder, so rigid even, that the one thing somehow is the other, is always a connection in grammar. (*RFM,* I, 128)

The grammatical character of the propositions of logic and mathematics does speak for the fact that they are not statements of fact at all, and that they rather limit the very nature of the empirical facts. So we could say that the grammatical propositions are the rules for the use of language in general: That is, 'the mathematical proposition has the dignify of a rule' (*RFM,* I, 165). This is alll to show that the propositions of logic and mathematics do not claim to describe anything factual: they rather define what is to be called factual. This makes them lay down the limits of empiricism. Wittgenstein explains this further in the following passage:

> The limits of empiricism are not assumptions unguaranteed, or intuitively known to be correct: they are ways in the which

we make comparisons and in which we act. (*RFM,* VII. 21)

Thus, the grammatical rules do make a difference to the way we use language and describe the facts in the world. They constitute the way we use language and describe the world. Therefore, the rules of grammar cannot be contingent like the empirical propositions. Thus, Wittgenstein has made it clear that logic and mathematics prescribe the rules for language which accords to them their status of solid and unassailable rules (*RFM*, I, 165).

In view of the above considerations, it is difficult to say that Wittgenstein has made mathematics an anthropological and empirical phenomenon. It is not the case that he has made the necessity of the propositions of logic and mathematics dependent on the human nature as Putnam alleges. All that he has done is that he has related them to the way we use language and the way we act. This does not make them empirical since there is the dividing line between the empirical and the non-empirical fixed by these propositions themselves. If the propositions of mathematics and logic were empirical, then the whole distinction between empirical and logical would collapse. If Putnam's interpretation were right, then the whole of logic and mathematics would consist of factual statements and that too the statements depicting the behaviour of mankind. But one can see that Wittgenstein cannot dream of making logic and mathematics such contingent phenomena.

4. Rules and normativity

We are, thus, led to believe that Wittgenstein's philosophy of logic and mathematics has a strong sense of normativism[17] in it which is manifested in the notion of grammar. Grammar has a larger presence in his philosophy of language in general and of logic and mathematics in particular. The reason is obvious: there is the centrality of rules in the discourse of logic and mathematics. Rules of logic and mathematics have a peculiar status in our language which is unlike that of the empirical propositions. That is why for understanding the nature of the rules we have to look to the grammar of the logico-mathematical discourse. Wittgenstein explains the concept of rule in the following passage:

---

17. See Hans-Johann Glock, 'Normativity and Necessity' in the *Cambridge Companion to Wittgenstein,* ed. Hans Sluga and David G. Stern, Cambridge University Press, Cambridge, 1996.

> .... What compels us to proceed according to a rule, to conceive something as a rule? What compels us to talk to ourselves in the form of the language we learn?
>
> For the word 'must' surely expresses our inability to depart from this concept (Or ought I say 'refusal'?). (*RFM,* IV, 30)

He adds:

> By accepting a proposition as self-evident, we also release it from all responsibility in face of experience.
>
> In the course of the proof our way of seeing is changed — it does not detract from this that it is connected with experience.
>
> Our way of seeing is remodelled. (*RFM,* IV, 30)

In this way we can see that Wittgenstein is interested in the self-evident character of the logical and mathematical propositions such that we have the sense of following a rule in pursuing the logical and mathematical proofs. We do feel that in logic and mathematics we are not embroiled in the game of describing facts but of following the rules laid down in it. We are surrounded by normative structures that compel us to perform certain actions.

Wittgenstein is fond of characterising the propositions of mathematics as the norms, or patterns that we follow in course of doing mathematics. These are deposited in language as 'standard measures' (*RFM,* I, 165). Mathematics is as such 'a measure, not thing measured' (*RFM,* III, 75). It 'determines a path, lays down a path for us' (*RFM,* IV, 8). All these expressions have the point of making it clear that the rules matter in mathematics as laying down the normative structure of language and, thus, of determining the conceptual connections.

Wittgenstein is interested in the fact that the grammatical rules of language in general make room for the normative elements that have a decisive role to play in the language-games. The language-games are the ways we use language and, therefore, there must be rules which make them possible. It is in this sense that Wittgenstein harps on the rules in language. These are called the grammatical rules in the sense that they help explain how language functions. This is reflected in the following passage:

> To accept a proposition as unshakably certain-I want to say means to use it as a grammatical rule: this removes uncertainty from it. (*RFM*, III, 39)

The rules are such that they are antecedent to the truth and falsity of the propositions that follow from them. In that sense they are unlike the propositions that describe the facts. They are like the paradigms that are laid down in language:

> the proposition provided by means of the proof serves as a rule — and so as a paradigm. For we go by the rule. (*RFM*, III, 28)

There is, therefore, in language a tract created for the purpose of use of language. The paradigms are the tracts in language. Wittgenstein explains :

> I want to say that the *must* corresponds to a track which I lay down in language. (*RFM*, III,30)

The logical 'must' corresponding to a grammatical rule signals the fact that rules are laid down for the purpose of language-use. They do not exist prior to the language-game; they occupy a place in the language-game.

5. Why there is no 'full-blooded conventionalism'

Wittgenstein's concept of the logical 'must' as something laid down in language creates the impression that whatever is taken as logically necessary in language must be created by the linguistic community. That is, it is presumed that the rules of language-game must be at some-time or other consciously laid down and followed by the members of the linguistic community. In that case, the rulers are just conventions or customs available in language. The conventionalists in general tend to believe that all that is in logical necessity is the conventions which regulate the use of language. There is nothing necessary in the propositions of logic and mathematics which cannot be squeezed into the conventions of language. Dummett interprets Wittgenstein's philosophy of mathematics as a form of 'full-blooded conventionalism' in the following way:

> Wittgenstein goes in for a full-blooded conventionalism: for him the logical necessity of any statements is always the

> *direct* expression of a linguistic convention. That a given statement is necessary consists always in our having expressly decided to treat that very statement as unassailable; it cannot rest on our having adopted certain other conventions which are found to involve our treating it so.[18]

What Dummett attributes to Wittgenstein in the name of full-blooded conventionalsim is the view that the necessary truths in logic and mathematics are so-called because of the way they function directly as the conventions of language. That is, the necessary truths are so-called because they are treated as necessary and not because they are in fact necessary. Their necessity is a matter of our decision and are entirely dependent on what we do with them. Dummett continues

> If we accept the proof, we confer necessity on the theorem proved; we 'put it in the archives' and will count nothings as telling against it. In doing this we are making a new decision, and not merely making explicit a decision we already made implicitly[19].

This seems to be in conformity with what Wittgenstein has said in so many places in his writings especially in his *Remarks*. For example, Wittgenstein says that 'the proof places this decision in a system of decisions' (*RFM,* III, 27). Besides, he goes to the extent of saying that

> in mathematics we are convinced of *grammatical* propositions; so the expression, the result, of our being convinced is that we *accept a rule*. (*RFM,* III, 26) (italics original).

Thus, there seems be textual evidence in favour of the view that the rules of language are at best conventions we have ourselves accepted.

But the question is: Has Wittgenstein really conceded that there is nothing necessary about logic and mathematics and that everything is so conventionally arranged that the so-called logical necessity is ultimately a misnomer? The full-blooded conventionalist is not committed to logical necessity *per se,* since he is convinced that it is we who make a proposition necessary in our language; we deposit it in the archives of language. That is the only explanation of why we

---

18. Dummett, 'Wittgenstein's Philosophy of Mathematics', p. 124.
19. *Ibid.*, p. 125.

have necessary propositions in logic and mathematics. However, Wittgenstein does not say in the banal sense that necessity is our creation, or that we have made the logical propositions necessary. What he is arguing for is the fact that the necessary propositions are in language as the rules of grammar. They are inexorable and are binding on us in the sense that we cannot think of what their opposites would be (*PI* Sec. 251). That is, we cannot conceive of what it would be for a grammatical rule not to hold good in a certain language-game. Can we think of the language-game without taking the necessary rules which make it possible?

Necessity, according to Wittgenstein, belongs to the rules of logical grammar of language since without them no language can work, nor can we make any move in language without following those rules. Thus, we are constrained to obey the rules that are embedded in language. Just as the language-games follow certain rules as a matter of necessity, so are we constrained to follow those rules in playing the language-games. In this sense, necessity is imposed on us as constitutive of our language-games and forms of life. Wittgenstein writes:

> What has to be accepted, the given, is-so one could say-forms of life. (*PI*, II xi, p. 226)

Stroud is right in saying that the necessity of the rules we follow does not lie in our accepting them as conventions but in our being so constituted that we cannot but accept them as they are formulated by us. Stroud's argument is that the ultimate source of necessity lies in our forms of life and not outside us. He says:

> The ultimate appeal in seeking a "foundation" for our procedures of calculating, inferring, and so forth, can only be to "ways in which we make comparisons and in which we act" That is all that an account of the "foundations" or "source" of logical necessity can achieve.[20]

That is to say, the only way to explain logical necessity is to locate them in the human forms of life, that is, in how we are constrained to calculate and infer in logic and mathematics. There are no other ways in which we can act at all if we do not follow the rules as they are given to us.

---

20. Stroud, 'Wittgenstein and Logical Necessity', p. 300.

Stroud has denied that there are any alternative forms of life which we can conceive intelligibly. We can definitely imagine what possible forms of life could there be. But that does not mean that we can make any form of life an intelligible alternative to ours. They do not constitute a

> a set of genuine alternatives open to us among which we could choose, or even among which we could have chosen.[21]

That is why to say that we could have chosen to follow a different set of rules of grammar sounds hollow because we could not say what it would be like to follow a different grammar. The necessity of the rules of our grammar follows from the possibility that we do not know what it would be like to be different sort of human beings who follow a different sort of grammar.

Dummett's attribution of full-blooded conventionalism does not hold good precisely for the reason that the necessary truths of logic and mathematics are not the direct expressions of our conventions and decisions. Our conventions and decisions themselves presuppose the truths of logic and mathematics. Besides, the full-blooded conventionalist view assimilates the truths of logic and mathematics to the truths of natural history thereby reducing the former into contingent truths.[22] But this is refuted by Wittgenstein in the following passage:

> But the logical "must" is a component part of the propositions of logic, and these are not propositions of human natural history. If what a proposition of logic said was: Human beings agree with one another in such and such ways (and that would be the form of natural-historical proposition), then its contradictory would say that there is here a lack of agreement. Not, that there is an agreement of another kind. (*RFM*, VI, 49)

6. Why communication does not (cannot) breakdown

Dummett's worry is that our following rules has no necessity about it except that the rules are taken as necessary for a limited purpose and that makes them subject to possible breakdown. The whole

21. Stroud, 'Wittgenstein and Logical Necessity', p. 296.
22. See Steve Gerrard, 'A Philosophy of Mathematics Between Two Camps' in *The Cambridge Companion to Wittgenstein*, ed. Hans Sluga and David G. Stern, pp. 182-6.

exercise of rule-following is contingent upon the fact that we make rules and adopt them for certain purpose. This spells disaster, according to him, so far as communication is concerned. Dummett writes :

> If Wittgenstein were right, it appears to me that communication would be in constant danger of simply breaking down.[23]

That is, if the rule-following is contingent upon our decisions then it is almost certain that we can never be sure whether we are following the correct rule. We will be constantly guided by a Deity as it were at every step of our rule-following. Thus, there can arise situations where we can never be free from doubts about the steps we take in rule-following.

Kripke's sceptical[24] interpretation of Wittgenstein follows Dummett's line of thought in claiming that our rule-following has no solid foundations except in the communitarian agreement to accept a rule for a certain purpose. Kripke further claims that no amount of collective agreement can avert the sceptical doubt that we may fail at every step in following the correct rule. This is because we are constrained at every step to appeal either to memory or to a previous decision to confirm our future step in following the rule. But our appeal to either may go wrong in coming to a decisive conclusion. We are inevitably on the verge of a collapse in matters of rule-following.[25]

Both Dummeet and Kripke have missed the point that Wittgenstein himself has tried to keep rule-following safe from the dangers of collapse since he is in need of a solid ground for rule-following in the very forms of life we have. The agreement that both admit to be crucial for rule-following is not an agreement, for Wittgenstein, 'in opinions, but in forms of lifer' (*PI* Sec. 241). That agreement is solidly based on the way we live and act, that is, in the very forms of life. That is all that we are trained to do and so there could be no choice before us in following the rules. Wittgenstein very

23. Dummett, 'Wittgenstein's Philosophy of Mathematics', p. 130.
24. See Saul A. Kripke, *Wittgenstein on Rules and Private Language*, Harvard University Press, Cambridge, Mass., 1982, pp. 7-53 for his sceptical interpretation of Wittgenstein's concept of rule-following.
25. *Ibid.*

aptly says:

> Disputes do not break out (among mathematicians, say) over the question whether a rule has been obeyed or not. People don't come to blows over it, for example. That is part of the framework on which the working of our language is based (for example, in giving descriptions). (*PI* Sec. 240)

That is to say, the rule-following is a part of the framework which constitutes language-use and, therefore, there is no question of our going wrong in following a particular rule if that is constitutive of our form of life.

Wittgenstein is not oblivious of the fact that there is a strong sense of compulsion in rule-following in view of the fact that we cannot but follow the rule already made internal to our thought and language. Following the rule *R*, for example, is binding on us if *R* is the rule we cannot but follow and if *R* is laid in the structure of our thought and language. So

> When I obey a rule, I do not choose.
> I obey the rule *blindly*. (*PI* Sec. 219) (italics original)

That is true of all cases where the rules are not of our making and are cumulatively deposited in our language and thought. There is no sense to the idea that I make my own rules, or that the community itself is responsible for the rules. Such rules do not matter in the long run because they themselves presuppose other rules which have no communitarian origin. The communicatiran rules, thus, have no ultimate logical significance; there must be other rules which have a logical grounding in our forms of thought and life.

If we are satisfied that there are primary rules which need no justification or further grounding, then they must be the rules that we follow 'blindly' and not the rules that are derivatively there. The rules of logic and mathematics constitute the bedrock rules that we are bound to follow without questioning. It is in this sense that Wittgenstein talks of the bedrock we reach in our search for the rules that we cannot justify:

> If I have exhausted the justifications I have reached the bedrock, and my spade is turned. Then I am inclined to say: "This is simply what I do". (*PI* Sec. 217)

We, thus, feel that we have nothing more to worry about which rule or rules we are following because such rules already are part of our logical heritage. We cannot simply disown our logic and mathematics because they constitute our way of thinking and being what we are.

Our communication depends upon our agreement on the rule-following and language-use which is imposed on us as a matter of our linguistic heritage. We are committed to that heritage because we have been trained in it and have internalised it as our own thought. In that case there is no escape from following the rules which are part of our linguistic heritage, e.g., rules of logic and mathematics. The hardest of the rules are the rules of logic and mathematics and they constitute the way we think and live. Here there is no question of our ratifying them in order to follow them. Ratification is presupposed rather than stated in our discourse:

> the agreement of ratification is a precondition of our language-game, it is not affirmed in it. (*RFM,* VII.9)

That is, there is no question of our making sure that we agree in following the correct rule. We are already in the business of following the rules made available to us which we accept without choosing.

Thus, Dummett's major charge that Wittgenstein's radical conventionalism results in the breakdown of the rule-following and the language-use does not hold good in view of the fact that Wittgenstein has enough space for the solidity and necessity of the rules in our language. Language itself is a standing guarantee against the possible breakdowns as it is language which takes care of itself. The sceptical worries are misplaced because they are unnecessarily worries about things which need no justification.

> The danger here, I believe, is one of giving justification of our procedure when there is no such thing as a justification and we ought to have said: *that is how we do it*. (*RFM*, III. 74)

7. 'Language must speak for itself'

The conventionalist worries have bothered the interpreters of Wittgenstein because of the fact that they have not noted Wittgenstein's rejoinder to their worries when he says that language needs no justification and that it 'must speak for itself' (*PG 3).* It is to be noted that throughout his later writings Wittgenstein is struggling against those who believe that language can be given a foundation. He is of the opinion that language needs no foundation as it is well-founded in its grammar and that there is no extra-grammatical reality that can provide a foundation for it. That is to say that not only language, but also grammar itself is autonomous.[26] That is, for both language and grammar, there is no need of providing extraneous considerations about how they work. Just as the language-games are played spontaneously without our choice (*OC*, 559) and so are not in need of justification, so also the rules of grammar are *sui generis* and do not await anybody's sanction and ratification. The rules of grammar are not accountable to any reality outside themselves. Wittgenstein writes:

> Grammar is not accountable to any reality. It is grammatical rules that determine meaning (constitute it) and so they themselves are not answerable to any meaning and to that extent are arbitrary. (*PG* 133)

That is to say that the rules of grammar do not have an origin outside language and that they do not wait for human ratification. The human conventions themselves do not explain the meaning of the grammatical rules. Grammatical rules are the source of meaning and so there is no prior meaning to which they are accountable. This is Wittgenstein's firm response to those who believe that grammatical rules themselves are conventions and are in need of constant ratification.

Wittgenstein defends the autonomy of language in view of the fact that there is nothing outside language that can provide an anchor to it; there is nothing that can make language a dependent reality. What we call reality is itself a category in language as it is language that provides the framework for making the reality intelligible. In the same way, the rules of grammar are autonomous because they cannot be justified by appealing to reality outside language. Grammar is accountable to language but not to reality because the grammatical rules are meant for understanding language and not for achieving something extra-linguistic. This makes the rules of grammar arbitrary in the sense that these have no non-linguistic purpose whereas the

---

26. See P.M.S. Hacker, *Insight and Illusion*, Clarendon Press, 1972, chapter VI, pp.156-66 for discussion on the autonomy of language and grammar.

rules of 'cookery', for example, have. Therefore, the rules of cookery are not arbitrary whereas the rules of grammar are. Wittgenstein explains:

> Why don't I call cookery rules arbitrary, and why am I tempted to call rules of grammar arbitrary? Because I think of the concept "cookery" as defined by the end of cookery, and I don't think of the concept "language" as defined by the end of language. You cook badly if you are guided in your cooking by rules other than the right ones; but if you follow other rules than those of chess you are playing another game; and if you follow grammatical rules other than such and such ones, that does not mean you say something wrong, no, you are speaking of something else. (*PG* 133)

Wittgenstein is, thus, claiming that the rules of grammar have autonomy to the extent that they are free of extra-linguistic purpose and are in that sense self-contained. They are not dependent on what the world actually is. The 'arbitrariness' of grammar is an euphemism for their independence from reality.[27] The notion of "arbitrary" as Wittgenstein uses it does not stand for anything that is based on fancy or personal preference. It means something which is not dictated to by anything external to it. Consider the following remarks:

> We have a colour system as we have a number system.
> Do the systems reside in our nature or in the nature of things? How do we prove it — Not in the nature of numbers or colours. (*Z*, 357)

Further:

> Then is there something arbitrary about this system? Yes and no. It is akin to what is arbitrary and to what is non-arbitrary. (*Z*, 358)

It is arbitrary to the extent it is independent of reality and is self-contained. But, at the same time, it is non-arbitrary because it is not a matter of taste or fancy. As Wittgenstein puts it:

---

27. See C. Wright, *Wittgenstein on the Foundations of Mathematics*, Duckworth, London, 1980, pp. 385-94.

> Compare a concept with a style of painting. For is even our style of painting arbitrary? Can we choose at pleasure? (The Egyptian, for instance.) Is it a mere question of pleasing and ugly? (*PI*, IIxii, p. 230)

Now we are tempted to ask, why are the rules of grammar not dependent on reality? Do they cease to be autonomous if they are applicable to reality? The question of independence arises precisely because the rules are not meant to be read off from reality. Had they been so read of, they would cease to be grammatical and so necessary. Because the rules are necessary, they have to be independent of reality; otherwise they would be contingent.[28] The following remark about necessity must be considered in this connection:

> The only correlate in language to an intrinsic necessity is an arbitrary rule. It is the only thing which one can milk out of this intrinsic necessity into a proposition. (*PG* 133)

That is to say that there is nothing that we can find in necessity that is not already in the rule itself. The rule carries its own necessity and, thus, there is nothing beyond the rule to derive it from. In this sense the rules can be called arbitrary if by that we mean that they are self-contained and self-justifiable.

The autonomy of the rules of grammar does not preclude such rules from being applicable to reality. In fact, the rules provide the scaffolding of the world. How the world is to be described in language is determined by the rules of grammar. Thus, the autonomy of the rules and the facts of nature do not conflict; there is a metaphysical harmony between grammar and nature. Wittgenstein writes:

> If the formation of concepts can be explained by the facts of nature, should we not be interested, not in grammar, but rather in that in nature which is the basis of grammar? Our interest certainly includes the correspondence between concepts and very general facts of nature (such facts as mostly do not strike us because of their generality). But our interest does not fall back upon these possible causes of the formation of the concepts; we are not doing natural science, nor yet

28. Cf. D.F. Pears, *Wittgenstein*, pp.133-9 for his view that necessity, according to Wittgenstein, has no backing in reality and that it is out and out based on the linguistic facts available in the human community.

> natural history — since we can also invent fictitious natural history for our purpose. (*PI*, II xii, p. 230)

In the same context, he further says:

> Like everything metaphysical the harmony between thought and reality is to be found in the grammar of language. (*PG* 112)

Thus, both grammar and nature are in harmony to make our talk of reality possible. Grammar makes our contact with reality possible in language.

8. Logical necessity and the forms of representation: towards a transcendental account

The fact that rules of grammar are constitutive of our ways of thinking has something deeper to tell about the nature of the necessary truths. These truths are such that they resent the forms of representation of the world. In this sense, grammar must be correlated with reality in that the latter is made intelligible in the forms of the former. As Wittgenstein puts it, 'grammar tells what kind of thing anything is' (*PI* Sec.373). This is to say that the grammatical truths have also a function in representing reality. But this is not to mean that the grammatical truths are in any sense descriptive statements about reality. In fact, Wittgenstein makes a clear-cut distinction between the empirical statements describing reality and the logico-mathematical statements constituting the framework of such descriptions.

The framework of descriptions is laid in the grammar of our language in the sense that the rules of grammar themselves define what would be the conceptual connections through which the facts in the world could be represented. For example, the rules of logic and mathematics define what the logical possibility of the world is, that is, they tell us how things would behave in the world. They anticipate not what the actual world is, but how the world would logically be. Thus, there is a distinction between the necessary rules of descriptions and the descriptions proper. Regarding necessary truths in mathematics D.S. Shwayder has to say the following:

> . . . successful mathematising would expose and confirm the conceptual connections which obtain in our everyday and scientific ways of thinking and talking. Mathematics, like

> metaphysics, is, according to this, the conceptual investigation of necessary connexions.[29]

This way of looking at mathematics does reiterate the fact that mathematical propositions or rules are reflective of the deep conceptual connections in our thought and language. Hence, they can easily be spotted to be revealing the way we think and use language. Thus, they play a constitutive role with regard to our understanding of the world; they provide for the apparatus for describing the world.

The way the mathematical and logical propositions function in language have much to reveal about their constitutive function. They are constitutive in the sense that they account for the sense of the propositions about the world — the propositions that say what the world is. The necessary propositions of logic and mathematics, however, show the logical features of the world. It is because of this showing function that the rules of logic and mathematics are said to constitute the 'method of representation' (*PI* Sec.50) of the world.

This account of the logico-mathematical propositions and the grammatical rules could be called transcendental in the sense that it brings out the necessary structures of language and thought. The grammatical propositions show the logical structure of language and the world. Wittgenstein says the following about the grammatical, propositions in general:

> A proposition may describe a picture and this picture be variably anchored in our *way of looking at things, and in our living and acting*. (*RFM*, IV, 36) (italics added)

The grammatical propositions are such that they represent the basic features of our forms of life such that those features cannot be detached from our way of thinking. This is a Kantian conclusion, and, therefore, Shwayder may be right in saying: 'Wittgenstein's philosophy was Kantian from beginning to end'.[30] For, according to him, Wittgenstein offered a transcendental account of logic and mathematics. In Shwayder's words:

---

29. D.S. Shwayder, 'Wittgenstein on Mathematics' in *Studies in the Philosophy of Wittgenstein*, ed. Peter Winch, p. 67.
30. *Studies in the Philosophy of Wittgenstein*, p. 66.

> Logic and mathematics are methods for the "transcendental" demonstration of the logical, essential properties of our "civil" (nonmathematical) ways of thinking and talking about the world.[31]

Paul Bernays seems to endorse this view in the following passage:

> A certain approach to the Kantian conception is embodied also in Wittgenstein's view that it is mathematics which first forms the character, "creates the forms of what we call facts". . . . In this sense Wittgenstein also strongly opposes the opinion that the propositions of mathematics have the function of empirical propositions.[32]

Now it may be asked : does Wittgenstein endorse Kant's view of mathematics in preference to the Platonic view? It is no doubt true that Wittgenstein is dissatisfied with Platonism in mathematics and logic. But this did not lead either to conventionalsim or to the empiricist view of mathematics and logic. He did not espouse intuitionism either, in spite of his sympathy for Kant's and Brouwer's constructivist mathematics. He remained stationed in his anti-Platonist platform showing deep inclinations towards a grammatical view of logic and mathematics which commits him to necessary truths that are true in all human forms of life.

The idea of searching for the fundamental sources of our conceptual connections in our forms of life, that is, in the way we act and think, could be characterised as the transcendental account of the normative structure of our thought and language. This is exactly the project which Kant[33] initiated and which Putnam[34] is urging on us while defending the view that there are necessary *a priori* truths in our conceptual structure because without them we cannot explain the meaning and truth of our language. According to Putnam, it is

---

31. *Studies in the Philosophy of Wittgenstein*, pp. 74-5.
32. P. Bernays, 'Comments on Wittgenstein's *Remarks on the Foundations of Mathematics in Ludwig Wittgenstein : Critical Assessments*, vol.3, p. 167.
33. See Kant, *The Critique of Pure Reason,* tr. N.K. Smith, Macmillan, London, 1929, Introduction.
34. See Putnam, 'Why Reason Can't be Naturalised' in *Reaslism and Reason* (*Philosophical Papers,* vol. 3), pp. 229-47 for his defence of necessity of the norms in our discourse.

difficult to explain away the *a priori* reasons from our discourse because we cannot maintain the rationality of our conceptual system if there were no norms or standards for evaluating our discourse. It is this thrust of the project that makes Putnam's search for norms and Wittgenstein's rule-following considerations Kantian in spirit, if not in letter. Wittgenstein is clearly demanding that the norms and the necessities are the forms of our understanding and language-use; they are the limits of our thought and language. As he puts it:

> There is no doubt at all that in *certain language-games* mathematical propositions play the part of the rules of description, as opposed to descriptive propositions. (*RFM*, VII, 6) (italics original)

These rules of description are the channels laid for the way the descriptions have to be made. They are the *a priori* truths which our descriptive language itself presupposes.

Wittgenstein has, thus, held that there are necessities in our language and thought which are deeply laid in our forms of life. Hence, his emphasis is on grammar and the grammatical rules. But this itself need not be construed as a concession to conventionalism because he is not making logic and mathematics the products of conventions. All that he is claiming is that there is nothing in logic and mathematics that is not related to human thought and life. In that sense they are human phenomena. But thereby they do not become empirical phenomena. They still retain the character of being grammatical and, thus, are normative and *a priori*.

The grammatical account retains the virtue of the transcendental[35] account in the sense that now the necessary rules of language are taken as the *a priori* presuppositions of our thought and language; they are the forms of representation that determine or limit the empirical language in which we interact with the world.

---

35. For a defence of the transcendental point of view in Wittgenstein, see Jonathan Lear, 'Transcendental Anthropology' in *Subject, Thought and Context*, ed., P. Petit and J. McDowell, Clarendon Press, Oxford, 1986, pp. 267-98. See also R.C. Pradhan, *Language and Experience : An Interpretation of the Later Philosophy of Wittgenstein*, Anu Prakashan, 1981, chapter 5 for a transcendental account of Wittgenstein's concept of logical necessity.

10

Wittgenstein's Philosophy of Language

A Feminist Response

Shefali Moitra

In this paper the focus will be both on *Tractatus Logico-Philosophicus* (*TLP*) and *Philosophical Investigations* (*PI*), without providing an exegetical account of Wittgenstein's philosophy of language. We shall begin straightaway by examining the possible feminist reactions to the received interpretation of these two texts.

Needless to say feminist positions are heterogeneous. One particular position cannot be identified as the feminist one. For the convenience of discussion two structural modes of feminism have been chosen for the purpose of examining the 'fit' between Wittgenstein's philosophy of language and feminism. Feminism in general terms is described as an opposition to patriarchy. 'Patriarchy' has different connotations in different cultures. A minimalist account of patriarchy would be to say that

> patriarchy prioritises male concerns/virtues in every area of investigation and simultaneously marginalises/silences female concerns.

The capacity for analytic thinking, abstraction and reason are generally equated with male virtues and the corollary role models of being culture-builders, theory-makers, abstract problem-solvers, are also attributed to men. Women, on the other hand, are perceived as the possessors of virtues like care, love for the concrete, and a propensity towards relatedness as opposed to abstraction of any form. Feminists of various genres are united in pointing out how *difference* leads to *discrimination*. How the prioritisation of one set of values/concerns leads to cultures which are negatively biased towards women. The minimalist feminist programme is to oppose discrimination whatever be its form.

In the present discussion two structural modes of feminism will be juxtaposed with Wittgenstein's philosophy of language. The programme taken up by the liberal feminist is one of inclusion. The radical feminist rejects this stance since it is pro *status-quo*. They, therefore, prescribe a restructuring of philosophy. A brief explanation of the respective programmes of the liberal feminist and the radical feminist will help clarify their relation to philosophy.

The liberal feminist complains that issues closely associated with women's experience like birthing, mothering, caring, abortion, adolescent pregnancy, pornography are neither acknowledged nor sufficiently discussed as important philosophical issues. Liberal feminists focus on identifying feminist issues which have been marginalised, they also concentrate on pushing for their inclusion into mainstream philosophy. Inclusion is executed by selecting an existing accredited philosophical framework like, existentialism, marxism, psychoanalysis and applying its investigative tools and conceptual schemes to the neglected feminist issues. The grievance against mainstream philosophy in this case, is one of omission. The feminist goal will be achieved once all the excluded topics are included. The liberal feminist sees the patriarchal bias as a case of gender-injustice.

The radical feminist by contrast sees the feminist agenda as one of fighting errors of commission. Mainstream philosophy is accused of using tools of investigation as well as conceptual schemes which pose to be gender-neutral but which are actually committed to one or the other form of patriarchy which excludes women's experience and all that is associated with being a woman and, therefore, being non-philosophical. The post-modern, post-structural stances represent this feminist position fairly well. These feminists critique reason from a gender perspective. Psychoanalysis as well as right-based ethics are also common targets. So their target is one of radical reconceptualisation of philosophy from a feminist perspective which claims neither to be exclusively male nor female but more representative of both. A radical theory may lead to a position of anti-theory on the ground that theories belong to hierarchical models of investigation and, consequently to closure, — activism is the sole agenda for these feminists. The second possibility is one where theories are critiqued with an aim to restructure concepts and categories and, by implication, logic and language.

It would be an interesting exercise to examine the ways in which a liberal feminist could possibly relate to the *TLP* or the *PI* from their inclusionist agenda. A point to be remembered is that all feminist agenda are necessarily political. Critiquing the power structure which leads to male supremacy is the focal point of feminism. So, if philosophy is seen as having a formal abstract core and a contextualised periphery, then the power games will be located at the periphery alone and the feminist must confine his / her critique to this zone exclusively. But, if power is perceived as omnipresent — sweeping over form and content, core and periphery, then the radical feminist has a point. This point is well brought out by Katherine Pyne Addelson when she writes

> To dissolve the separation between knowledge and social organisation of cognitive authority requires that feminists jettison, the old assumption that knowing is a matter of beliefs of conceptual schemes of individuals. . . .[1]

By now the impossibility of the radical feminist's being attracted by the *TLP* must be amply clear. They cannot accept that 'A proposition has one and only one complete analysis' (*TLP* 3.25). But then could a liberal feminist push for the inclusion of her agenda into the *TLP* model of language and silence? Strictly speaking 'No'. All normative questions remain outside the limits of language. 'It is clear that ethics cannot be put into words' (*TLP* 6.421). If this proposition is to be taken seriously then discrimination must be suffered. There is, however, another option open to the liberal feminist within the *TLP* model. Ethical questions could be included in naturalistic terms or in some other positivistic mode.

The saying-showing demarcation apart, there is much in the *TLP* that could be accepted and applied to feminist issues. To give an example, while discussing the abortion issue the liberal feminist could subscribe to all the following propositions of the *TLP* and to

---

1. Katherine Pyne Addelson, 'Knowers/Doers and their Moral Problems', in *Feminist Epistemology*, ed. Linda Alcott and Elizabeth Potter, Routledge, 1992.

many others in the same text:

(a) 'What can be said at all can be said clearly'. (*TLP* Preface)

(b) 'A picture agrees with reality or fails to agree'. (*TLP* 2.21)

(c) 'It used to be said that God could create anything except what would be contrary to the laws of logic'. (*TLP* 3.031)

(d) 'A proposition has one and only one complete analysis' (*TLP* 3.25)

(e) 'The world is independent of my will'. (*TLP* 6.373).

The liberal feminist could appropriate any one of these Tractarian propositions because they all subscribe to the view of the *Blue and Brown Book* that 'What one wants to say is 'Every sign is capable of interpretation but the *meaning* mustn't be capable of interpretation. It is the last interpretation' (*Blue and Brown Book,* p.34). Each of the above propositions, taken separately or jointly, refute the position attributed to the *PI* by many a commentator. They hold that the *PI* position is that understanding is always interpretation.

Whether meaning-understanding is always interpretive or not is a much debated point with respect to the *PI*. The inclusion agenda of the liberal feminists requires a conceptual scheme, a scaffolding into which their agenda can be included. The scheme or scaffolding itself is necessarily seen as being gender-neutral. The scaffolding metaphor is present in the *TLP* and in Wittgenstein's later works. In *On Certainty* he writes about the 'scaffolding of our thoughts'. (*OC*, 211) Both Tushar Kanti Sarkar[2] and Pranab Kumar Sen[3] speak of Wittgenstein's continuous allegiance to a universal and inviolable world picture, 'the element in which arguments have their life' (*O.C.*, 105). Those who hold such a strong continuity thesis between early and later Wittgenstein argue that the scaffolding in the *TLP* was the logical form and that of the *PI* a 'human form of life'. However, it may be seen, 'it is the inherited background against which I distinguish between true and false' (*O.C.* 94). Acknowledgement of the

2. *Knowledge Truth and Justification,* Allied Publishers in collaboration with Jadavpur University, Calcutta, 1992.

3. 'On a Gentle Naturalist's Response to Scepticism' in *The Philosophy of P.F. Strawson*, ed. Pranab Kumar Send and Rook Rekha Verma, ICPR, New Delhi, 1995.

heterogeneity among feminists even within the liberal tradition can very well be accommodated within this fixity of a logical form or within a human form of life. Different permutations and combinations of the liberal feminist position are possible without disturbing the scaffolding. The feminist agenda can seek to rectify the patriarchal bias by pushing its agenda of more and more inclusion. For this a structural adjustment is not required. To use a Strawsonian metaphor the periphery will simply be readjusted and the core will be kept intact. The margins of the periphery, in this case the marginalised feminist issues, will, thus, be made visible and transformed into a viable content for philosophical discussion. In the *TLP* the transformation of the invisible into the visible or from the margin to the focus will take place within the broad regulative principle that 'language determines thought'. The move from the invisible to the visible or from the margin to the focus will happen under slightly different conditions. In the *PI*, the language-games played determine the structure of the language. The full picture is that in the *TLP* language is embedded in a fixed logical form and in the *PI* thought and language-games are embedded in a form of life.

The liberal feminist could argue that oppression takes place at the level of practice, — i.e., through the practice of exclusion. Ignorance could be a plausible cause for this or it could be the result of a power-game. As Langton[4] would argue, rational practice may be at fault but not reason. In spite of the recognition of the role played by power and the play of context these feminists may remain committed to Wittgenstein's pronouncement in *O.C.* 'Some propositions seem to underlie all questions and all thinking' (415). The question of what these foundational propositions may be has been variously answered by Russell and Strawson. Russell in his *Problems of Philosophy* speaks of unchanging instinctive beliefs and in *Scepticism and Naturalism*[5] Strawson speaks of the 'natural limits within which, the serious operations of reason can take place' (p. 51). Sen tries to emphasise the acceptance of such foundational beliefs by saying that 'the question we can ask about the particular move is not a question we can ask about the rules themselves'.[6] But

---

4. Rae Langton 'Beyond a Pragmatic Critique of Reason', *Australasian Journal of Philosophy,* vol. 71, No. 4, Dec., 1993.
5. P.F. Strawson, *Scepticism and Naturalism.*
6. *Philosophy of P.F. Strawson*, p. 275.

then that is precisely what the radical feminist wants to do. Both the particular move within the rule as well as the rule itself are put to question.

The rational practice which presupposes a difference between core and periphery, margin and focus is embedded in a tradition of two-valued logic. Val Plumwood in her 'Politics of Reason: Towards a feminist practice'[7] iterates this point. She holds that this kind of logic entails a rational practice of stereotyping or homogenising of the two members of a dualism, e.g., man and not-man are treated as homogeneous categories. The second convention related with this rational practice is the denial or minimisation of continuity between the two members of the dualism.

Val Plumwood's criticism of two-valued logic is a widely accepted criticism among radical feminists. Allegedly these logical rules lead to particular moves within the limits of a rule and these moves are discriminatory. The debate between the liberal and the radical feminist could be highlighted with reference to this point. The former asks for *remedial practice* of rules and the latter for *remedial rules*. Pushed to its logical consequence the radical feminist position requires a structural change which can by no means be accommodated by the *TLP* model which prescribes the same scaffolding for all possible worlds, the *TLP* rejects all structural changes. The question is, 'Do the radical feminists intend to go to the extent of demanding structural changes at the level of a 'human form of life'?

One way of rejecting the closure of a structure would be to opt for structural anarchy where 'anything-goes'. Under anarchic circumstances the feminist aim of reorganising power equations could be nothing but a pragmatic one. 'Anything-goes' as long as it serves the purpose of breaking the patriarchal hegemony by allowing a feminist distribution of power, it is to be remembered, not a feminine distribution of power. The radical feminist perspective should not be equated with some form of matriarchy. Replacing patriarchy by matriarchy would merely mean a shift from a top-down to a bottom-up one. Whereas the feminist programme is a more radical one, it aims at an equitable acceptance of the male and female perspective. They argue that this change of perspective calls for a total reorientation. The 'anything-goes' position is an anti-theorist position

7. *Australasian Journal of Philosophy, op. cit.*

taken up by many activists and in philosophy by thinkers like Richard Rorty. Rorty's stance is brought out clearly in his article titled 'Wittgenstein, Heidegger and Lanauge'.[8] Here he even interprets Wittgenstein as a successor of the American pragmatic tradition of John Dewey. Many disagree with Rorty's understanding of later Wittgenstein as a pragmatist.

In addition to the radical agenda of the activist we must also examine the radical feminist agenda which demands a structural change by the introduction of a new logic and a new language. We have noted that an activist agenda can be accommodated by a pragmatist interpretation of later Wittgenstein. Radical feminists who demand a structural change are addressing some very complex questions of rule-following, and conceptual schemes. Val Plumwood's work is a case in point.

Plumwood is opposed to classical two-valued extensionalist logic. Relevant logic holds great hope for her because it interprets negation in a way that can, she feels, overcome the stereotyping of either member of a dichotomy. Relevant logic also avoids the extentionalist demand for radical discontinuity between two members of a dichotomy. Without going into the technicalities of this logic and without examining the premises it makes we could ask whether the replacing of one scaffolding by another is permissible in later Wittgenstein. There is no reason why it should not be. We know of his oft-quoted remark from the *PI* that there is no preconceived idea of crystalline purity in language and also his further remark in the *PI* 'It is possible to be interested in a phenomenon in a variety of ways' (*PI* 108).

When we look at the scaffolding in a variety of ways are we not changing a form of life? Is this not tantamount to that Wittgenstein calls 'changing a bank of a river'? Wittgenstein refers to the river-bank metaphor in *O.C.* Both Sen and Strawson object to situating the river-bank or the scaffolding metaphor in a relativistic context.[9]

One alternative way of avoiding a relativistic interpretation of form of life could be by speaking of changing forms of life within a diachronic slice of time, where permanent means relatively

---

8. *Essays on Heidegger and Others, Philosophical Papers*, vol.2, Cambridge University Press, 1991.

9. *The Philosophy of P.F. Strawson*, p. 276.

permanent. Many have gone for this explanation of later Wittgenstein's position where necessity is not a-historical and relative is not momentary or solipsistic.

For the radical feminist the question is how different is the difference they are aspiring for, i.e., how different is their perspective from the patriarchal one. If it is radically different then how can they communicate their position to those with whom they want to share the power with — the people they want to transform and also, how do they communicate this stance to those whom they want to empower? The situation is further complicated when the patriarchal form of life has been internalised. Wittgenstein focuses on this point when he says

> we learn this when we come into a strange country with entirely strange traditions, and what is more, even given a mastery of the country's language. . . . If a lion could talk we could not understand him. (*PI*, p. 223)

It seems implausible that feminists can engineer a radical conceptual shift in one sweep. The internalisation of the patriarchal system poses a serious constraint and the other constraint is posed by the fear of a total communication breakdown. The two constraints are no doubt closely related to one another. One way of avoiding this impasse would be to sail on 'Neurath's raft'. The question is, could a radical feminist do this without slipping into a liberal feminist position? Let us try to make a case for such an escape route for the radical feminist. In a sense Derrida does use the same boat for post-modernist purposes.

Recently much work has been done on how a Wittgenstein can be a Derridian or how one can make room for polysemia within the limits of a given form of life. The necessity of polysemia was acknowledged by Aristotle. But it attains a new dimension in the hands of Derrida. Simon Glendinning[10] has persuasively argued for the correlation between the Wittgenstein programme and the Derridian one. Both sought clarity but not at the cost of openness and freedom. Wittgenstein writes 'An indefinite sense — that would really not be a sense *at all*' (*PI* 99). The radical feminists need to

---

10. Glendinning, *On Being with Others : Heidegger-Derrida-Wittgenstein*, Routledge, London and New York, 1998.

establish that their position has a definite sense, yet the sense is not just another mode of closure — a bottom-up stance. A complicated proposal indeed! A Derridian reading of Wittgenstein may provide helpful clues for solving the problem. Later Wittgenstein provides fertile ground for the working of the Derridian proposal. How this is so could be outlined with the help of a selective account of Glendinning's exposition of the problematic.

Derrida argues that this notion of *dissemination* helps retain polysemia and at the same time avoiding the pitfalls of closure on the one hand and anarchy on the other. We shall quote Glendinning on this point:

> Thus, while language itself constantly invites or incites us to conceive 'meaning' in this way, the necessity of 'play' ensures that any putative 'unity of meaning' is *a priori* 'dispersed' in advance. In his (Derrida's) writings, 'dissemination' is the concept through which this dispersal of the 'seme' (unit of meaning) is affirmed. The concept of dissemination is thus opposed to the classical concept of polysemia. In an affirmation of the 'play' which, according to Derrida, marks *all* conceptual identities.[11] (For Derrida's own account see *Limited Inc.* North Western University Press, Evanston, 1988)

In *Acts of Literature*[12] Derrida writes that in its operational sense 'play' refers to 'the spacing between the pieces of an apparatus (which) allows for movement and articulation'. Wittgenstein echoes this notion in his *PI* when he says that in sign-games the functioning of signs is 'not everywhere circumscribed by rules' (68) and again in *Zettle* where he says 'The rules of a game may well allow a certain freedom, but all the same they must be quite definite rules' (*Zettle,* 441) Glendinning suggests that

> this means that the 'the urge to understand' the essence of the world is at once 'an urge to misunderstand' the structure and functioning of our language. In short, the idea of achieving complete clarity about the world 'as such', the

11. *On Being with Others : Heidegger-Derrida-Wittgenstein,* p. 81.
12. *Acts of Literature,* Routledge, London and New York, 1992, p. 64.

> idea of containing or limiting 'the world' within a horizon of intelligibility or significance which escapes 'looseness', simply cannot be achieved.[13]

Later Wittgenstenian texts make room for a dynamic account of the emergence of concepts and their gappiness. Room is available for 'play' and pressure to transform the conceptual space by shifting the foregrounds and the backgrounds. If concepts themselves are gappy then the changing of configurations from patriarchy to feminism may not require a quantum leap. Nor should a change imply that further changes of configurations will be ruled out for all future times. Neurath's boat could keep afloat and through the gaps in language the radical feminist could keep pushing for changes that entail structural adjustments and all this could happen within the Wittgenstenian system.

13. Glendinning, p. 92

11

The Language of Face
Wittgenstein on Cinema

Sanil V.

Is cinema a language? Both Semiotics and Hermeneutics hastily answer in the affirmative. No such quick response can be expected from Wittgenstein. This is not because cinema is never a subject-matter for his reflection on language. As Kripke has shown, Wittgenstein made all simple answers to the question whether a certain set of marks or behaviour constitute a language, impossible. Wittgenstein inaugurated an enigmatic conception of language with a profound discovery — there is no fact to the matter of language. We cannot begin with an idea of language formed on the basis of the so-called ordinary or natural languages and see whether cinema fits into that idea. No such idea is readily available.

Wittgenstein used this very enigma — 'whether X is a language' as the clue to the nature of language.[1] He faced language at the threshold of its intelligibility as language. He rejected the available accounts which anchors language in reality, intention or on public

1. Wittgenstein explicitly uses this strategy to investigate dream language. Is there a language of dreams? Wittgenstein's first response is in the negative. But he acknowledges our felt need to treat dreams as if they speak to us. "What is intriguing about a dream is not its causal connection with events in my life etc., but rather the impression it gives of being a fragment of a story". (Wittgenstein L, *Culture and Value,* ed. G.H. Von Wright, tr. Peter Winch, Oxford: Blackwell, 1978, pp. 68-9). This puzzlement is a symptom of language. "Think of how puzzling a dream is. Such a riddle does not have a solution. It intrigues us. It is as if a riddle is there. This could be a primitive reaction". (Wittgenstein L., *Last Writings on the Philosophy of Psychology*, ed. G.H. Von Wright *et al.*, (Chicago: University of Chicago Press), 1982, vol. 1, Sec. 195.

consensus. He lets the enigma shine in silence and throw light on its own sources within language. This forecloses the possibility of extending an available philosophy of language to cinema. Instead, we may ask: is there an aspect of the enigma of language to which cinema responds well? The answer might lead us to cinematic conception of language which illuminates not only the language of cinema but also the cinema of language.

Wittgenstein's reflections on various non-linguistic phenomena like pictures, memory, dreams and faces exemplify this strategy. The relevance of these reflections cannot be restricted to a philosophy of perception or of mind. They don't aim at generalisations of the sort 'pictures are like language' or 'language is like pictures'. Instead, they show that language doesn't escape the spell of picture, dreams and faces and this spell works through the language-like appearance of the latter. Wittgenstein discovers a relationship of mutual presup-position and capture between these visual phenomena and our verbal behaviour. Our task is to introduce films which are essentially audio-visual into the web of these relationships.

Saying and seeing: The pussle of aspects

Wittgenstein's thought was captivated by both the idea and phenomenon of picture. Early Wittgenstein gave us a picture theory of language whereas the later one gave us a language theory of pictures. In *Tractatus Logico-Philosophicus* 'picture' refers to a transcendental isomorphism between language and reality.[2] 'Picture' answers the question how can we have a logic given the fact that we have a world. It is as if, the pictures equip the blind words with visibility and the mute world with speech so that we say what we see and we see what we say. But having identified language with speech, 'picture' refers to a domain of exclusive seeing which speech can only pass over in silence. The picture which can only be seen, nevertheless, makes speech possible. At the same time, *Tractatus* demands us to burn all bridges and ladders between the domains of saying and seeing so that they don't cross over into each other's domain disturbing the order of saying and the clarity of seeing. This paradoxical relationship between saying and seeing underlies what is popularly known as the 'picture theory of meaning'.

2. Wittgenstein. L., *Tractatus Logico-Philosophicus*, tr. D.F. Pears and B.F. McGuinness, London : Routledge & Kegan Paul, 1961.

In *Philosophical Investigations* language is no longer transcendentally anchored in reality.[3] The picture of isomorphism is shattered but the picture itself persists. Here Wittgenstein investigates the nature of our verbal and non-verbal behaviour towards pictures and realises that our experience of picture is inextricably tied up with language. He discovers an original link between saying and seeing. This link constitutes language as essentially an audio-visual phenomenon. Saying and seeing are woven together in practice. Practice here is an audio-visual assembly of sayings and seeings. Wittgenstein finds that not only the puzzle of ducks and rabbits but a whole range of visible phenomenon like dreams, memory, the colour of letters and the fatness of Wednesday are caught up in the web of such a verbal and visual network. This is the picture theory of the Later Wittgenstein. Here language is already cinematic.

Film theory has already exploited Wittgenstein's idea of aspect to illuminate the perception of cinematic images. However, these discussions are limited to issues about the viewer's psychological responses to film image. In the idea of aspect they fail to notice a radical clue about the audio-visual nature of cinema.

The idea of aspect brings out the diversity of games which goes under the common name 'seeing'. Wittgenstein brings out three conceptually different types of seeing — aspect dawning, continuous aspect perception and aspect blind seeing. He uses the paradoxical picture of the duck-rabbit to illustrate these ways of seeing. When asked about what we see in that figure we would say we see now a duck, now a rabbit. We don't say that we see a pattern of lines, shapes and colours which we interpret as a duck or rabbit. We spontaneously respond to the picture by saying 'this is a rabbit, this a duck'. Of course, every picture is made up of a certain arrangement of lines, colours and shapes. In the puzzle picture it is the same arrangement of lines that appears now as rabbit and later as a duck. This paradoxical experience of seeing a duck exactly where we saw a rabbit a moment ago is called noticing an aspect.

> I contemplate a face, and then suddenly notice its likeness to another. I see that it has not changed; and yet I see it differently. I call this experience 'noticing an aspect'.[4]

---

3. Wittgenstein, L., *Philosophical Investigations,* tr. G.E.M. Anscombe, Oxford: Basil Blackwell, 1958.

4. *Ibid.*, p. 193.

Those who are incapable of manifesting such paradoxical experience and see only an arrangement of lines which need to be interpreted are aspect blind. One can manifest the paradoxical experience of aspect dawning only if he doesn't treat a picture as a blue print of the object it represents but stands towards it as he does towards the object itself.

> In some respects I stand towards it (picture-face) as I do towards a human face. I can study its expression, can react to it as to the expression of the human face.[5]

This mode of perception is called continuous aspect perception.

By distinguishing these three modes of seeing Wittgenstein destroys two myths — the myth of the innocent eye which has an unmediated access to the given and the myth of the ideal tongue which speaks exactly what it sees. Wittgenstein draws the distinction between aspect seeing and blind seeing by referring to the verbal behaviour that accompanies the experience of seeing. Seeing is inextricably linked to the representation of what is seen. However, as Wittgenstein demonstrates, the concept of representation of what is seen together with the concept of what is seen are very elastic.

The dramatic turns in aspect perception cannot be explained by invoking changes either in the perceived object or in the organisation of psychological images. For Wittgenstein, the criterion for visual experience is the representation of what is seen, But the puzzle of aspect dawning is that the alterations in our visual experience cannot be expressed in a representation of what is seen. We cannot explain the change of duck picture into rabbit picture by tracing our fingers over the contours of the figure because the figure has not changed. However, we are inclined to speak about this experience as if in the blink of an eye the duck disappeared and the rabbit leaped in. But materially nothing has changed.

> The expression of a change of aspect is the expression of a new perception and at the same time of the perception being unchanged.

The paradoxical experience of aspect dawning is characterised by the attitude of the viewer which is manifested in the fine shades of verbal and non-verbal behaviour he exhibits. This attitude is

5. *Philosophical Investigations*, p. 194.

exemplified in the nature of the description we use to convey the discovery of aspect dawning. We might convey the dawning of the rabbit aspect in a duck-rabbit picture by a cry of recognition, 'It is a rabbit' or by pointing out to other pictures of rabbit or to a real rabbit itself. But these references are not expected to convey any extra or optional information about what we see in the figure. The description or representation of what is seen which accompanies aspect dawning is not a report on what is seen. This description or representation is the only possible expression of what is seen. From here we should not jump to the wrong conclusion that the representation 'It is a rabbit' is a wordless cry. The cry at its very birth is consoled and tamed into a meaningful order of words. But the words instead of waiting to speak to us flow into the very experience they are expected to attest. As Wittgenstein says

> Hence the flashing of an aspect on us seems half visual experience, half thought.[6]

Aspect is neither word nor a picture. It appears in the gap between the word and the image, separating them and linking them.

> Aspect dawning is characterised by the observer's felt need to employ a representation which might otherwise refer to subjective visual experience — to one way of seeing the figure — as if it were a report of new perception.[7]

A representation is used as a description in certain contexts, but not in all. The concept of seeing is used in certain contexts to refer to the movement of eyes traversing shapes and lines, not all always. But Wittgenstein asks

> Is it, then, so surprising that I use the same expression in different games. And sometimes across games?[8]

Just as the same figure without undergoing any material change becomes a duck now and rabbit later, the representation of what is seen also elastically stretches from description to cry.

---

6. *Philosophical Investigations*, p. 197.
7. Mulhall, Stephan, *On Being in the World*, London:Routledge, 1990, p. 11.
8. *Philosophical Investigations*, p. 188.

> But here is the problem: a cry is which cannot be called a description, which is more primitive than any description, for all that serves as a description of the inner life.
>
> A cry is not a description. But there are transitions. And the words ' I am afraid' may approximate more or less, to being a cry. They may come quite close to this and also be far removed from it.[9]

Thus, the elasticity of saying and the plasticity of seeing preserve the meaningfulness of utterances across language-games and the identity of the visible across apparitions.

The visibility of aspect needs to be distinguished from that of picture, if we characterise the latter in terms of resemblance with what is pictured. Wittgenstein explicitly makes this distinction in his discussion on attributing the experience of pain to others.

> It is a misunderstanding to say 'The picture of pain enters into the language-game with the word 'pain'. The image of pain is not a picture and this image is not replaceable in the language-game by anything that we should call a picture. The image of pain certainly enters into the language game in a sense; only not as a picture.
>
> An Image is not a picture, but a picture can correspond to it.[10]

The visibility attached to the sentence 'he is in pain' is not that of the contortions of skin we notice on the face of the one who is in pain. Such 'superficial changes' constitute the picture of pain and not its image. Those who try to imagine the pain of others on the model of one's own pain or vice versa see only the picture of pain. He would see the other face as an assembly of separate parts — eyes, nose, lips, skin etc., — when arranged in certain manner corresponds to the experience of pain and in another manner corresponds to happiness. But one can see the image of pain even if the other doesn't betray any sign of pain. The image of pain need not be attested by tears. The sentence 'he is in pain' bears the image of pain on its face. Cinema displays the image and not the picture.

9. *Philosophical Investigations*, p. 189.
10. *Ibid.*, p. 101.

The physiognomy of words

Wittgenstein finds the concept of aspect important because of its connection with the concept 'experiencing the meaning of a word'.

> For we want to ask `what would you be missing if you did not experience the meaning of a word?[11]

The earlier discussion on pictures shows that we manifest the experience of seeing the aspect by employing sayings. Now Wittgenstein shows that language itself can be the object of aspect seeing. When we experience that 'Wednesday is fat' as opposed to a lean Tuesday or 'jiggery pockery' is funny or 'e' is yellow or when we use a word to mean in different ways by using them in isolation or by using a certain intonation or when we feel that a word sounds hollow when repeated many times we are treating language as an object of seeing. These 'queer' experiences cannot be explained by causal/ psychological accounts or by invoking notions like conventions of use or mastery of rule.

We attribute linguistic understanding to someone if he uses the word in the appropriate way and responds appropriately to its use by others. However, this can take place even if he is incapable of experiencing the meaning of words.

When I say 'Wednesday is fat' I am not referring to a psychological experience nor to the conventional uses of the word 'fat'. Here we are using the word 'fat' in a different meaning. If asked what do we really mean here by 'fat' we can't answer by pointing to Wednesday and Tuesday. We can explain meaning only by saying more about fatness and by pointing out the examples of fat people and fat books. These definitions and examples fix the primary meaning of the word 'fat'. This primary meaning allows us to use the 'same word' 'fat' in a secondary meaning as in 'Wednesday is fat'. Here the secondary meaning is not metaphorical. We cannot paraphrase what we want to say in any other way than by using 'fat' which has a certain primary meaning. Here the identity of the meaning is ensured not by fat people nor by the intention of the speaker nor by the auditory or graphic identity of the word 'fat'. The primary meaning is assimilated onto the face of the word. The word has a physiognomy which manifests its meaning.

11. *Philosophical Investigations*, p. 214.

> The familiar physiognomy of word, the feeling that it has taken up its meaning into itself, that it is actual likeness of its meaning — there could be human beings to whom all this was alien.[12]

What is visible about a word is not he object it refers to nor its graphic properties but its face. There is no fact to the matter of language. All that it has is its face. It is the visibility of this visage which finds its perfection in cinema.

> The physiognomy of the words allows us to say
>
> I feel as if the name Schubert fitted Schubert's work and Schubert's face.[13]

Here we are not referring to a naïve resemblance between names and the objects they name. 'Fitting' here refers to a smooth assimilation of the contexts of its use to the name itself. It is as if Schubert the individual, the composer, his works, its performances, recollections all have left the world in which we could have encountered them and migrated on to the face of the spoken word 'Schubert' where they allow themselves to be seen.

Here we should avoid the fallacies of both descriptivist and anti-descriptivist theories of meaning. The former takes the name as a condensed description. For descriptivism, names are bearers of meaning and they refer when they satisfy the cluster of descriptions which constitutes the meaning. Here the fit between the word 'Schubert' and Schubert's life and work is the fit between the descriptions about Schubert and the state of affairs which satisfy them. Discursive knowledge about Schubert and his works will enable us to experience the meaning of the word 'Schubert'. But anti-descriptivism would remind us that in some possible world Schubert might not have composed 'Die Winter Reise'. Schubert might not have studied under Michael Holzer. All the works which bear the signature of Schubert might have been composed not by Schubert but by Schumann. The name 'Schubert' will continue to refer even if all the descriptions associated with it are false. Hence, the anti-descriptivist would argue that, what we experience on the face of the name cannot be the meaning of the cluster of descriptions which are

12. *Philosophical Investigations.*

13. *Ibid.*, p. 215.

made about Schubert. However, having purified the reference of names from the meaning of descriptions, the anti-descriptivists fail to account for our felt experience of meaning occasioned by names. He might even argue — at least on some occasions Wittgenstein might seem to agree with him — that such special experiences associated with words are chimerical and are not constitutive of the meaning.[14]

The word Schubert is expressive. It has a face. We recognise 'Schubert' on the face of his name. We feel that if he had another name we might have failed to recognise the face of Schubert. Suppose in some possible world Schubert had a different name and had composed same music and led a similar life, we expect that he takes up 'Schubert' as his pseudo-name.[15] Imagine that Schubert's name was Shoe-lace. His music would have sounded funny to our ears. If it is discovered that the person to whom we refer with this name did not do any of the things we ascribed to him, we might stop experiencing Schubert's face and music on the face of the word 'Schubert'. Or we might continue to use that name to refer to whoever satisfies some of the descriptions we associate with the name 'Schubert'. Neither of these would make sense unless, in the first instance, we experience that the word has a face.[16]

Here we see Wittgenstein's profound non-descriptivist theory of

---

14. Kripke Saul, *Wittgenstein on Rule Following and Private Language,* Oxford: Blackwell, 1982, p. 46.

15. Psuedo names and nick-names reveal something significant about proper names. Often nick-names stick to the object more than proper names. On nick-names Adorno and Horkheimer observe:

    Even though laughter is still the sign of force, an outburst of blind and callous nature, it also has within it the opposite element: In laughter, blind nature precisely becomes aware of itself as such and therewith renounces destructive force. This double meaning of laughter is akin to that of the name and perhaps names are nothing but frozen laughter, as nick-names still are today — the only names in which something of the primordial act of name-giving lives on. (Adorno, Horkheimer, *Dialectics of Enlightenment,* New York, 1972, p. 77).

16. Here we must guard against cultural relativism. It is true that someone who comes from a world where there are no rabbits and pictures would fail to notice the rabbit aspect. A non-Western listener of music might fail to experience the meaning of 'Schubert'. Instead, he might experience the fit between 'Swathi Thirunal' and his compositions. Wittgenstein is probing the conditions of possibility of having such experiences whose content might very well be relative to cultures.

language which avoids both descriptivism and anti-descriptivism. Words find their objects not through descriptions and interpretations. Words bear their meaning on their faces. Words and meanings are related through a primitive reaction. This non-descriptivism is unlike the anti-descriptivism of Kirpke, which sends descriptions on a holiday with the trifling task of 'picking out objects' for naming. Wittgenstein combines the partial truths of both descriptivism and anti-descriptivism. For the anti-descriptivist descriptions have only a heuristic role in fixing the reference of names. They serve the purpose even when the referent fails to satisfy the descriptions. Wittgenstein circumscribes describing as a specific language-game and shows that what appear to be descriptions are often moves in other language-games. However, Wittgenstein gives due credit to descriptions when he notices that even a cry takes recourse to descriptions. Our response to the experience of meaning is half cry and half description.

The 'experience of meaning' cannot be explained in terms of resemblance between words and objects or in terms of psychological experience. The word 'meaning' is not used here in any metaphorical sense. No reference to the mastery of rule or use can account for it. As we have said, someone who has mastered the rule for using a word may still fail to experience its meaning. No additional rule needs to be learned to make sense of 'meaning' in 'experience of meaning'. It is the same word 'meaning' which has been used here, though with a new meaning. Here noticing this new sense of 'meaning' is like noticing the dawning of the rabbit aspect in the puzzle figure. We experience the same word but as different. This paradoxical experience of 'meaning' is the 'experience of meaning'. Here we see the aspect of the word. But, just as the rabbit aspect is not constituted by the lines of the figure, the word-aspect is not constituted by its auditory or graphic form. There is nothing more to the identity of meaning than its aspect that dawns on the word.

Though the meaning of a name is not determined by the descriptions associated with it, the experience of meaning cannot be dissociated from such descriptions. This paradox is better exemplified by words which are used as stereotypes — woman, muslim, etc. These descriptivist would argue that these descriptions which are complicit in doing injustice to the object must be replaced with another set of correct descriptions. However, he does not tell us how would the new set of descriptions emancipate the same object who was the victim of the old descriptions. The anti-descriptivist would insist on freeing the meaning of name from any descriptions whatsoever and on handing it over to what the name rigidly refer — the essential woman, essential muslim, etc. But he doesn't tell us anything about the economy of descriptions which actually surround the name and its disastrous effects on the object.

The user of stereotypes are least perturbed when we tell him that the actual women or muslim do not fit the descriptions used to refer to them. He will readily agree that perhaps most of the women he finds around are strong and intelligent and muslims, patriotic and kind. He would maintain that these strong, intelligent women are not the real women. He uses the stereotype to refer to the real object. What is the difference between the invocation of the real object by the anti-descriptivist and by the 'stereotypist'. The anti-descriptivist says 'a woman is a woman'. The stereotypist also says 'after all a woman is a woman'. Who/what is the real woman? The real muslim? The real object?

The real woman is that which necessarily satisfies the descriptions. What is the ground of this necessity? It is nothing but the name 'woman' itself. The real woman is someone who satisfies the descriptions because she is a woman. The woman is she who carries the stigma of the name woman. The object woman is not a complex or rich essence which is in excess of all descriptions. It is only an effect of the name itself.

The name confers a certain illusion of necessity on the contingent fit between descriptions and objects. Descriptions are about something. From here we shall not conclude that something is rigidly designated by names even if it fails to fit the descriptions. All objects are objects under some description or another. A name designates a description-object complex. Which description-object would a name designate is contingent. Today, perhaps the word 'woman' refers to a complex made of descriptions like weaker sex, obedient wife, sacrificing mother and of objects like raped women, burned wives, undernourished mothers. Tomorrow this word 'woman' might be hijacked by a different set of descriptions and objects. A certain description-object fit gets the appearance of necessity when its is tied around the peg of a name. It is economy of meaningful descriptions which demands a meaningless name as its support.

No essential features of the object can guarantee the identity of the object which the names designate. The only support of the identity of the object and the unity of the field of meaning is the name itself. There is no mysterious object X which the name refers to irrespective of the vagaries of the descriptions. It is not that the object X is too rich to be exhausted by descriptions. In fact, the object is too poor. It is nothing. A void. For Wittgenstein 'the experience of meaning' is grounded in a 'primitive reaction' with which the game of language begins. This primitive reaction is not ostensive definition or description. 'The primitive reaction may have been a glance or a gesture, but it may also have been a word'. 'Meaning is the effect of a primitive performance by which a gesture, a glance or a word cuts through the void of the object X. A radical non-descriptivism grounds the identity of the object on the primitive act of naming.

For Wittgenstein the inaugural gesture or word is the half visual and half language of the aspect. The aspect is language traversing the void of the object X. The original linguistic act is an act of 'choosing and valuing words' which makes us attached to our words. It is the word itself qua word and not its auditory or graphic qualities, nor the descriptions attached to it nor the object it represents nor the ways of using it that gives it a face.

This primacy of word does not imply any linguistic or cultural relativism. This needs to be emphasised because many interpret Wittgenstein as grounding meaning in some unreflected or pre-reflective linguistic/cultural consensus on the use of words. Here we might misinterpret the 'experience of meaning' as the ready to hand availability of certain word for a certain practical accomplishments. This is a travesty of both Wittgenstein's notion of meaning of words and Heidegger's notion of ready to handedness of practical involvement with the world.

Here we should also keep in check a vulgar conception of the 'public' which has followed Wittgenstein's critique of private language. Neither the deliberated consensus of a group nor the pre-reflective identity of a life form make a public. The public is not an omniscient observer who robs us of our private lives and fantasies. The public is not a treasury or authority of rules which the private users of language are compelled to draw upon. A Kripke's Wittgenstein shows, there is no vantage point neither private nor public from where the identity of a rule, use or meaning can be stabilised. He debunks the myths of the private-inner and the public outer. The solution to the question of meaning lies on the surface — the face of language. The aspect which is neither word nor object but both, which is neither what is spoken nor what is seen but both, which is half thought and half experience, half report and half cry traverse this face. It is the object correlate of the primitive reaction that inaugurates language.

Wittgenstein says

> If God has looked into our minds he would not have been able to see there whom we were speaking of.[17]

This is not merely because meaning is not in our heads. Even if God were to look elsewhere, say in the public sphere or 'in the public mind' he wouldn't see that either. But if God were to look, what would he see? He would see nothing but the word — the brute simple, mundane fact or face of the word. The experience of meaning dawns on us not when the word 'meaning' totalises across all shades of meaning and fixes it as its field of reference. In fact, the perpetual slipping of the meaning of meaning comes to a halt against an empty, performative 'use'. The word 'meaning' or 'Meaning' or 'mEaning' represents only the non-sense and the contingency of any 'meaningful' signifier. Paradoxically this fragile signifier will come to be the locus of the totalised field of meanings. The word represents within the conditions of utterability the fragility of every specific act of utterance. Hence, the primitive reaction is self-reflective. To display its meaning word needs a face. The availability of self — the first person makes a surface into a face. Wittgenstein teaches us that this self is not a mysterious entity, a depth hidden behind the surface. It is an apparition which traverses the surface. On this surface, words smile and objects speak.

Often we think that the visual dimension of cinema is capable of showing what language can only imperfectly describe. Wittgenstein does not allow any such easy commerce between the spoken and visual. He knows that words are the wrong currency to exchange for pictures. What makes a set of marks or behaviour language is not any fact about them but the face they acquire. This is the face on which we directly experience meaning. It is the visibility of this visage that cinema raises to a greater degree of perfection. In cinema this face coincides with a surface — the surface of the screen where seeings and sayings encounter each other.

---

17. *Philosophical Investigations*, p. 217.

This visible face is beyond phenomenology and semiotics. For Phenomenology the visible is mute meaning which language will soon raise to the order of speech. For Wittgenstein the murmur of visible is only the effect of the enigmatic relationship between the visible and language. The face resists phenomenological reduction. As pure surface it doesn't conceal any depth of meaning for Hermeneutics to unearth through interpretation. The face as the bearer of identity defies the structuralist semiotics which dissolves the identity of meaning into a system of differences. The referential dimension of the primitive linguistic reaction of the word and glance disrupts the systems of internal differences. The idea of aspect, if thought beyond phenomenology and semiotics, yields the idea of image which Wittgenstein distinguishes from picture.

Art makes the 'this' of ostensive definition which hopes to build bridges between saying and seeing to tremble like the rigid designator of a magnetic compass gone mad when taken to the poles. Paintings of Klee, Magritte, Kandinsky, Duchamp and Wahrol witness the tough exchanges between the text and the figure where the sharp edges of language cut the picture open, releasing the image.

Great cinema shows us the difference between the image/face and pictures. The image dawns at interstices of sayings and seeings. The sound track is not meant to give voice to the visible improvements of character. The cinematic image arises where all natural relationships between the spoken and visible dimensions — of resemblance, isomorphism, isotopism, symbolism, causality — are broken. Here I can only mention a few examples of this apparition. Eisentsein's Juxstaposition of the 'written cry' of Mutineers and their faces in Battleship Potemkin, Orson Wells' deep focus shots which pierce through different slices of time in Citizen Kane, Alain Resnais's parallels between events within and outside history in Hiroshima mon Amour, Ozu's indifferent spaces which allow speech and objects to drift apart in Tokyo Story. . . ; all of them witness the birth of the image from the difficult liason between the spoken and the seen. This image which can both be heard and seen is the face of language. If cinema has a language it is the language of face.

12

Exploring the Grammar of Emotion Words

G.P. Ramachandra

WITTGENSTEIN'S philosophy of language throws much light on problems in the philosophy of psychology. According to Wittgenstein, one of the great sources of confusion in philosophy is the tendency for words to make us look for counterparts. Emotion words are an example. Most people think of emotions as ontologically real entities. They think that a situation evokes an emotion-say, joy — in a person and this in turn causes the characteristic bodily manifestations of the emotion in question. This view is emphatically rejected by Wittgenstein.

> But 'Joy' surely designates some inward thing. No. 'Joy' designates nothing at all. Neither any inward nor any outward thing.[1]

Emotion words are not denoting words at all; they are function words. In the case of joy, for example, the ontologically real elements are the situation, which enters the person's life as something elating and the bodily manifestations. The situation and the bodily manifestations are criteria for talking about joy, for evaluating the situation. A cloudless sky, sunshine etc., are criteria for talking about good weather, good weather is not something existing independently of these conditions, whose existence is to be inferred from them. Good weather is not a distinct something; instead, 'good weather' is a term we use to evaluate a situation.

1. Ludwig Wittgenstein, *Zettel*, ed. G.E.M. Ansocmbe and G.H. von Wright, tr. G.E.M. Anscombe, Basil Blackwell, Oxford, 1967, 487.

We need emotion words to impose order and meaning on what would otherwise be isolated acts, to provide a practical guide in living our lives. An experiment carried out by a scientist called Hebb in the late nineteen forties and discussed by Robert M. Gordon, a philosopher of psychology, shows that this is true even of our experience of apes. In this experiment, some chimpanzees were studied over a period of years. Initially, their behaviour was described in anthropomorphic terms of behaviour and attitude. And it was found that they could be handled safely by a newcomer. Then, for two years, records were kept of the apes to bring out behavioural differences without any anthropomorphic concepts (e.g., 'anger', 'hostility') being used. It was impossible, it was found, to learn which apes could be approached safely, by whom, and in what manner.

> All that resulted was an almost endless series of specific acts in which no order or meaning could be found.[2]

By using anthropomorphic concepts, it was possible to quickly and easily describe the peculiarities of the individual animals, and with this information, a newcomer could handle them safely. Hebb said that the 'objective' descriptions missed

> some order or relationship between isolated acts that is essential to the comprehension of behaviour.[3]

> Emotion words provided 'an intelligible and practical guide to behaviour'.[4]

Emotion words are necessary tools for living; they are not indicators of anything hidden. This is the philosophical conclusion to be drawn from Hebb's experiment. But Robert M. Gordon does not see the matter in this way. He says that Hebb's account enables us to see or surmise the divergent 'states' that may lie 'beneath' outwardly similar behaviour.[5] Talk of 'states' and being 'beneath' can be dangerous if we hypostatise these concepts, which are purely notional.

Wittgenstein's rejection of the counterpart theory of meaning is

---

2. Cited in Robert M.Gordon, *The Structure of Emotions: Investigations in Cognitive Psychology*, Cambridge University Press, 1987, p. 2.
3. *Ibid.*, p. 4.
4. *Ibid.*
5. *Ibid.*

a part of his philosophy of language and this paper will draw on this principle. But it will use another principle of his philosophy of language as well — his distinction between material and grammatical propositions. Material propositions are propositions which are about the world, about phenomena and they are the propositions of the natural sciences and the social sciences. Philosophical propositions are not about the world; they are about language in one way or another, they are grammatical. But Wittgenstein seems to have used the word 'grammatical' in more than one way. Philosophers introduce linguistic innovations, thinking they are making statements about phenomena, when all they have done is to decide to use words in a new way; such propositions give no information about the world. Wittgenstein calls them 'grammatical' and they are endemic in philosophy. But he also calls 'grammatical' propositions which are of a somewhat different sort. These are propositions which are contained, as it were, in other propositions, which are logically implied by them, which also give no information about the world. There are criteria for identifying them. There is no procedure for verifying or falsifying them. They have no antithesis; we cannot imagine what it would be like for them to be wrong. For example, if it is true that '*A* is the cause of *B*', then it always will be true that '*B* is the effect of '*A*'. Again, if it is true to say of a patch on the wall that it is blue in colour, it will always be true to say that it is not green in colour. Or if it is true to say that my mother's mother is still alive, it will always be true to say that my maternal grandmother is still alive. We are concerned with grammatical propositions in this sense here.[6]

If emotions are not real entities, if emotion words are function words, it follows that any attempt to give an account of emotions in their own right must fail; we can give an account of situations and bodily manifestations only. And it is a fact that those who attempt to describe emotions end up advancing grammatical propositions in the second sense mentioned above, they end up talking in tautologies and extended tautologies, they end up exploring the grammar of emotion words. The present paper will demonstrate this by looking

6. For a discussion of grammatical propositions, see W.E. Kennick, 'Philosophy as Grammar and the Reality of Universals', in the Alice Ambrose and Morris Lazerowitz, (eds.), *Ludwig Wittgenstein : Philosophy and Language*, George Allen and Unwin, London, 1972, pp.140-85. But Kernnick focuses almost exclusively on grammatical propositions in the first sense.

at two such attempts — Saam Trivedi's article 'The Emotions — Some Preliminaries' and parts of Robert M. Gordon's book, *The Structure of Emotions.*[7] Neither of them succeed in saying anything significant about emotions and this is exactly what we should expect to happen if emotions are not real entities and a philosopher tries to give an account of them, assuming that they are.

We turn now to Saam Trivedi's article. Let us look at his definitions first. He says that emotions 'standardly' are 'complexes consisting of two components : (i) an affective element consisting of affects or feelings as well as (ii) a cognitive element, consisting typically of evaluative beliefs, thoughts, judgements, imaginings, and the like.[8] By virtue of this cognitive, emotions have intentionality.

It is difficult, he admits (a significant admission) to give a very precise account of affects, but very roughly, affects are the non-cognitive, non-intentional part of emotion and involve a 'what-it-feels-like' aspect. They involve 'raw feels'[9] or inner psychological affects of pleasure and pain. They may also involve physical or bodily affects, which are affects themselves, and not just manifestations of inner psychological affects. He says that psychological affects are best seen in cases of intense emotions.

The cognitive element involves an evaluative belief that a certain judgement is true and that it is good or bad; and this evaluative belief causes the resulting emotion. A person who feels intense grief upon her mother's death has a belief that it is true that her mother is dead and that this is bad; and this causes the emotion of sadness, and its constituent affect in the person. An act of judgement takes place, but it happens 'below the level of our consciousness',[10] that is, we are not aware that we are making it. Such judgements cause and are indeed part of the emotion.

It is evident that Trivedi has not got beyond this initial definitions of affects or feelings. Since 'affects' and 'feelings' are synonymous terms (he acknowledges this) one does not explain what an affect is

---

7. Saam Trivedi, 'The Emotions : Some Preliminaries', *Journal of the Indian Council of Philosophical Research,* vol. XV, No.3 May-August, 1998, pp. 87-95, and Robert M. Gordon, *op. cit.*, pp. 1-85.

8. Trivedi, *op. cit.*, p. 87.

9. *Ibid.*

10. *Ibid.*, p. 88.

by saying that it involves a 'what-it-feels-like' aspect; this is equivalent to saying that a feeling involves a 'what-it-feels-like' aspect. Since he has already separated affects from beliefs, which he says are cognitive and intentional, he is repeating himself when he says that affects involve 'raw (i.e., non-cognitive) feels'. He also says that affects involve inner psychological affects of pleasure and pain. Since an affect of feeling is necessarily psychological or inner, this can be rewritten as 'an affect involves an affect of pleasure and pain' in other words, that feelings are either pleasurable or painful. This is a grossly reductionist thesis which fails to do justice to the richness and nuances of our emotional life. Trivedi's assertion that psychological affects are best seen in cases of intense emotions can be rewritten as 'feelings are best seen in cases of intense emotion', which in turn, cannot easily be separated from 'feelings are best seen in cases of intense feelings'.

Trivedi also says that affects or feelings may also involve physical affects or bodily reactions. It is true that feelings or affects involve bodily reactions, in the sense that certain kinds of bodily reactions are criteria for talk in about certain kinds of feelings. But there is no point at all in violating convention by calling these reactions 'physical affects'. Convention permits us to call them 'effects' (a very similar-looking word, be it noted) of emotions but this convention expresses a philosophical confusion; they are the outcome, not of 'inner states' but of situations which have certain kinds of significance for us, or, to put it in another way, by 'inner states'; we mean the ways in which situations enter our lives. Trivedi tries to use the example of drowsiness to prove that bodily reactions are themselves affects, and not just manifestations of psychological affects, but what the example of drowsiness really proves is that bodily states need not be manifestations of psychological states, not that they cannot be. We may, however, readily agree with him when he says that bodily reactions are easier to describe than psychological ones. This is because the bodily reactions are ontologically real.

Trivedi fails equally to give a genuine account of the cognitive element in emotions. He says that a cognition consists typically of beliefs, thoughts, judgements, imaginings and the like. Here the word 'consists' is not being used in an empirical way, to tell us what something is made of, as, for example, in a sentence such as 'A molecule of water consists of a combination of two atoms of hydrogen to one atom of oxygen'. It is being used of members of a linguistic category, except for imaginings, which are not properly called cognitions. Trivedi is really telling us how the word 'cognition' is used by philosophers (nobody else uses it) except in the case of imaginings, where his grammar goes wrong. He says that emotions have intentionality by virtue of the cognitive element. This again is not an empirical remark. It is not a case of one set of circumstances making another possible, for example, the stomach digesting food by virtue of the juices it secretes. It is a case of one form of words being contained in another. Whenever we say that somebody is cognisant, we can say that he is cognisant of something; cognition is always intentional. Similarly, a thought is always a thought of something; a thought is always intentional. One has to scratch something, one cannot just scratch, while one just yawns, one cannot yawn anything. Such propositions give no information about phenomena. They do not state empirical facts. However, while 'yawn' and 'scratch' denote something concrete which we can describe, 'cognition' and the members of its category like 'thought', as also the various emotion words, are function words, which do not denote anything; we use them to evaluate state of affairs. We cannot describe them in the sense of saying anything about them in their own right; we can describe a thought, for example, only by describing that of which it is a thought. Trying to give an account of 'feelings' and 'cognitions' in their own right is like trying to give an account of 'butness' and 'andness' in their own right and it is small wonder that Trivedi fails in the attempt.

Trivedi maintains that when someone experiences intense grief upon her mother's death, she believes that it is true that her mother is dead, and that this is bad. But this is another case of one form of words being contained in another. Whenever one says truly that someone is affected for the better or the worse by something, it will be true to say that someone believes that something is the case and it is good or bad. I say 'form of words' and not 'usage' because the normal use of 'believe' is utterly different. It is used in situations where it would make sense to say someone does not believe, where we would be giving information.

Dr. Trivedi holds that these beliefs involve judging evaluatively 'below the level of consciousness'. This obviously means that we are not aware of these acts and there is no need to infer them either. Trivedi seems to think of judgements as mental clicks happening offstage or onstage. Actually, the concept of judgement is evaluative, not designative. We apply the term 'good judgement' to certain kinds of behaviour and withhold it from others. If I say that somebody is a nice fellow, there is no point at all in looking for a separate something which the word 'niceness' designates.

Trivedi says that emotions 'standardly' have a cognitive element, which give them intentionality. 'Standardly' seems to mean 'usually' and this remark is probably true. The emotions we experience are usually connected with some situation. But there is such a thing as undirected fear. Again, when we are cheerful, we are not cheerful about anything in particular (a grammatical remark, cheerfulness is a mood).

Trivedi states at one point that on account of his explanations, the difference between emotions and affects or feelings is clear, affects or feelings

> are necessary but not sufficient for emotions, for they lack the cognitiveness and intentionality involved in emotions.[11]

This is not an empirical statement like

> A temperature of 100 degrees Centigrade is necessary but not sufficient for water to boil; ground level air is pressure is also necessary.

It is an analytic triviality which restates his original definition of emotions as affects or feelings and cognitions. If we say that a room consists of an upper half and a lower half, it will follow inescapably that the lower half is necessary but not sufficient for the existence of the room.

Trivedi is concerned to distinguish emotions from desires, emotions from beliefs and emotions from moods. Since he is dealing with different kinds of evaluative concepts (comparable to 'niceness', 'stupidity' and 'bravery') and not different kinds of phenomena, he fails again to say anything of substance about them in their own right. For example, he says that

> Beliefs lack the affective component of emotions, a component which is so essential and distinctive to emotions.[12]

---

11. 'The Emotions: Some Preliminaries', p. 90.
12. *Ibid.*, p. 91.

This only means that when we say that we believe that something is the case, we do not mean that that something affects us.

Trivedi is also concerned to distinguish emotions from moods. He says that moods, unlike emotions, are non-intentional. Depression, for example, is not focused on anything in particular, although it may be caused by a particular event. This is not an empirical statement like 'Heart disease is not a communicable disease'. We can at least imagine what it would be like for heart disease to be communicable (e.g., we can imagine bacteria travelling from one person to another). But when we say that someone is in a mood, it is never possible to say correctly that the mood has a focus. Actually, moods have other criteria as well: duration (we cannot say that someone was in a mood for a few seconds. Although we can say that he was angry for a few seconds) and the fact that the behaviour in question was not exactly what we expected (we cannot say of someone who we say is in a mood that his behaviour was exactly what his surroundings called for). All we have, when we talk about moods, is acts of a certain sort, which have no focus, which occupy a certain length of time and which are unexpected in some way or other.

Trivedi thinks he is advancing material propositions when his propositions are actually grammatical; he is only drawing out certain expressions which are embedded in other expressions. His use of words like 'complex', 'component', 'consist of,' 'constituent', 'constitutive of', 'element' and 'causing the emotion' suggests strongly that he is thinking of emotions as entities. But even more significant is the fact that he thinks his redundant propositions are worth advancing. This suggests that he thinks he is making empirical discoveries of some kind.

Let us turn next to parts of Robert M. Gordon's book *The Structure of Emotions*. Gordon, whose discussions focus on emotion words followed by 'that' clauses, talks of a remarkable dichotomy he has discovered. If a person is glad, unhappy, amazed, etc., that *p*, then he knows that p, whereas if a person hopes, fears, etc., that *p*, he does not know that *p*. He calls the first group of emotions 'factive' emotions and the second group 'epistemic' emotions. In factive emotions, a person emotes that *p* only if he knows that *p*, where the dummy word 'emotes' is replaced by glad, unhappy, amazed, etc. Here '*S* emotes that *p*' presupposes that *S* knows that *p*. In epistemic emotions, '*S* emotes that *p*' only if *S* does not know that *p* ; these emotions are knowledge precludes.

This distinction is really one between 'certainty' and 'uncertainty' emotions and Gordon is making a song and dance about linguistic inter-connections. He says that '*S* is amazed that *p*' implies that '*S* knows that *p*' but '*S* is amazed that *p*' is equivalent to *S* is amazed at the fact that *p*'. Whenever we say truly that '*S* is amazed that *p*', it will be correct to say that '*S* believes that *p*'. Naturally, since amazement is a certainty emotion. But since that '*p*' is equivalent to the fact that *p*', *S* is believing a fact, and if *S* believes a fact, he necessarily knows it. (This is not, of course, the ordinary use of 'know' and 'believe' but never mind.) On the other hand, '*S* hopes that p' is equivalent to '*S* hopes that the possibility that *p* will be confirmed' (hoping is an uncertainty emotion) and since it is a possibility that is in question, it will never be the case that '*S* knows that *p*'.

Gordon points out that in the case of epistemic emotions, concepts like 'confirming', 'bearing out' and 'proving to be true' can be applied but not in the case of factive emotions. How could it be otherwise? Since epistemic emotions are uncertainty emotions, these concepts can get a grip, and since factive emotions are certainty emotions, they cannot. The implications Gordon draws out are inexorable, but the inexorability is grammatical.

Gordon also says, in connection with positive emotions, that '*S* is delighted that *p*' only if *S* has a favourable attitude towards *p* and wishes it to be the case that *p*. Regarding negative emotions, he says that '*S* is afraid that *p*' only if *S* has an unfavourable attitude towards *p* and wishes it not to be the case that *p*. Once again, Gordon is only bringing out linguistic implications. If we say truly that *S* is delighted that *p*, it will always be true to say that *S* has a favourable attitude to *p*, and *S* wishes it to be the case that *p*, and if we say truly that *S* is sad that *p*, it will always be true to say that *S* has an unfavourable attitude to *p*, and wishes it not to be the case that *p*.

Gordon concludes that wish-satisfaction and wish-frustration are involved in positive and negative emotions. Wish-satisfaction and wish-frustration have certain characteristic effects on human beings, which words like 'glad', 'sad', etc., denote. Although Godron says at one point that he is trying to bring out logical differences, he fails to keep this consideration in mind and tends to think that he is talking about phenomena. The above formulation is an example, because Gordon's use of the concepts of cause and effect suggests that he is thinking of wish-satisfaction and wish-frustration on the one hand, and gladness, sadness, etc., on the other, as independent psychic constituents.

That Gordon is talking about phenomena becomes more obvious when he discusses negative and positive emotions, using anger and pleasure as examples. He says that when *S* is angry about the fact that *p, S* not only believes that *p*, but wishes it not to be the case that *p*, and *S*'s wish is frustrated.

> What is causing *S* to be angry is the belief and the wish in combination; it is . . . the wish-frustration that is causing *S* to be angry.[13]

In regard to the positive factive emotions, he takes pleasure as the example. When S is pleased that *p, S* believes that *p*, and wishes it to be the case that *p*, and the pleasure arises from the wish-satisfaction. Elsewhere he talks of the 'belief dependence'[14] of the emotion.

Gordon is transferring linguistic implications to the structure of the world. His language implies that a three-stage process, involving four distinct entities, is taking place: belief and wish come together to produce wish-frustration which in turn causes *S* to be angry. The reality is that '*S* is angry that *p*' is consistent with certain other sentences. Whenever it is true to say '*S* is angry that *p*', it will be true to say that '*S* believes that *p*' and '*S* wishes it not to be the case that *p*'. When it is true to say that *S* has been angered by something, it will be true to say that a wish-frustration caused *S* to be angry. But these would be vacuously true statements, with no counterparts in the structure of the world. What is really happening is that a situation enters *S*'s life as something angering, and *S* reacts with anger-behaviour, and we talk of *S* being angry.

Let us take a concrete example. Suppose that after *S* wrote a paper for a seminar, the seminar convenor writes to *S*, withdrawing the invitation. The letter will enter *S*'s life as something enraging and *S* will react by scowling, uttering rude words and throwing the letter into the waste-paper basket. The letter and the behaviour will be ontologically real and are criteria permitting talk of *S*'s anger, but the word 'anger' will not denote anything. One could talk of *S* 's belief that the invitation had been withdrawn and *S*'s wish that it had not been, of

13. Gordon, *op. cit.*, pp. 52-3.
14. *Ibid.*, p. 47.

the belief and the wish coming together to produce wish-frustration and wish-frustration causing *S*'s anger, but all this says nothing more than that the letter withdrawing the invitation made *S* angry. 'Belief', 'wish', 'wish-frustration' and 'anger' do not denote entities and 'coming together', 'producing' and 'causes' do not denote processes. Gordon's formulation is a mere exercise in redundancy.

Discussing factive emotions, which are neither positive nor negative, Gordon says that if *S* is surprised about the fact that *p*, then at the time that *S* came to be certain that *p*, *p* was contrary to *S*'s expectations — which is pure grammar.[15]

Gordon discusses epistemic emotions next, taking fear as the example.[16] If *S* fears that *p*, he wishes it not to be the case that *p*. Second, if *S* fears that *p, S* is neither certain that *p* nor certain that not-*p*. This is tautologus. Whenever we say correctly that *S* fears that *p*, it will be correct to say that *S* wishes it not to be the case that *p*. And epistemic emotions being uncertainty emotions, if *S* fears that *p*, he necessarily is not certain that *p*, and not certain that not-*p*.

Gordon appears to recommend (with special reference to anger) the following analysis of the causation of emotions.[17] The subject hears *S* utter *U*. The primary cognition then takes place, that *U* is an insult by *S*. This makes the subject angry with *S* about *U*. This, in turn, causes a general physiological arousal in the subject and an impulse to strike *S*. This leads to a secondary cognition — that the general arousal and the impulse are caused by the primary cognition that *U* is an insult by *S*. This secondary cognition causes an act of labelling — 'I am angry with *S* about *U*'. The act of labelling leads to the subject having an angry feeling, which, in turn, causes him to strike *S*.

Gordon is certainly, or almost certainly, thinking of distinct, successive, ontologically real stages — eight of them, in fact. The subject hears *S*'s insult and strikes *S* — but there are six intermediary stages. Actually, these putative states are idle hypostatisations, usually (but not always) hypostatisations of grammatical derivations. There are really (or need be) only two stages — the subject hears *S*'s insult and strikes *S*.

15. Gordon, *op. cit.*, pp. 54-5.
16. *Ibid.*, p. 68.
17. *Ibid.*, pp. 105-6.

One could talk of a primary cognition that *U* is an insult by *S*. But it would be an idle grammatical derivation, and should not be misconstrued as a reference to a second and subsequent 'inner' event; we give no additional information when we make such a statement. All that happens is that *U* enters the subject's life in a particular way, as something insulting and infuriating — and these two adjectives do not denote two separate ingredients in what is head; the remark enters the subject's life as an integral whole. Gordon's cognition is not only idle but incompletely defined — it is infuriating as well as insulting.

Gordon says the primary cognition causes the subject to be angry with *S* about *U*. But being angry is not a succeeding third event. All that happens is that *U* enters the subject's life as something infuriating and insulting, and this is one criterion for talking about the subject being angry. 'Being angry' is not a separate inner occurrence. As we saw, being angry is supposed to lead to a general physiological arousal and an impulse to strike *S*, which in turn leads to the secondary cognition that the arousal and the impulse are caused by the cognition that *U* is an insult by *S*, which in turn causes an act of labelling ('I am angry with *S* about *U*') which again causes the subject to have an angry feeling, which causes him to strike *S*. When someone strikes someone else because of an insulting and infuriating utterance, there probably always is a general physiological arousal (increased heartbeat rate, etc.) but it is wrong to assume that the striking is necessarily preceded (at several removes) by a physiological arousal and, equally, it is wrong to think that the striking must be preceded (at several removes again) by a impulse to strike. Why cannot the arousal and the striking happen together? This appears to be a fallacious material proposition, and not a grammatical derivation. The physiological arousal and the impulse are supposed to cause the secondary cognition that both are caused by the primacy cognition that *U* is an insult by *S*. In fact, if the subject is so worked up as to strike *S*, he probably will not be aware of his physiological arousal. It appears that there is no grammatical derivation here; it is not possible to say, whenever someone is physiologically aroused on account of an insult, that he is aware of his arousal, and is aware that it is due to the insult. As we saw, there need not be an impulse to strike prior to the act of striking, but if there is an impulse, it will always be true to say that the impulse is caused by the state of being angry with an offender about something; this is a grammatical derivation. Moreover, there is no ontologically real act of labelling, which happens after the subject hears *U* and before he strikes *S*, which is necessary if *S* is to be struck. *U* enters the subject's life as an infuriating and insulting utterance by *S*; *U* is already labelled, as it were, and there is no need for a separate act of labelling. We cannot talk of a grammatical derivation here. Whenever S's utterance *U* enters someone's life as something infuriating and insulting, it will be true to say that the subject attributes his anger to *S*"s utterance *U*. But what makes this a necessary truth is the utterance and not the bodily changes. Gordon has made another fallacious empirical claim. This alleged act of labelling is supposed to cause an angry feeling, which in turn causes the subject to strike *S*. But this means that being angry (the third stage) and having an angry feeling are two different things, which is certainly a paradox. All that is veridical in Gordon's schema are the utterance, which enters the subject's life in a particular way, and the physical and behavioural changes. Everything else is an idle construct.

Gordon distinguishes between emotions, which are passive, and actions, which are not.[18] His argument is quite exceptionally complicated and difficult to follow but it appears to include the following claim. When an action is performed for a reason, it is always possible to speak of its 'desirability characteristic',[19] that is, that it serves a purpose. In the case of emotions, this is never possible. It is tautologous to say that all purposeful action serves a purpose. On the other hand, when we say that someone is experiencing an emotion, what is meant is that he is undergoing something and the idea of an undergoing necessarily excludes that of doing something for a purpose; these concepts occupy different grammatical spaces, as it were. Someone who murders his wife in a fit of jealousy is certainly not passive, and we may say (although very artificially) that his emotion motivated the action, but the 'desirability characteristic', the quality of serving the subject's purpose, belongs necessarily to the purposeful action and not the undergone emotion. We can press the point a little. When one says that emotions are not 'performed for a purpose', one is not making an empirical point; this is not a statement like 'Breathing is not done with one's hands'. Emotion words are evaluative words, they do not designate anything real. It is

---

18. Gordon, *op. cit.*, pp. 121-7.
19. *Ibid.*, p. 123. The expression is G.E.M. Anscombe's, which Donald Davidson reproduces in a passage cited by Gordon.

a question of a grammatical rule governing the use of a purely functional term; a comparable statement would be 'The concept of courage is not that of a man'. What is veridical in the above case is the situation and the jealousy behaviour (such as the man murdering his wife, which is purposeful, and his brooding and giving black looks, which are not), and these are the criteria permitting the use of the function word 'jealousy'.

Gordon's language, like Trivedi's, suggests that he is thinking that his propositions are empirical ones. But, as with Trivedi again, the very fact that he thinks his redundant propositions worth advancing is even stronger evidence that he assumes, even if only implicitly, that he is engaged in a scientific sort of enterprise.

The present writer has criticised in detail elsewhere the view that emotions are ontologically real.[20] The thrust of this paper is not to combat that misconception but to show — by looking at concrete examples and drawing on two principles of Wittgenstein's philosophy of language — that attempts to describe emotions lead nowhere.

One final point. Someone might object that we do in fact often talk abut emotions, our own and those of others. The answer to this is that when one does this, one is not really describing emotions in their own right. The expression 'talking about emotions' could refer to one or more of three things. Firstly, one may identify emotions. For example, one may say 'He is terrified', 'I am disappointed' and so on. Secondly, one may use metaphors to express an emotion. Examples are Nehru's comment upon the assassination of Mahatma Gandhi:

> The light has gone out of our lives and there is darkness everywhere[21]

and Hitler's reaction in 1918 on learning, when recuperating in a military hospital, that Germany would accept an Armistice:

> Darkness surrounded me as I staggered and stumbled back

---

20. G.P. Ramachandra, 'Do Feeling-Nouns Designate Anything?' *Journal of the Indian Council of Philosophical Research*, New Delhi (forthcoming).

21. Cited in M.J. Akbar, *Nehru : the Making of India*, Viking, Harmondsworth, 1988, p. 435.

to my ward and buried my aching head between the blankets and pillow.[22]

Thirdly, one may describe a situation. For example, Nehru went on to say:

I do not know what to tell you and how to say it. Bapu, as we called him, the father of the nation, is nor more[23] (the language is factual, except for the expression 'father of the nation').

And Hitler went on to write:

So all had been in vain. In vain all its (the war's) sacrifices and privations, in vain the hunger and thirst for endless months, in vain those hours that we stuck to our posts though the fear of death gripped our souls, and in vain the deaths of two millions who fell in discharging this duty.[24]

An identification is not, of course, a description. Again, when words are used metaphorically, that is, in a secondary and not in their primary sense, as 'light' and 'darkness' are used here, no true description is being given. And when one describers a situation, one is obviously not describing emotions *per se*. But a more fundamental point is that although it is correct to talk about identifying emotions and expressing emotions through metaphors, one is really talking about situations in both cases. When one says 'He is terrified', one is really evaluating a situation (his behaviour in a particular context). When one is using a metaphor to express an emotion, one is really capturing the impact, which a situation has upon oneself. The metaphor is a gesture, a response to a situation and not a description of an inner event, just as Hitler burying his head between the blankets and pillow was a gesture, a response to a situation, and not a description of an inner event.[25]

---

22. Adolf Hitler, *Mein Kampf*, Jaico Publishing House, Bombay, 1988, p.176.
23. Akbar, *op. cit.*
24. Hitler, *op. cit.*, p. 177.
25. On this point, see the chapter 'The Musicality of Language', in Paul Johnston, *Wittgenstein : Rethinking the Inner*, Routledge, London and New York, 1993, pp. 101-32.

The Contributors

Suresh Chandra is retired Professor, Department of Philosophy, University of Hyderabad, Hyderabad.

Srinivasa Rao is Professor, Department of Philosophy Bangalore University, Bangalore.

Nizar Ahmed is Lecturer, School of Social Sciences, Mahatma Gandhi University, Kottayam.

Amitabha Dasgupta is Professor, Department of Philosophy, University of Hyderabad, Hyderabad.

S. Panneerselvam is Professor, Dr. S. Radhakrishnan Institute of Advanced Studies in Philosophy, University of Madras, Chennai.

P.R. Bhat is Professor, Department of Humanities and Social Sciences, IIT, Bombay.

Ganesh Prasad Das is Reader, Department of Philosophy, Utkal University, Bhubaneswar.

Sadhan Chakraborti is Lecturer, Department of Philosophy, Rabindra Bharati University, Calcutta.

R.C. Pradhan is Professor, Department of Philosophy, University of Hyderabad, Hyderabad.

Shefali Moitra is Reader, Department of Philosophy, Jadavpur University, Calcutta.

Sanil V. is Asst. Professor, Department of Humanities and Social Sciences, IIT, Delhi.

G.P. Ramachandra is Professor and Director, School of International Relations, Mahatma Gandhi University, Kottayam.

Index